Muddy Shoes

A Ministry In the Mud and Dirt of the Horsetracks

Norman Evans

"LOVE ONE ANOTHER"
John 13: 34
[photo by Norm Evans]

The horse is "Tony Be Quick," owned by Fern Taylor,
Indiana foaled, Ohio raced. The cat is "Andrew," out of
"Feisty" by "Unknown Prowler," Florida bred, Ohio foaled.

This Book is Dedicated to:

My Wife, Florence L. Evans,
My Encourager, My Cheerleader, My Love and
My Friend,
Mother of our Three Children, One Whose Prayers for me
are Ever Before God.

Race Track Chaplaincy of America, Inc.

National Ministries, American Baptist Churches
of the United States

The Ohio Baptist Convention

All of Whom Trusted Me to Do God's Will in
Whatever Task I Was Asked.

And Thousands of My Racetrack Parishioners.

Acknowledgements

M Y THANKS TO: My wife Florence and our extended family for support and encouragement: My racetrackers who changed my life: My support and encouragement from Race Track Chaplaincy of America, and my fellowship with brother chaplains all over the country: the Rev. Dr. John Sundquist, Executive Minister of the Ohio Baptist Convention during most of my chaplaincy, and later head of our ABCUSA International Ministries: the Rev. Dr. Daniel Sommer, President of the Ohio Council of RTCA and President of RTCA for some fine years! [I worked closely with both of them:] my nephew, Sidney Soderholm and a friend, Blanch Swaim, who started me on computer use: Dave Eddy, proof reader extraordinary, who made me realize how much has changed and how much I'd forgotten since English 101 back in 1942: My personal Internist, doctor and friend, Dr. Barbara Krenzer, who saved my life several times, and Dr. William Berkery, Cardiologist and dear friend, who is trying to keep me alive at least until this book is published: Judy and Horace Ivey for manuscript reading to let me know if I was "on track:" fellow residents of Hallmark Nursing Centre and the staff who ask all the time how the book is coming, and the nurses who keep warning me not to overdo [actually, I've never had so many women telling me what to do, but all in all, I kind of like it:]

Foreword

I moved to Columbus, Ohio, from Pennsylvania, in the summer of 1972 to serve as the pastor of Lincoln Baptist Church. That fall I attended the Ohio Baptist Convention where Dr. Joseph Chapman, Executive Minister of the O.B.C. introduced the Rev. Homer Tricules, an American Baptist missionary, who was serving as a Race Track Chaplain in New Jersey. Homer shared with the assembled group his work as a Race Track Chaplain. I was fascinated by his description. It sounded to me like a literal fulfillment of the Great Commission — to go into all the world. The "backside" of the racetrack was a "world" within our world and I was convinced that Christ had died for the citizens of that world as well as the world around it.

Dr. Chapman had presented the ministry of Race Track Chaplaincy of America to us with the hope of starting such a ministry in Ohio. I expressed an interest in helping with the work of the chaplaincy in Ohio. Before I knew it I was on my way to River Downs, a thoroughbred track in Cincinnati. There I met a Race Track Chaplain, Kelly Blanton. Kelly was serving temporarily as chaplain until a fulltime chaplain could be appointed. Kelly was a great help in understanding what a chaplain does and how a Christian can work effectively in an industry that is based on gambling. After my day with Kelly I thought God was calling me to help, where I could, in this ministry. I became a member of the Board of the Ohio Division of the Race Track Chaplaincy of America. Our task was to hire a full-time chaplain. Dr. Chapman already had a man in mind. His name was Norm Evans and within a few weeks Norm was on the Ohio scene. The pages of this book are largely the story of Norm's work.

Within a year Dr. Chapman retired and I was asked to serve as President of the O.D.R.T.C.A. The first ten years were relatively easy years due to the work of Norm Evans, the chaplain for the Ohio Division. Norm raised the money for the ministry through the racing industry and the churches of Ohio. Norm developed the ministry on the tracks of Ohio and did the ministry work on the tracks. His wife, Florence, was supportive of his work. Florence was called the "cookie lady" on the tracks of Ohio. She made the best cookies to share with the "backsiders."

A few years after the ministry was established in Ohio I was asked to serve as the president of the national R.T.C.A as well as continue as executive director of the Ohio Division. At the national level I discovered a wonderful group of dedicated Christian lay people, ministers and denominational executives. All were committed to the ecumenical, evangelistic ministry to the racing industry. In fact, this unique group, in my mind did not fit into the term interdenominational. I coined the phrase "transdenominational" as a better description of what we did together. In general terms the American Baptists represented the geographic part of our country described as Northeast and Midwest. While the Southern Baptists represented the Southern states, the Assembly of God had most of the Western part of the United States. These groups also represented distinctly different cultures in our country, but we all came together in a common cause of reaching the racing industry for Christ. The people on the racetracks to whom we minister are largely "itinerate," traveling between race-meets. So, our chaplains had to go where their "flock" went. Although there were distinct cultural and religious difference in our organizational make-up there was a great amount of "mixing" of chaplains from one culture into another. This largely happy experience was due to the nature of the industry to which we ministered. The work of R.T.C.A. and Norm Evans, in particular, I believed from early on, that as exciting and fulfilling as the work was, I could never be a chaplain. The work of a Race Track Chaplain is just too difficult. At the same time, I owe a great debt to the ministry. When I became discouraged in the pastoral ministry because nothing was happening, I could look at the work of Race Track Chaplaincy and realize that God was indeed doing a mighty work of grace in a world largely forgotten by His church, but not by Him.

Friday, January 16, 2004
Poneto, Indiana
Rev. Dan Sommer

Preface

It has been twenty-six years since I first met Chaplain Norm Evans. Norm, then and now, qualifies in my book as worthy of inclusion in any list of "most unforgettable characters."

Norm is a big man whose long muscular arms seem to extend from his heart. He greets you with an embrace, warms you to your core, and pulls you into the warm embrace of God's grace.

"MUDDY SHOES" tells the surprising story of a part of our world that few people know; the backside of the thoroughbred racetracks. There live a fast paced, incredible people bound together by their love for horses. If church people see the track at all it is the frontside. Out back is another world: a bustling migrant community of horsemen and their families. A village walled off and by in large from the rest of the world.

"MUDDY SHOES" is the story of their lives and the story of the big man they call Chaplain. Real stories of real people invigorated and stained by the mud of the backside.

Norm Evans has walked the last three decades of his life with muddy shoes pointing to one who was born in a stable on the backside named Jesus. It is Jesus who understands best those who live on the backside of life. His embrace has the power to bring hope and life at its fullest, - even on the backside.

January 14, 2004
Sawyer, Michigan
Dr. John A. Sundquist

Introduction

A HISTORY OF Race Track Chaplaincy of America, HORSES, HOOFBEATS AND HALOS, by John C. Hillhouse, Jr. [available through RTCA, {310} 419-1640,] P.O. Box 91640, Los Angles, CA 90009, at $8.00 per copy] told the general history of RTCA and many of its divisions. Not every division responded and a book of this sort has to leave out most of the personal stories and experiences of the Chaplains themselves. As one of those on the history committee, I felt that events of those on the "cutting edge" of the ministry needed flesh and blood stories to round out our history.

Any one of our chaplains, past or present, could be writing this. Coming in at the beginning, I have heard many of my fellow chaplains tell tales that would evoke emotions from joy to tears. I can only tell of those that happened to me and will never be forgotten. Sometimes actual names will be used, sometimes names will be changed. But all those written about were real people.

I speak of "the cutting edge." A knife has a cutting edge. We are on the cutting edge of ministry, where the gospel of Jesus Christ is presented in the market place of the world.

On a knife, the cutting edge is constantly resharpened, wearing away the steel in the process. We leave part of ourselves on those to whom we minister, and they leave their mark on us. We are worn down in the sharpening, but also constantly renewed by the Holy Spirit.

For those of you who might not be familiar with RTCA, we minister on the "Backside" of horsetracks across the country. On every track there will be 1,500 to 5,000 people involved with the support of horses in a host of job classifications. Some of them have to cool down a "hot horse" before they can buy breakfast; some are actual millionaires, but you might not know it by looking at them. Most work seven days a week and would not be welcomed in church if they were able to go. Some are from the community, but most are transient. They have all the problems of those outside the track, but here they are concentrated on 100 acres, more or less. They call themselves "trackers," and see themselves as a people tied by a common bond – the horse. They work and live inside the fence; everyone else is "outside." The fence is not to keep them in; it is to keep the others out.

The "Frontside" of the track is the glamorous part, where the Grandstand and Clubhouse are set on the track. It's where the jockeys in the silks of the owners come out to parade their mounts for all to see and where the horses race to the yelling and excitement of the crowd. The people there, for the most part, are folks who can go to church if they wish, and are not forced to work in the grime of the Backside, every day of the week with the horses.

We chaplains usually have an office, normally a tack room or a spot in the rec room or other place they can find for us, to use as a base or to counsel. However the bulk of ministry takes place on our feet, in the shedrows, barns, at the rail, in the track kitchen [cafeteria], horseman's office, racing secretary's office, jock's room, and in fact every place that employees can be found, from Backside to Frontside. Occasionally, someone from the Grandstand will seek out a chaplain, but our ministry there is mostly muted; most of those who pay to get in already have a chance to go to church, yet we keep aware of those in need. Many trackers live on the track, in a tackroom or a stall near the horses, and often dormitories are provided. If the chaplain lives on the track with the trackers, and many do at least part of the time, acceptance is rapid.

Race Track Chaplaincy was a new idea in January of 1976 at Thistledown in Cleveland OH when I first arrived. I was under suspicion. There were those who said, "Watch out! He may be an undercover FBI man or something!" But that first week was a bitter cold spell, and after a week, the same one who had posted the warning said, "He must be what he says he is, because an FBI type would have stayed across the street in the Holiday Inn"

We chaplains have come from all types of backgrounds. I was a farm boy, as I will relate later, and I knew horses. But one of my colleagues came from New York City, a former gang member who had been converted under Nicky Cruz. I was with him at Las Alemedos in California when he started his ministry during a quarter-horse meet. He asked me in an aside, "Norm, what are these 'quarter-back' horses anyway?" The things we share in our backgrounds are a knowledge of Jesus Christ as our Savior, a call to ministry, a love of people and a non-judgemental way of ministry. We can learn to love the horses.

Contents

DEDICATION xii

ACKNOWLEDGEMENTS ix

FOREWORD...xi

PREFACE xv

INTRODUCTION xvii

CHAPTER 1
  SCARY SITUATIONS 25

CHAPTER 2
  TRUSTING GOD AND GETTING READY..............41

CHAPTER 3
  MEETING PROBLEMS HEAD ON...........................51

CHAPTER 4
  DIVERSITY ON THE TRACK 63

CHAPTER 5
  REACHING OUT FOR CHRIST................................73

CHAPTER 6
  CHAPEL SERVICES ON THE RACETRACK........103

CHAPTER 7
    SPREADING THE WORD 113

CHAPTER 8
    MOLDING YOUR ATTITUDE 131

CHAPTER 9
    THE GOSPEL IN HORSE STORIES 139

CHAPTER 10
    A MISSIONARY TO THE CHURCHES.................145

CHAPTER 11
    ROUNDING UP LOOSE HORSES 153

CHAPTER 12
    MESSAGES FROM THE TRACK 159

CHAPTER 13
    BUT HOW ABOUT ALL THAT GAMBLING?......167

CHAPTER 14
    THE GREATEST JEWISH JOCKEY 177

CHAPTER 15
    CHRISTIAN PRESENCE 183

CHAPTER 16
    ADVENT FROM THE TRACK...............................191

CHAPTER 17
    SAMARITANS AMONG US?.................................197

CHAPTER 18
    RUNNING THE RACE...203

CHAPTER 19
    TALKING TO THE ANIMALS 209

CHAPTER 20
    SPIRITUAL WARFARE ON THE TRACK 223

CHAPTER 21
    THE EXTRAS ON THE TRACK 227

CHAPTER 22
    WORKING WITH TRACK SECURITY.................245

CHAPTER 23
    A DANGEROUS BUSINESS 253

CHAPTER 24
    FIRE! 263

CHAPTER 25
    PAST, PRESENT AND FUTURE...........................285

CHAPTER 1

Scary Situations and a Call to Enter Them

"I Came To You In Weakness And Fear..."

[Paul, II Timothy 2:15]

"W hich way, Lord? Quick!" I needed my answer in seconds, and I got it! I was a new missionary, going to my first day among a new people, and how do I get there?

We think of missionaries as people of great faith, going fearlessly into the world with the banner of Christ. In my case, I felt like Paul when he told the Corinthians he came, "In weakness and fear, and much trembling. [I Corinthians 2:3] But Paul came as called, and God gave him strength in spite of his fears. I entered the Race Track Chaplaincy of America, feeling like Paul, but going anyway.

We had moved to Grove City, Ohio on December 29, 1975, to start a new work at Thistledown Racetrack in

Cleveland. My new Ohio Council and I met for the first time on January 2, 1976. My appointment was a three-way deal: RTCA had accepted me and approved my position, The Ohio Baptist Convention had approved me and was to stand behind me, and the National Ministries Board of The American Baptist Churches of the USA had appointed me a missionary . I still wondered if God had not gotten the wrong computer printout!

My position was made clear at the meeting. Unlike most of the chaplains, my Sundays were to be available to the churches of Ohio, or elsewhere as opportunity presented itself. This was to help in raising funds for the ministry, and all my gratuities were to be turned back to the OBC to extend my expense account. RTCA had contacted the tracks and horsemen and their contributions were to go to our treasurer, who was the OBC treasurer. National Ministries gave us some "seed money" to get started. It was a confusing arrangement but I was told that if it did not work out, the OBC would help me get a church! I left two churches by faith that God had called me, and I did not feel that God would let me down, or that I would let Him down. But I was still scared!

Thistledown was about 120 miles up the pike from Grove City. We had chosen to live in Grove City, just south of Columbus, in the center of the state, because Beulah Park was in Grove City, and River Downs was about 100 miles south near Cincinnati. By living close to one track, we were about equidistant from the other two, and near the center of the state to travel to churches.

On January 3,1976, I left home, with packed food, a gallon of ice-tea, a sleeping bag and prayer. My Volkswagen bus with its air-cooled motor put out little heat, but my prayers were fervent. On the beltway, I saw a sign that said, "Thistledown – Next Two Exits." I turned off on the first exit, hoping to find signs to lead me to Thistledown. Then I came to a fork in the road with no signs! I was praying at the time, "Lord, Please help me! There were no courses in seminary to prepare me for work on the backside of the tracks. You've brought us 500 miles from our home and friends, and — Quick, Lord, which road do I take to get to the track?"

At that very moment, an old pickup truck passed me, with a few bales of hay in the back! "Thanks, Lord," I said, and followed the truck to the track gate!

I parked my rig and got out near the guard shack. I did know that you had to show a license to go in, so I walked to the shack and pronounced, "I'm Chaplain Norm Evans, just coming in!"

The guard at the desk looked up in amazement and sputtered, "Chaplain! You're in the wrong place!"

So much for a warm welcome. My initial fear of a brand new situation with people who were supposed to be difficult was not helped.

I asked how to get to the manager's office, and was directed out the Horseman's gate and into the main gate. At the grandstand, I asked an usher where the manager's office was, and he took me to the door. As we approached, Manager Mike Mackey was just getting there. The usher called out, "Mr. Mackey, the chaplain is here." He looked around with a startled look, put his hand on the doorknob and told me to come in.

At his desk, I introduced myself as he sat there, drumming his fingers on the desktop. Finally, after a long pause, he spoke. "I didn't know you were coming. I don't know where I'm going to put you. The track is frozen, the union is on strike, the horsemen are upset because we can't race and everything here is in an uproar."

My mind went immediately to Paul's words to Timothy; [II Tim. 4:2]

> "Preach the Word, be instant in season and
> out of season."

Only I rephrased it in an urgent, silent prayer as I quickly looked up: "Lord, I'm here to preach the Word, but it's out of season, and it's up to You to be instant!" Frankly, my stomach was now in knots.

"Come with me. We'll at least get you licensed and I'll introduce you in the Racing Secretary's office." Downstairs we went and I was fingerprinted, mug shot and registered, while Mr. Mackey was explaining his dilemma.

The Stall man spoke up and said I could use his office on the Backside. He took me over and I found a tackroom that had a desk and chair in it. I got the lay of the area, locating the track kitchen, the Horseman's Benevolent and Protective Association's office [HBPA], the bathroom area, which was about 100 feet away from my room. Then I realized there was another area of Backside beyond the far turn [over 3/8ths of a mile away] called "Tin City." I called it a day. That night I slept on a pastor's couch in his house. The next day, after a morning on the track, I bought a cot and moved into the office.

At daylight, I drove to the track, showed my new license badge, and started my new ministry. The first job was to get to know people. So, whether in the track Kitchen or out in the barns, I would walk up to folks and introduce myself. "Hi! I'm Norm Evans, the new track Chaplain!"

It worked pretty well. I met people and got their names. Sometimes I had to ask again, but I made a real effort to remember names. On the first or second day I met three men walking toward me. I did the usual greeting and extended my hand. Two of them took my hand and gave me their names, but the third stuck his hands deep into his pockets, lowered his head with a shake and walked around me.

The next morning I saw that man in the track kitchen, sitting at a table, elbow on top, holding a coffee cup. He was a long ways from there in his mind, just staring into space. "Ah, here's my chance!" I thought. I sat down opposite him.

His eyes refocused, saw me and the response was immediate. "NO! NO! NO!" I put my hands up to show him I would not intrude, got up and walked to another table, but I admit to being embarrassed and a bit distressed as his voice carried to all corners.

The Backside [where the horse barns are] was a sloppy mess. With its dirt "streets," it was dusty when dry, but snowy or raining, it was a muddy mess. Most days your shoes or boots were covered with mud. In my first week I was wearing rubber overshoes because of the snow and mud. Over in "Tin City," to leave one barn, you had to walk on a 2X6 placed from the barn sill over an especially obnoxious puddle of water, mud and horse manure. You guessed it! I stepped off the plank one morning and went in over my overshoes. I tromped the half-mile back to my tackroom to change my shoes and socks and found the Stall Manager there. When I told him what had happened, he disgustedly called maintenance and told them to get a truckload of gravel to that barn immediately!

That Sunday, I was introduced at a church's evening service as a "veteran of one week as a race track chaplain." I spoke and asked for questions afterward. The very first question asked was, "How far is a furlong?" One week had not been long enough to answer that one. I quickly replied, "About two partridge flights! Next question." I learned the next week that a furlong was one-eighth of a mile, which would be about four partridge flights! If you never "put up" a partridge, you'll just have to take my word for it.

However, the next question was, "Are there specific things you want us to pray for?" So I told them about a man who would not shake hands with me and who warned me away from him in the kitchen. I wanted contact with that man and they promised to pray that it would come about. Talk about odds, the poor man did not know what he was up against!

I returned to the track Monday morning and that afternoon walked into the kitchen. At a table for four sat my man, flanked by Slim on one side and Big John on the other. They were in conversation, so, when I approached the table, I pulled the extra chair back about two feet to signify I was not butting into their talk. They continued for a short while, then Slim said, "Come on in, Chaplain!" So I pulled into the group. I let things flow for a minute, until I had gotten my man's name from his badge.

I looked across to him and asked, "Where are you from, John?"

He jerked a bit, then decided to answer. "I was brought up on a dairy farm in Pennsylvania, but spent most of my life logging with horses in the West."

I nodded with a smile. "I farmed and milked cows for twenty years in New York, plus years of 4-H dairy before that."

"You did?"

"And I'm a Certified Tree Farmer with 300 acres of forest."

"You are?"

"And I've used draft horses on the farm and pulled a few logs with them as well."

"You did?" After that, he could not stop talking. Later, I asked him about that time in the kitchen. I told him he looked as if he were a thousand miles away. He was, thinking about a son whom he could not see, and he blamed a minister for the family breakup. Getting him to talk about it began to help. We became good friends.

He came to my services and, while I cannot say he gave his heart to the Lord, he listened intently. A while later he decided to make a change. He would leave the racetrack and go south to find a more permanent job on a big horse farm. He was an avid reader and used to buy second hand books of high educational value. We passed books between us.

Just before he left, he asked me to come to his tack room. He looked embarrassed as he said, "I always wanted one of these Irish Fisherman's sweaters, so I bought one. It's really too hot to wear in the shedrow, so I wish you'd try it on and see if you could wear it." He had tears in his eyes as he gave it to me.

My fears of being in an unfamiliar place did not disappear all at once. In fact, I'm not sure when the butterflies in my stomach stopped coming from apprehension and turned to anticipation! Surely, there was not much anticipation that first winter in Thistledown! My room had one electric heater in it. Most of the tackrooms where people slept had an extra, illegal heater with cardboard stuck to the walls, but I could not modify my room, for it was still the Stall Man's office. The snow blew in under the door and around the window. I usually went to bed in my sleeping bag soon after 6:00 P.M., just to keep warm! I could not read, because my hands got too cold. It was good for prayer time and sleep.

Introductions were to have been easier, as Salty Roberts, RTCA's founder and a tracker himself, was to have been there for my first week, to introduce me to people he knew. But Salty had been recently injured and was unable to come. Salty had been a fixture on racetracks all over the country and was well known. I had known him since the mid-1960's when I was involved with the Tri-State Coordinating Council of Race Track Ministries.

As chairman of that organization, I had gone back and forth to Race Track Chaplaincy of America, based in Florida, and had worked out a merger of our two groups. We became the Tri-State Council of RTCA. They had incorporated and we had done much homework as to purpose and practice, so we each had an equal contribution to make.

But now I was on my own! An Ohio Council had been formed, but it was too early for them to even know what life on the Backside [the barn area] was like. Conditions were primitive and the cold that winter penetrated you night and day. I found out that most of the grooms were so cold that winter that they were getting together to rent rooms in a nearby cheap motel. I stuck it out and it paid dividends.

Some of the trackers were suspicious of a chaplain coming to be with them. Most of them had never heard of a chaplain on a racetrack. In fact, most churches seemed to shun the trackers or fight the tracks. As I mentioned in my Introduction, rumors flew that I might be an undercover FBI man or a fed of some kind! Finally, Dakota, a pony man, said, "He must be OK and what he says he is! If he was FBI he would have a room across the street instead of staying here with us!" Trust developed. I had to earn it. I lived with them. I made a point to be out when it rained or when it snowed. They had to be out there, so I would be with them. More than once I was asked why I was out in weather like that and my reply was always, "Because you have to be out in it!"

Why I was there on the racetrack as a chaplain needs explaining. I did not "just" decide to go into the ministry and become a racetrack chaplain. I do not want this to be an autobiography, but an understanding of some things from my life is necessary to understand this unusual calling.

At the age of nine or ten, I heard the Rev. Lewis Brown, a Baptist missionary to what was then the Belgian Congo, speak in my home church, the First Baptist Church of Georgetown, NY. I was fascinated by his message. I also realized for the first time, that while I was being raised in a Christian home and was a faithful Sunday School student, I had to decide for Jesus as my Savior in a conscious commitment. No one is "born" a Christian. One has to "become" one. Rev. Brown gave an invitation and some of my friends went forward. One of them spoke to me about going up, but I whispered that I already had decided for Christ. That was not actually the truth. The real reason was that I stammered so badly that it was difficult to talk. It was extremely embarrassing to talk, especially to strangers.

Before I went to bed that night, I was on my knees, asking God to forgive me for not going up, and for Jesus to come into my heart. I asked Him to be my Savior. At the very moment that I asked Christ into my heart, I heard the voice of God within me, saying, "I want you to be My missionary!" I was scared to death! How could a scared kid who stammered even be considered as a minister or missionary!

That hung over me for years. I did not tell anybody else, except that once my mother told me gently that she had always hoped that I would be a doctor. I actually burst out crying, when I blurted out, "I can't! I have to be a minister!" Even in high school, when guidance people helped us to make decisions about the future, I put down "Ministry" as my choice, although I still stammered to an embarrassing degree.

I was able to get through my speech at graduation without trouble [It was not hard to be in the top ten percent of your class when there are only eleven in it] but I knew exactly what I was going to say. Before graduation night, I would go up on the hill in back of the house, a quarter-mile from anywhere, stand on a stump, and with a loud voice, go over it time and again. But for normal talk, I could only be fluent when I was mad or singing, and it did not seem appropriate to go through life always in one or another of these modes. Only after my freshman year at Cornell starting in the fall of 1942, just before I turned seventeen [which was a horrible year of stammering] did I decide that something had to be done.

I gained confidence in my ability to carry out a task, and I prayed mightily that I might be able to talk. It worked! [Now they have trouble getting me to shut up!] I am still a shy person inside, but I am outgoing now because I cannot serve my Lord adequately and remain shy. It's just a matter of doing what has to be done no matter how hesitant you feel! I will address this later as I come to training new chaplains for the racetrack. [Chapter 8]

By the time I was finishing high school, however, I had decided that my childhood call to the ministry and missions was childish imagination. After all, Rev. Brown was a missionary and I must have picked up on that since the call came so soon after hearing him. At Cornell, I was in the College of Agriculture, and the farm back home was calling me. I loved cattle and had sold my thirteen head of registered Guernsey cattle in the summer after high school graduation to go to college.

When my freshman year was over at Cornell, I worked full-time for my father in the potato farm business. In the spring of 1943, Dad's partner on the dairy farm decided to quit and take a job back in Akron, OH in a rubber plant. He had worked there before and, with the war taking so many of their younger workers, they made him a good offer to return. In March, I moved my recently purchased bunch of registered Holstein heifers to the farm and joined them with the young stock of Dad's. The herd began to grow.

Florence was my high school sweetheart and we married in June of 1946. We were actually in first grade together, although when people ask how we met, I like to tell them it was at a Travel Agency. She was looking for a vacation and I was the Last Resort!

By the fall of 1958, we had three children and a good dairy. I was looking forward to repainting the big barn my Grandfather Brown had built and putting on it, "Norman B. Evans & Sons." I loved farming and I loved cows! That fall, my pastor asked me to preach on Laymen's Sunday, the third Sunday in October. It was not the first time I had preached, but that sermon had far reaching effects – on me!

I had been active in my First Baptist Church of

Georgetown. I'd been a Sunday School teacher before I was 20 and a deacon soon after. I had served on the Board of Christian Education, was the Youth Group leader with Florence, had served the Madison Baptist Association in a couple of positions, and had been president of the Otselic Valley Sunday School Association. In short, I had done a pretty good job of hiding from God in His church!

After the sermon, I was complimented in the usual fashion, but I was disturbed. After our noon meal, my Dad and Mom came up and got all three children to take them for a ride. My hired man had Sunday evening off, so I headed for the barn about 2:00 P.M. There were a lot of chores to do with close to a 100 head of Holsteins. All afternoon, God spoke to me. No one else could have heard, but it rang through my head that He wanted me in the ministry. I prayed right back, "Lord, I can't go into the ministry! I have a wife and three kids!" "Lord, I can't go into the ministry! I have a farm and a mortgage!" "Lord, I can't go into the ministry! There's no way I can swing it!" And no matter what I said, no matter how I rephrased it, He kept right on telling me I was going to go into the ministry, that my excuses did not matter. I even offered Him one of my sons, hoping He would take a substitute. And He kept on telling me that it was "me" He was talking to.

What an uneasy afternoon and evening! Finally, about three-quarters through with the milking, I took the head off a Surge milking machine with my right hand, poured the milk out into the strainer over the milk can with my left, and just stood there on the barn floor. "Alright, Lord, I give up. I'll go into the ministry, but You will have to open the doors!"

Immediately, I had relief. There was actually a joy! It lasted almost a minute. By the time I had the milking machine on the next cow, I thought, "What is my wife going to say about this?" We talked about our decisions, and here was one I had just made that would affect her, and our three children in life changing ways! If she were upset, it would complicate everything! Scary thoughts and scary decisions!

I finished milking and had everything done about 7:30 p.m. I dawdled around before going into the house! How was this going to work out? Sunday night supper was on the counter and stove. I filled my plate and went into the front room where Florence sat crocheting in her rocker. I sat down across the room from her, supper untouched. "Well, I might as well get it over with. No better time than right now!" I thought to myself. I looked at her across the room and blurted out with no preliminaries, "Honey, what would you say if I was to go into the ministry?"

Her hands never stopped moving. She just looked up and said, "Nothing you could do would please me more!"

I just looked up and said, "Lord, that's opening the door a little quicker than I expected!" Florence had graduated from Baptist Institute for Christian Workers in Philadelphia in '46, the year we were married. She always felt that she should have been in some kind of Christian service when we married. So this was fulfillment for her!

Jumping temporarily ahead to 1976 because there is a post-script to my two calls to the ministry, I was in Ohio, working as a missionary on the racetracks under ABCUSA/ National Ministries, as well as the Ohio Baptist Convention and Race Track Chaplaincy of America. There had been no ceremony or anything to indicate that I was a missionary, just correspondence. In October, the Ohio Baptist Convention held its annual meeting in Cleveland. There I was called up to the platform where Bob Fisher of National Ministries commissioned me as a Missionary. I knelt as Bob, Stan Borden of the Cleveland Baptist Assoc. and Joe Chapman of the Ohio Baptist Convention put their hands on my head and prayed for me at my commissioning. While I was on my knees and my eyes were closed, I heard God's voice ringing in my head. "I told you that you were going to be My missionary!" I went back to my seat beside Florence speechless and with my eyes full of tears. It had been about 40 years since my childhood call to be a missionary. God means what He says!

Checking out my options for finishing my education for the ministry, I found that I could go back to Cornell on a part-time basis, commuting the 60 miles from farm to school, three days a week. So, in the fall of 1959, I started back to college to make up the three years that I lacked to graduate. It meant long days, both on the intervening days catching up on chores, and the days I went to Cornell, milking and hauling the milk to the station before breakfast, and driving 60 miles before 9:00 A.M. to reach my first class. Then, there was the drive home, which could get hairy during the winter in Central New York, and chores to help finish after I got home.

I learned to absorb lectures while taking notes, for there was seldom time to study with milking cows and all the chores and assorted field work that goes with a large [for that time] herd and a large farm. Close to three hours were spent in the car each day of classes, and it seemed that more and more churches wanted me to fill a pulpit as they found out via the grape-vine that I was headed into the ministry. I have often said that I farmed seven days a week, went to Cornell three days a week, and preached one day a week. The weeks were longer then and I was a lot younger!

One day in a particularly hard growing season stands out in my mind as extra long and strenuous. We'd had had no hired man since spring. All my crops had been planted at night, for it seemed with my days at school that I could get the ground ready before dark, but had no time to plant until night after milking and supper. I told my professor of Agronomy that I was now "planting by the moon" "What!" he exclaimed. Then I told him laughing that it was the only time I had to plant!

Summer was haying time. We were short handed, with only our two boys and myself to do all the work. Tim was twelve that year and Mark was nine. I mowed the hay, Tim did all the raking, and I baled when it was ready. We had three big, old, sixteen-foot flatbed trucks, each fitted with a drawbar by the drivers seat to fasten to a ground-driven hydraulic bale lifter, which picked up the bales and threw them over the truck racks. Tim would drive the big trucks and steer the loader onto the bales. Mark was on the truck-bed, moving the bales into even layers, building them seven tiers high. As the load got high, he would build up the front, back and off side of the load, leaving a space in the middle that was out of reach of the bale thrower. When they got that far, I'd come over from baling and throw up the bales needed to finish the load. They could unload at the barn onto a bale conveyor.

Haying was slow because we had no crew. When second cutting was ready, I stopped mowing first cutting to cut the second, which was finer and richer than the first. We stopped haying to get the grain harvested, and then returned to haying. Silo filling time came in the fall and we halted haying to put up the ensilage. By this time I was back at Cornell in the fall semester. One field of hay remained to be cut in October. I had mowed and then raked it, then had to leave for Cornell instead of baling. The forecast was for a clear day and a clear night, so I told the boys that when I got home and milked, we would bale that last hay.

On the days when I had classes, I had to get up at 3:30 A.M. in order to get chores and milking done, haul the milk to the station in town, wash up, change clothes, eat breakfast and be ready to leave for Ithaca at 7:30 A.M. On days when I had a lab class, I might not get home until 6:00 P.M. This day I arrived at 6:00, expecting to run right into the house and change clothes to milk, but the two boys were standing by the milkhouse door waiting for me. "We've already done the milking, Dad!" they announced with pride."

"You have?"

"Yeah, look in the milk-cooler!" So I looked, counted the cans, lifted some covers to see if they were full [they were] and turned to hug them. They had never milked alone before but they had done the job! With grins, we all got ready for the last hay job of the season. We even had a full moon and no dew that night, so we baled and loaded until all three trucks, two wagons and a pickup truck were filled and inside the barn. About 10:30 we went into the house for supper. I was <u>dead</u> tired, my head ready to fall into my plate, when little Mark piped up, "C'mon Dad, let's get going!"

"Going? Going where?"

"There's a few more bales up there. Let's go get 'em!" With spirit like that, a man can be real proud of his sons. I think I can say that my kids put me through college.

It was also a fun time. I enjoyed making friends, I enjoyed the opening up of new fields of study, and I enjoyed the repartee with both fellow students and professors, some of whom were younger than I was. An inexplicable happening occurred down on the Arts Campus in an Overview of History Course. We were seated in a half circle type of amphitheater lecture room, with tiered seats and a door at each end on the upper row of seats. The professor did not like dogs in his classes and Cornell was famous for its roving dogs of every breed and type, either going to class with their masters or fraternity "brothers," or wandering the campus or halls. This day, Prof. was lecturing on the Daniel Boone era and, since I was going on an outing that afternoon, I was wearing a fringed buckskin shirt. In the middle of the hour, someone opened a door and let in a huge hound. He stopped the professor from being heard with baying that would have done credit to a hound about three feet behind a "coon" heading for a tree! The dog ran baying around the back of the amphitheater to the center aisle, where he turned and came baying down to the front row of seats where I was seated. There he stopped and sat, with his wet jowls and slobber on my hand and notebook, looking into my eyes with a look of hound-love and with his tail beating a tattoo on the floor. Everybody, including the professor, was laughing. I took him by the collar and escorted him to the other door to put him out. As I returned to my seat everybody clapped. My face was very red. Nobody would believe me later when I said I had never seen that dog before! They all thought he must belong to the old Daniel Boone type student from the hills. Why he came to me is still a mystery!

It took me four and a half years to complete the three years of Cornell that I lacked and I graduated in January of 1964. I had started as one of the youngest freshmen and graduated as one of the oldest seniors! In fact, the local Mid-York-Weekly printed my picture on graduation with the caption, "Evans graduates after 22 years!" Some folks are slow to learn. During my first semester back in 1959, a student in the next seat in a class asked me if I was a graduate student. I replied that I was a part time sophomore, having matriculated in 1942. "My gosh!" he said. "That was year I was born!" I used to feel that being with young folks helped keep me feeling young.

CHAPTER 2

Trusting God and Getting Ready

**"Do your best to present yourself to God as one
approved, a workman who does not need to be ashamed
and who correctly handles the word of truth."**

[Paul, II Timothy 2:15]

My last two semesters before graduation from Cornell
were a time of physical and spiritual testing. What I
learned I will never forget. And while it happened to me, I
hope it can help others.

My back had bothered me for years, but what is a dairy
farmer to expect without a pipeline milker or a milking
parlor? You are up and down about three times to each cow
and when the milking machine is taken off, it's heavy with
milk! Things came to a head in the fall of 1962. I went to
doctors, osteopaths and chiropractors, trying to get relief.
Cornell had a medical service and they gave me an exami-
nation there. I was told to go to a specialist in Syracuse and

had a three-month wait to get a visit. He, in turn, told me I had a disk problem that would get really bad in anywhere from three days to three years. He told me what to look for in symptoms that would make a return call imperative.

Soon after I was dragging my left leg and could not move it except by swinging my body. Severe pain came with the leg problems as a calcium growth on a vertebrae was pressing the spinal nerve and sciatica made the leg helpless and like a thee-foot long toothache. Successful surgery took place in March of '63 and I came home with instructions of no lifting more than fifteen pounds. That would have been fine, as long as I did not milk cows and handle loaded milking machines.

I had been trying to sell the farm for several months, hoping to sell together the farm, the herd I had spent 20 years building, and the machinery in one sale. An appraiser had come from Cortland to give me a fair price. I had a buyer that I had promised first chance to buy, and he knew that my back was bad. He'd held off as it got worse, hoping I would come down in the price, which I had. He still waited. In the meantime, I had promised my young hired man an extra month's salary if he would stay with me until the farm was sold. He came to me one day with tears in his eyes. He'd been offered a good job three farms up the road, where the farmer friend of mine had had a heart attack. He was also about to get married and his fiancee wanted to stay near Georgetown. He was concerned about how I would make out, but the new offer was perfect for him. He got my blessing.

The next morning I was back into the milking, with my threen-year old son Tim, my only help. We were milking 62 cows with milking machines, [before pipeline milkers that carried the milk directly to the milkhouse]. In fact, we were still using milkcans, as I had put off investing in a bulk tank because we were about to sell. Production was high, with thirty-seven, 40-quart cans going to the milk station in town every day. Two of the cows were giving over 100 pounds of milk apiece each day. This boils down to the fact that I was lifting far more than fifteen pounds over and over each milking. Morning and evening milkings went pretty well, though I knew my back hurt. The morning after the first day of milking again, I had only milked a few cows when I was doubled over and could not straighten up. In pain, I had to stop. I drove to town and roused a boy out of bed to bring back to help Tim. Then I went to bed, gradually straightening my back. It took 45 minutes to ease myself straight. I went out and let the boys load the cans onto the truck so I could take the milk into town. Unloading was hard, but I stuck to it. Things got worse as the days went by. One morning I could hardly make it onto the truck. Once there, I hurt so much that I could hardly move a can. Another milk hauler came up behind me and unloaded my cans for me. I was able to get the empty cans back on board, but by the time I was on the way home, I was in agony.

I was hurting so much there were tears in my eyes. I prayed out loud in tears and anguish, both physical and spiritual. As I turned onto Lebanon Road, a quarter-mile from home, I was telling the Lord, "Father, I heard what I thought was Your voice, telling me to go into the ministry. Trying to follow that call I have gone back to college to study in preparation for seminary to prepare for the ministry. Now I'm almost unable to keep going; the farm is almost sold but my buyer is holding off because I'm almost at the end of my rope! Lord, **what am I going to do?**" At that very instant, as I went up the last hill before the farm, a "finger of fire" wrote across the road in front of me, from one shoulder to the other, the word, **"TRUST."** The beginning of the first "T" faded as the last "T" was spelled, and it was gone as I drove over the spot where it had appeared.

Talk about shock! I was stunned! "Alright Lord. Forgive me for not trusting. I will trust You for everything. Please help me trust and keep going. Thank You! Thank You! I'll start right now!" Those few seconds of my life are indelibly burned into my memory. What happened next proved beyond a doubt that what I had seen was a message from God.

I pulled into the yard. My son came to the truck. "What do you want me to do now, Dad?"

I told him to take the empty cans off the truck, put them on the racks in the milkhouse, wash the milking machines, scrape off the barn floor and put sawdust down. "I'm going to take the tractor and go mow some hay."

"How are we going to get it in, Dad?"

"I don't know, but it's past time we should have started, and we have got to trust and go ahead." I took the tractor and mower and started up the farm road. It bounced enough on the farm road that I had to drive it in low gear because of the pain. You can make what you wish out of the Biblical number "seven," but when I started mowing, I started on a seven-acre field of alfalfa, with a seven-foot cutter bar, and went around seven times. I'll leave the interpretation of that to someone else. When I came around that last time, Tim pulled up with the farm car [farm kids learn to drive early] to tell me that someone had called from Cortland to say they wanted to buy our farm, and that they had to know within 24 hours!

I started to laugh uncontrollably. Talk about TRUST-ING! Less than two hours had passed since the vision on the way home, and here was the answer to my prayers! I was laughing so hard with sheer joy that Tim was worried. "What's the matter, Dad?"

"I've got a lever! " I shouted, which made no sense to him. I had to explain that the assessor had told a farmer in Cortland that I had a farm to sell. He and his wife had come up in the early spring and I had showed them the farm and buildings. I felt I was honor bound to let my first buyer prospect make up his mind before I dealt with them, and they wanted only the farm: they had their own dairy. Their wanting to buy at this time was the lever that would push the first prospect into an immediate decision.

"Tim, put up the cutter bar and bring the tractor down the hill. I'll take the car. I've got a phone call to make!" I called my lawyer and confused his secretary I was so excited. "Call Dan and tell him to fish or cut bait!"

"What? What does that mean?"

"It means that if Dan has not come to terms with me within 24 hours, I've sold the farm to someone else!" He came to terms at once! TRUST! God had everything planned all the time, but I had a lesson that has come back to me many times! There are lots of Bible verses that tell us to trust God, and I could quote many of them, but that day I really learned what it meant to trust God in EVERYTHING!

We rented the house next door and moved there for a year. I recovered enough to serve the Madison Baptist Church in Madison, NY for a year while I finished my last semester at Cornell and prepared to go for my master's degree at a seminary. I picked Eastern Baptist Theological Seminary in Philadelphia, after checking out a couple of other seminaries and attending a prospective student's weekend at Eastern.

One of the seminaries we visited, before we settled on Eastern, was Andover Newton Theological Seminary in Boston, MA. There I talked with Dr. Cubby Rutenber at supper. The conversation went from spiritual things to a hobby of mine. I wanted to know what these professors of higher learning would think of the old country custom of dowsing for water. Prof. Rutenber wanted to see it work, so we went out on the campus and I showed him where the water pipes were buried. Little did I know then how he would remember that night!

Before we moved, we purchased a travel trailer and took a six-week tour to California and back. We had miracles on that trip, too, or we would not have made it back. However, that is not part of this story, except that God's Mighty Hand was upon us, still teaching us to trust Him in all things, and that He was preserving us for His work in the future.

Some may wonder why I was spending all these years in study, at Cornell and then Eastern. My denomination, The American Baptist Churches, USA, had passed a resolution some years before, that beginning at a certain date, ordination should not take place without four years of college and three years of seminary, or the equivalent. Before that date, it was up to the ordaining church or association of churches to decide on the qualifications of each person they choose to ordain into the Christian ministry. Ordination meant that recognition of any person regularly ordained would be honored in any other ABC church in the country. A minister friend had suggested to me when I was starting at Cornell, that I should apply for ordination before that deadline, so as to save a lot of time. My reply was immediate; that I did not want anyone in the future to think I had taken a shortcut. I was determined to study to be the best that I could be. I'm glad I went the full course, and I was in the pastorate all the time anyway.

I started my study at Eastern in the fall of 1964. I had thought that the Lord would find me a nice county church where I could serve as a student pastor. Was I ever shocked to find myself serving the Bethany Baptist Church in Camden, NJ! For those not knowledgeable about the area, Camden is across the Delaware River from Philadelphia. I read in a magazine once that, "Camden was the arm-pit of Philadelphia." Coming across the Ben Franklin Bridge from Philly, your first smell of Camden came from the Campbell Soup factory right under the NJ approaches! Strange smells in Camden were not unusual. There was a rendering plant with lots of smoke and smell that I had to go by every day. It ran day and night. Later it was raided, for the bloodmeal smell had covered the odors of the whiskey they made at night! Some city folk don't like the smells of a farm or race-track, but I still prefer them to the city smells.

Eastern was about 16 miles from our new place in Camden. It was necessary to travel on the Schuylkill Expressway most of the way. For a country boy, this was a horror! Locals called it "The Surekill Crawlway!" For three weeks, my stomach was so tied up in knots after traveling on it that I was afraid I'd get an ulcer. Since I realized that there ought to be an easier way of handling the situation, I figured out exactly which lane I wanted to be in and when to switch to another lane for the route I had to take. Then I just settled down to finding my "spot" and staying in it whether someone cut in front of me or not. Soon I could relax. The stomach settled down and the old farmer had done it again! Not too long after that that I could take on any of the wild folk who drove it every day!

The three years of seminary became five, as Bethany Baptist merged with Alpha Baptist at the end of my first year, and the merger called for a new building. I was deeply involved with planning and programming for the new build-ing and I had to cut my load at school. The new church organization was Hope Memorial Baptist Church and a new, round, 88-foot diameter building was put up at 36th and Hayes. When I graduated from seminary in 1969, the church was not yet finished, so I waited until December of 1970 so as to have a place for the ordination ceremony and celebration.

Seminary was a joy to me. As I studied, I could put into practice what I was learning. Besides, I was older than some of my professors, as I had been at Cornell. If this did not give me an advantage, I took it anyway! I had long ago told the Lord that if He was going to call me into the ministry in my old age, that I was going to enjoy it!

Dr. Thorwald Bender was a rather short man who taught Systematic Theology. He had been a farmer in his youth and a country pastor. We had a lot in common. One day he started the class lecture, as was his custom, with his elbows on top of a tabletop podium, hands clasped beneath his chin. As he talked, he would unclasp his hands to gesture. He slowed down, stopped and sniffed of his hands. Then he looked up and told us, "I picked some chrysanthemums this morning and, even though I washed my hands, the smell certainly lingers."

I spoke up from three rows back and replied, "I used to have the same problem Doc, after I had come in from the barn in the morning."

There were a few shocked gasps from some of the more genteel students, but Dr. Bender sniffed at his fingers again and said, "Yes, but of the two, I think I prefer the cow!" We farmers stick together.

Especially in my Christian Education classes [but in all of them they knew I was a farmer] I would inject a "cow story" to illustrate a point my teacher was making. One day I figured I had gone too far, as most of them brought a bit of laughter when I compared cows to people. I apologized to the teacher outside the door the next day, but she said, "Oh, no. I used one of your cow stories in a faculty meeting this morning!"

One girl in my Christian Ed. Classes was a bit of a snob; at least she had trouble with a country boy like me. My cow stories would always draw a grimace and an expulsion of breath to show her distaste for me. I ruined her [our] graduation exercises. Dr. Rutenber, who was receiving another honorary degree in that program, was our speaker. I watched him as he carefully looked over each person in the audience, nodding to people he knew, and who happened to be focusing on him. He came to the graduating class, all bedecked with caps and gowns, looking us over, one by one. When he came to me, he remembered that night about six years before when I had met him. His eyebrows went up and he gave me a smile and a wink. When he got up to speak, he greeted the audience as important speakers customarily do. The president, the dean, the faculty, the alumni, etc. Then he intoned, "And I greet the graduating class of 1969, including Norm Evans, who showed me how to find water pipes at Andover Newton!" I thought the girl who disliked my country ways was going to faint! She just sagged. Too bad, for I had just been trying to broaden her education!

I finished nine years in Camden and was happy there. Then I had a call that took me back to the Earlville and Randallsville Baptist Churches in NY. I had been interim pastor at Earlville for six months while I was still milking cows. Many a sermon had been worked on while milking or while driving a tractor! We had only been there a year, when the Rev. Dr. Joseph Chapman, Executive Minister of the Ohio Baptist Convention called to say they wanted me to come to Ohio and begin a new ministry there on the thoroughbred racetracks. I did not want to leave after so short a time of ministry, but eventually sixteen more months were to pass before things were ready in Ohio. We moved, just before the end of December in 1975.

CHAPTER 3

Meeting Problems Head On

"The Son of Man came eating and drinking, and they say, 'Here is a glutton and a drunkard, a friend of tax collectors and sinners.' "

[Jesus, Matthew 11:19]

"The racetrack! You'll sure hear a lot of swearing out there!" So I was informed when it became known that I was going to the racetracks as a missionary. And they were right. It was almost as bad as a junior high school!

Early in my first January at Thistledown, I was invited to the first meeting of the year of the Horsemen's Benevolent and Protective Association [from here on, the HBPA.] The president had just returned from racing in Florida, and he was very angry. Sometimes I have wondered about thoroughbred horses and their trainers. The horses are much higher strung than any other breed that I know of, and the thoroughbred trainers and workers seem higher strung than most people. Does one affect the other? Anyway, I had never heard so much swearing and yelling at a meeting in my life! A few of the men kind of looked over their shoulders at me while it was going on, presumably to see if I had passed out in shock. Some of them came over after the meeting to apologize to me for the swearing. I told them that I even used some of those words in my chapel services, but in a very different way, and invited them to come and see! Another said, "I'm sorry you had to hear all that, Chaplain." I responded by telling him that I had heard all those words before, but instead of worrying about what I heard, they should worry about what God heard.

My first chapel services were small but they grew. One afternoon, I decided to have a Bible study and passed out Bibles. When I had them all on the right page, I started a study. Everyone was following me verse by verse except Slim. He was running his finger down the page with a broad smile on his face, reading ahead and not hearing me at all. Suddenly he jumped to his feet and said, "Hell, Chaplain, listen to this!" and read us a passage that was especially good news to him. I grinned as he read it and silently prayed, "Lord, I hope You'll accept Slim's enthusiasm."

That first summer of 1976 at River Downs, I found when I arrived that a summer softball season was getting started. The teams had a rivalry that had been going on for years. Some trainers even put "ringers" on their teams by putting them on their "badge lists" [each trainer gives a list of workers to management]. The persons on the list are then fingerprinted, photographed and given a plastic badge, which is supposed to be in sight for security purposes.] The teams were all picked when I got there, but I innocently asked if I could have a team. The response was enthusiastic, as some of the better teams thought that the Chaplain's team would be "fresh meat." I put up a notice that I needed some players and I soon had a team. None of them were considered good enough to play for the regulars. I found that my team named themselves, "Rev's Rejects!"

They played with enthusiasm, but while we never won a game that summer, we had fun. One night we played the "Feed Men," a team consisting mostly of very tall and strong brothers and a father, who delivered horse feed every day and were as rugged as could be. Games were five innings in length, due to starting time and nightfall. We held the Feed Men to nothing for four innings, to everyone's surprise. The mother of the several brothers turned to me and asked, "Are you getting help from Upstairs?" I took off my hat, bowed and replied, "We have a Merciful God!" at which the spectators roared with laughter. Yes, we lost in the last inning, but had a good time.

We did win a game the second year against the "Starting Gate," and they were so ashamed that they disbanded and never played again.

I had realized that the evening games were places where I could meet more people and talk with them. One night there was a make up game between two good teams. I went and sat on a bench getting to know people and letting them know me. Suddenly I heard, "Chaplain! You've got to umpire this game! We don't have an umpire and you're the only neutral person here!"

I was shocked, as I am no ballplayer and knew only the major points of the game. "I don't know the rules! I can't umpire!"

"That's all right, we'll teach you the rules! Come ahead!" So, with misgivings, I went in back of the plate.

"Let's see, you count the balls on the left hand and the strikes on the right?

Thus affirmed, the game started. One of my troubles was, when someone hit the ball foul, I would follow the ball with my eyes and unclasp my fingers. Then I would have to ask the catcher what the count was. Very embarrassing. Soon there was a hit and a dash for first base. They looked at me as I raised my hands above my head and yelled, "Safe!"

The pitcher came off the mound and said, "Ah, Chaplain, I don't want to interfere, but usually, when someone is safe, the umpire bends and puts his hands out to the side, down low."

"Sorry, I'm a pastor and a chaplain, and I give the blessing and the benediction with my hands raised to Heaven."

"OK, team, we can go with that." Soon there was a hit to mid-field and a close play at second. The pitcher was there, the second baseman, and an outfielder or two as the runner slid into base in a cloud of dust. They all whirled to look at me.

"Sorry. Everybody was in the way. You'll have to settle it yourselves." Two men jumped off the bench, eager for a chance "to help settle it."

The runner got up before there was an argument, dusted the seat of his pants and announced, "I think I was out!" At the end of the second inning, the pitcher came off the mound and proclaimed in a loud voice, "Boys, we're behind! Let's get going," and attempted to try to invigorate his team with a long string of profanity.

I yelled back, loud enough to be heard in Kentucky across the Ohio River from the field, while pointing my finger at him. Both teams stopped dead in their tracks when I yelled. "Harry, you're teaching me the rules in this game, but you just broke one of the rules in God's Rule Book! That's a STRIKE!" with the appropriate right arm sweep down and out. Made my point. After the game both teams talked together, saying they had never had so much fun in a game before, and also agreeing never to ask the Chaplain to umpire again. I got a lot of backslaps that night, and Harry never met me again without telling everybody around us to "watch their language."

One time I walked up on three trainers discussing something. The one facing away from me was talking, while the other two smiled in greeting. As the talker turned to see me, I said, "Don, do you want that prayer answered?"

"What do mean, prayer?" he stammered with a look of astonishment at me.

"You just made a public prayer. You asked God to damn someone. Do you really want that prayer answered?" They laughed, but again my point was made without rancor as I hugged the talker in his embarrassment.

At River Downs that summer, a little boy, probably closing in on his fifth birthday, was most everybody's concern. He was the son of a trainer and his wife who had a few horses there. They let the child roam with no supervision. At that time, there were deep ditches draining the Backside. With horse manure, blowing dust and trash, the water was filthy. The boy wore nothing but a pair of shorts and was as dirty as the mud in which he played. His vocabulary, when told to get out of the unhealthy ditches by passing pony people or other folk, was well beyond the capacity of normal adults in being as dirty as the mud which covered him. The next spring, he walked up to me, dressed with shirt and shoes added to his wardrobe, pushed out his hand to me, and spoke in a solemn tone, "Chaplain, I went to kindergarten last fall and I want you to know that I've quit cussing!" I don't know who had gotten to him, but he stayed out of the ditches that year.

Early on in my first month in the racetrack ministry, I dropped into a seat at the breakfast table in the track kitchen at Thistledown, before daylight. Across from we was a man just starting to eat his eggs. My usual greeting to people I had not met was, "Hi! I'm Norm Evans, the new Chaplain at the track."

His jaw dropped. "What are you doing here with us sinners?"

"Oh, I'm a sinner too!" He looked at me in amazement,

his fork suspended halfway between the plate and his mouth. "I'm a sinner, but I'm a forgiven sinner! I'm here to tell about forgiveness." His eyes went glassy, food forgotten. He was digesting something far more important than food! In fact, that was all he could handle at that moment. His food was forgotten as we talked longer.

The racetrack people call themselves "Trackers." They see themselves as in a different world. They are a community within themselves, cut off from the world by the fences around the tracks and the security gates. The fences are to keep people out, not to keep them in, although the public might see the fences as enclosing horses and people who are strangers and may smell different. One trainer sat with me in the track kitchen after I had been there about a month. "Chaplain, how do you see us as different from people on the "outside?"

"Well, I find you more honest than folks on the outside." No one had ever accused this particular trainer of being honest before. He looked shocked.

"How do you mean?

"It's like this. When you swear, you swear in front of me, not behind my back." His face turned a bit red. "No, I mean it. A lot of people have two faces. They try to act pious before a minister, but that face is dropped when he goes away. Another thing, if a tracker has a problem, he looks me over, sizes me up, tells me he has a problem, and honestly describes it. In church, some folks are so double faced that they tell me their wife's sister's husband's brother has a problem, and we both know he is talking about himself. It's refreshing to be where things are out in the open, where I may be able to help!"

It is essential that a racetrack chaplain be "non-judgmental" at all times. Non-Christians almost expect us to judge them for everything and tell them what they are doing wrong. They may be doing something wrong, but they usually know it and don't need us to tell them. Florence went with me to the track when she could and was with me at Thistledown in the kitchen one day. Several trackers were with us. A good-looking pony girl was in the conversation and suddenly blurted to me, "I just can't figure you out!"

My astonishment showed as I said, "I thought everybody could figure me out!"

"I can't. The first time I met you and you told me you were the chaplain, I just knew you were going to ask me when I went to church last, but you didn't. You asked me my name and where I was from. The second time I saw you I just knew it was coming, but you smiled and talked to me about my work and family. You still haven't asked me, but *I haven't been to church in a long time!*" By being non-judgmental, loving people and getting them to talk about themselves, they become your friends and are ready to receive what you have for them. I became a tracker to them. I was a part of their society and <u>earned</u> their trust.

As I said in the beginning, I am an American Baptist, but I did not go onto the tracks as a Baptist. I was a Christian minister, conservative and evangelical if a title has to be put on me. [Actually, it all depends on where you come from. Up in NY's north-country are many Conservative Mennonites. Their Bishop told me once that they used to be Amish, but their group wanted to use electricity and machinery on the farms. They were then called "Liberal Amish" until they joined the Mennonite denomination. Here they were called Conservative Mennonites. I've been called Fundamental by some and Liberal by others. So such "brands" depend mostly on the angle of view of the "brander," and he or she can be on either end of the theological spectrum.] I was there to minister, to love, to help and to bring folks to a decision for Jesus Christ as their Savior. When people asked me on the track what denomination I was, I avoided it if I could. When I told them I was a Baptist, the exclamation was usually,

"But I thought Baptists were against more things than other churches!" [Which had to include racetracks with gambling.]

One day I had my hiking shoes on walking a shedrow, meeting people where they were and being conversational when I could, and I ran into an elderly man at the stall of his horse. It had just rained and the shedrow path was muddy and full of puddles, which could not be avoided. The trainer told me he was from Arkansas. When I told him I was the Chaplain, he started to rub his chin. His chin had about four day's growth on it, which makes rubbing your chin a sensory thing. [Sorry, ladies. You'll never know!]

"Are you a minister?"

"Yes, I'm an ordained minister."

"Where's you church?"

"You're standing in it!"

He looked at me in astonishment and then drew up his right knee. Slapping it, he said, "Well, there's one thing for sure, **you're no Baptist!**" I doubled up in laughter and then told him I was, indeed, a Baptist. He proceeded to tell me his story. Seems he married the daughter of a Baptist deacon back home, but the deacon was always bothered that his son-in-law was taking his daughter to the racetrack. To him the track had to be the abode of sinners, for everyone knew that gambling was there. One spring, the deacon came over to his farm and made a proposition to him. "Son, if you plowed that piece of ground over there, and prepared it for planting, we could go halves on a little cash crop. We could put in potatoes and I would hoe and care for the crop, and go halves with you on the seed and fertilizer."

"How much do you think it would cost me, Dad?"

"Probably about $50."

After a little thought, he responded, "Dad, if I took $50 out to the racetrack and put in on a mare, I'd know in a few minutes that I'd lost the $50 and I wouldn't have to wait all summer to find out!" Dad was not pleased.

Alcohol is as much a problem on the backside as it is in the rest of the world. The horses seem able to cope with it. I've seen horses that were dangerous for a sober man to handle and would act protectively to a groom that was semi-drunk. This is maybe the one job in the world where a person can get by without being sober! Horses seem to be able to sense a defenseless person, child or someone sick. Returning horsemen told me one spring of a mean stallion in Florida that had to be handled with utmost care when being groomed. He would kick and bite at every opportunity. One morning his groom had an epileptic seizure and dropped in the stall. The stallion straddled him, took him by his collar and moved him so that he was half out from under the webbing, and stood over him screaming until someone came running!

Practically every track chaplain has started an Alcoholics Anonymous group on the Backside. Some go to local groups wherever they go to race. Many come to the chaplain to ask for help. Many don't want help. But the racetrack is one place that will give a man a second, a third, or even more chances that they would not get on the outside. I well remember the day that a man was expelled by the stewards for excessive drunkenness. He was in bad shape. Trying to help him in his present state was rather hopeless, but I listened to him tell every Bible-story he was ever taught in a conglomeration; they were all mixed together from Adam to Herod. Later that afternoon I saw him wandering the road by the river on the backside of the track. Stopping to talk with him again, he asked for help, over and over. He was holding a can of beer in his hand. I told him that I could possibly help him if he really meant he wanted help. However, to show me he was serious, he should throw the beer can over his shoulder. He could not. He went back to the Kentucky side of the river and as one tracker told me later, "They had to throw him in the loony-bin before they could take him into detox!"

Later that summer I had a group of visitors to the track from a church in Illinois. We were sitting on a wagon with seats on the far-turn watching a couple of races, as they had a schedule to keep that would not allow them to visit the front-side. Several trackers gathered around us and entered into the conversation. I mentioned that the track gave people second chances where the church often did not, and told about the man just mentioned who had recently returned after his experiences in hospital and detox. He now had five horses under his care and was sober. I had just talked with him earlier. He told me, "Chaplain, when I saw a bird flying in the air, I used to think he might fall. It bothered me so much I had to get another drink! Now I am free again!"

The trackers around me added to the story, and I pointed to my friend Red, who was standing there with a can of beer. "Now Red used to have a lot of trouble drinking hard stuff, and I've got him down to beer, but I can't seem to get him off the stuff entirely."

He grinned at me and told us all, "Chaplain, would you believe that I've got a daughter in Kentucky who is a minister?"

"Sure," I said, "did you just see those horses that went around the turn? It's not always pedigree that makes a winner!" We all laughed and Red and I hugged each other.

I had started a pair of Brown Swiss bull calves for oxen in the early part of 1981. Since you cannot get ox-yokes from Sears & Roebuck any more, I had to make my own. A large beam had to be shaped by hand with primitive tools to make the yoke. Evenings in the River Downs summers often had me out in front of my tack-room or later my chapel trailer, working on an ox-yoke. Calves grow and it takes several yokes to keep up until they are grown. Invariably, two or three old alcoholics would drift by to watch and then ask if they could take over. Most expressed faith in Jesus

Christ, but had never let Him take charge of their lives. I'm glad I am not God, to make final judgment. Florence came to the last service at River Downs one year and I had announced her coming. She had been at Judson Hills Nursing Home in Cincinnati for recovery from a bad fall. When I brought her up to the outside service in a wheelchair, a whole line of old alcoholics came up to her, hats in hand, and told her they had been praying for her.

At Beulah Park one fall afternoon, I walked into the bar section of the track kitchen where several had gathered to watch the televised races. I greeted them, and one man, an African American, who was sitting at a table covered with empty beer bottles, turned to me and announced to all, "I'm sorry chaplain. I know I told you that I would see you at one o'clock, but I sat down to have a beer, and one led to another, and I forgot all about it!"

The one o'clock appointment was news to me, but I did not tell him so. I said, "Hey, maybe I've got a worse problem than you have!"

"How can that be, chaplain?"

"Well, you could stop smoking completely if you wanted to, right?"

"Sure!"

"You could stop drinking completely if you wanted to, right?"

"Sure I could, Chaplain!"

"Well, I weigh too much, but I can't quit eating! If you'll go to AA, I'll go to Weight Watchers!" He got up from his buddies and hugged me. How can I condemn someone with a speck in their eye when I have a 2X4 in mine. I will admit to burying more people with alcohol and smoking problems than overeating, but I know the side effects of being overweight.

River Downs once had a problem jockey named Billy. He was sick and drank hard stuff to excess. I had not been able to reach him, but one night he literally staggered to my chapel trailer after a service. A glass of liquor was in one hand. "Chaplain, I need help. I'm sick. I need help." One look told me he needed help from people who had been where he was and would not be conned. I knew I was in over my head if I tried to handle this alone, although I would have prayed for help and tried if other help did not show up. The Lord had timed everything to perfection. I looked up and a pony man drove around the corner. He had been in AA and offered to help when he could. I raised my arm with a finger pointing up and he wheeled right in. I turned to the guard shack a hundred yards away and with my arm and finger still raised, motioned to the guard, another AA man. He came running. As he ran, another car came around the corner and he saw my arm and pulled in. I had three AA men right there within about a minute! With a tough love from "being there," they took charge.

Billy was gotten into detox and the hospital, had surgery, and was recovering pretty well. I had called on him in the hospital regularly. My final day at River Downs I went to see him again. "Billy, when you were drunk, I did not try to talk to you about Jesus. You were too drunk, but I prayed for you. I've called on you here when you were in much pain and I prayed with you, but I knew you were hurting too much to think well. Now you are recovering, sober and out of pain. Are you ready to talk seriously about Jesus?"

He swung his feet out of bed, reached for my hand and said, "Yes, chaplain, I am!"

CHAPTER 4

Diversity on the Track

"...I have become all things to all men so that by all possible means I might save some..."

[Paul, I Corinthians 9:22]

The diversity of people on the Backside is amazing. I soon learned to say, "Good morning!" in eight different languages, although that was about as far as I could go. People were cheered to hear at least a couple of words in their home tongue, accompanied by a smile. There were some that spoke no English at all and a big smile with an English greeting worked wonders. Some words in return were in languages unknown, but they knew they were loved.

I tried to learn Spanish but I had a peculiar problem. Spanish is spoken differently in different Hispanic nations. There was Spanish from Cuba, Puerto Rico, Mexico, New York City, America's Southwest, Honduras, Argentina, Chile, Peru and other countries and areas. I would practice a phrase with one person, and then try it on another. "No, no!

Say it this way!" And in my confusion, I usually got it completely mixed up. Added to that, I do not have an aptitude for languages, maybe because of my stammering problem as a child. I had to develop a smile-sign language approach to some. And it worked!

Chico was from New York City. One summer I had a Spanish-speaking assistant from El Salvador. I figured he might get to Chico, but he was bewildered; "I can't understand him!"

A fellow Hispanic spoke right up. "Chico don't speak Spanish, he speak Puerto Rican!"

One very hot day I went by Chico with a greeting, and he replied, *"Mucho caliente, cappellan"*

"What's that mean, Chico?"

"Mucho hot. Verrry hot!"

"Right! *Mucho caliente*! I'll remember! *Mucho caliente, mucho caliente."*

The next morning it was not hot; it was raining. I got out my wordbook and thus prepared, went in search of Chico. Not finding him, I went into the track kitchen where I saw a friend from Chile sitting with a Mexican lad. I approached, took off my hat and bowed, saying, *"Buenos dias, Señor Santos! Mucho mohado!"*

"No, no, no, no! You no speak Spanish so good!" he yelled loud enough to get everyone's attention; "You no want *'Mucho mohado'*, you want *'Mucho awa,'* much water. He *'mucho mohado,'* " pointing to his companion, "He wetback!" Everybody roared with laughter. My efforts in languages were appreciated, and we all enjoyed the teasing about my clumsy progress. Oh, well, no *comprendo*!

Early on in my speaking to churches about my ministry, I had used Acts 1:8 as a text;

"But you will receive power when the Holy Spirit comes upon you, and you will be My witnesses in Jerusalem, Judea, and Samaria, and to the uttermost ends of the earth."

I pointed out the usual interpretation that Jerusalem was "our" city, Judea "our" area, Samaria that place where we did not go very often, and "the earth" meaning all our foreign missions. But Samaria had a special meaning. Samaritans were despised by the Jews, who considered them mongrels and beneath their station in life. Who have we despised? Who are our Samaritans? Where don't we want to go? The racetracks and racetrackers seem to be modern Samaritans to a lot of Christians, and Samaria therefore has come to be in our Jerusalem!

In the December, 1976 issue of *The American Baptist* magazine I reported on my first year on the Ohio tracks. Part of the article was a description of my life on the track and of the trackers themselves.

"Most of the people are unknown or shunned by church people. Many have stories of outright rejection by church people They are to many what the "publicans and sinners' were to the Pharisees. They are often lonely, with the problems and vices that go with it. Their culture and language are different, but they live as a community closed off from the rest of the world. A few from the outside enter it on their own terms; doctors and lawyers may walk their own horses. A few trainers and jockeys make a splash in the outside world. But there are many who live, work , eat and sleep on the Backside, never leaving except to move to another race meet [and many move in the back of a horse van.] Some can't read and write. Some are misfits, unable to cope anywhere else but in this supportive community, while some could make it anywhere. Millionaire or pauper, intellectual or simple, it's hard to tell them apart. All colors, all kinds, all in need of Jesus Christ, and neglected until now.

"I live alone in a 'tack' room during the meets in Cleveland and Cincinnati. Only in Grove City [Columbus area] can I live at home. I'm thankful for Florence – as one groom said, 'That wife of yours; she's in yo' corner!' She comes to the track as often as she can. [When she can't, she sends "care packages.] "If the way to a man's heart is through his stomach,' said one trainer, 'then the way to a man's soul is through Mrs. Evans's cookies!'

"It's exciting, exhausting and a new frontier. Some have come to 'church' for the first time in their lives and may not know that most preachers don't preach from a pool table! Many are being renewed in their childhood faith in Jesus, and some have accepted Him as Savior and Lord. All have a friend. The sick are visited and the injured comforted. Counseling takes place in my tackroom, leaning on a manure wagon, at the cafeteria table, in the rest room or by the winner's circle, early until late. I translate 'sheep' into 'horses.' I am a tracker, living among those I serve."

Grove City, Ohio, was one of those towns where trackers were very much looked down upon. I had supposed that my entry into Ohio had been publicized much more than it had, for when I showed up for a meeting of the Grove City Clergy, they were very flustered. They did not really know how to take me! Gradually they came to accept me, even coming to one morning breakfast at the ClubHouse! Yet when I set up a Grove City Clergy Day for them to see the ministry in action, only my friend, the Catholic priest dared to attend. Near the end of my years in Ohio, the Chairman of the Clergy group did recognize me in a statement he made at a meeting. On Easter Sunday that spring, quite a number of my racetrack "parishioners" were baptized in several of the Grove City churches. "Brothers, we have not realized the extent of Norm's ministry to us in our churches!"

But the prejudice was there, nonetheless. One morning early I got a cup of coffee in the track kitchen and sat down with a groom named Buddy. He looked out of sorts. "What's up, Buddy? I asked

"The people in this town are crazy! Last night I went to Judy's bar and had a beer and a sandwich for supper. Then, seeing there was no traffic on Main Street, I walked across to come back to the track. A cop car pulled up and told me I was jaywalking. So I says to the cop, 'let me walk back and go up to the light.' 'Nope,' he said, 'get in the car.' He took me to the station, booked me and wanted $10.00 for the fine. I didn't have $10.00! So he says I can make one phone call before locking me up! So I called Judy at the bar. She came up and paid my fine and drove me home! I can't wait until this meet is over and I'm out of here!" I cringed. He might have called me, but no church in town would have listened to his phone call.

Not that I would fault the police if they arrested a drunk and disorderly person, but they began to press the racetrackers too hard. One day after lunch a respectable blacksmith looked me up to tell me he had gone to the corner bar at Main and Park and had a sandwich and a beer for lunch. As soon as he left, two police on foot closed in from each side of the door and took him in for public drunkenness. He had horses to shoe and did not take the time to argue with the authority, but paid the fine and came to the track steaming. I told him to hang on, that I thought I could put a stop to this petty stuff.

I sought out the former mayor of Grove City, who was a lawyer and a horse owner. Finding him with his trainer, I told him about what was going on, [and I only mentioned a bit of it.] I gave him a message for the Chief of Police and any other town officials he wanted to tell. "Trackers are easy to identify with work clothes and an ID hanging on their shirt. But the police don't know me! If I hear of this happening one more time, I'm going to let my beard grow for a few days, put on old clothes and walk into the bar with fellow trackers. I do not drink, and I'll not have a beer, but I'll come out staggering just a little bit. If they pick me up, tell them it will be on television and I'll put an end to these shenanigans!" It worked. There was no more harassment of my trackers.

The depth of the prejudice ingrained in church people

was brought home to me with force when I spoke to a Men's group of a church in a racetrack town one night. After explaining my ministry and storytelling about my people and experiences, bringing in scripture and salvation in Jesus Christ for all people, one deacon stood up with a dark frown and fury in his face. He exploded with, "YOU MIGHT JUST AS WELL HAVE A MINISTRY TO <u>PROSTI-TUTES!</u>" When he expelled the "P" in "PROSTITUTES," he could have blown out a candle six feet away!

There was a stunned silence, and then all the men turned to me for my response. "Well, Jesus did," I replied with a shrug of my shoulders. The deacon looked at me with the proverbial "if looks could kill" expression and went out, slamming the door behind him. It did open up a discussion. Two of the men told the pastor, to his surprise, that they had been grooms at the local track. The angry deacon made my point better than I could have done, but I know he would have reprimanded Jesus for talking to the Woman at the Well!

As I worked with people of all backgrounds, I found that there was little problem in establishing a relationship. I had been a farmer and knew both work and riding horses, I had been in the city, I had traveled a bit, and I had a very eclectic set of interests and hobbies. I had an education, knew big words, and knew enough not to use them when a small one would do. [I eschew obfuscation!] People of all back-grounds from high to low, from east to west, were easy to know. Florence pointed out to me one day that all my experiences and interests were being used of God to reach people for Jesus. She then read Paul's words in the chapter title from I Corinthians 9:22, reading verses 19-23, where Paul literally became like the people he served in order to minister to them. I became a tracker, to walk with my people in all weather, just as God became incarnate in Jesus, that He might walk with us. It is a very humbling thought.

Diversity was pronounced in my people. For instance,

Larry was a groom. My first spring at Beulah Park I found him working near the far end of a certain barn, and you always knew when you were approaching his barn. The decibel level of track sound went up fast there, and most of it was Larry roaring at those around him. He was "intellectually deprived," to use today's politically correct language, but nobody used that term. He was an orphan, raised in an institution for those like him, and taken out in adulthood by a trainer who used him both on his farm and at the track.. He could not read, write or count, but could walk horses, "water off" [using a hose to fill the individual horse drinking buckets] when told, and "muck" stalls [no description is really needed for this.] He was teased by almost everybody who thought themselves superior in any way to Larry. Most of them knew better, but Larry was almost always mad and swearing a blue streak at the top of his lungs most of his working day.

My attempts to talk with him were rather futile, for either I could not understand Larry, or he could not understand me. So, I began to avoid his end of the barn when making my rounds. One morning about a week later, I was set to walk away again, when God's voice sounded loud in my head. "You are to minister to ALL My people, not just the ones you choose!"

I was stopped in my tracks. I prayed, "Lord, I'll try to get to Larry, but I need your help! You know what has happened when I've tried!" I kept trying until we all got to River Downs.

One night Larry came up to me and said, "Ol' Man," [he couldn't say 'Chaplain,' and it didn't do much for me, but under the circumstances it was acceptable.] "Got to go store." He had to say it three times before I realized what he was saying! Here was my opportunity to reach Larry! I thanked God right then and there, and told Larry to get in my van and we'd go to the store. We went up the hill to a business district, but every time I asked Larry if this was the store, he shook his head. Finally he pointed his finger and told me, "There!"

We went in together and wandered the aisles. He picked up what he wanted, went to the counter, laid down what he had, then reached in his pocket and took out a handful of bills and change, letting them take what was necessary and handing the rest back to him.

Larry had an uncanny knack of showing up at the end of a weekly chapel service [usually held in the outer office of the Racing Secretary's area] just as I said, "Amen," and we started on the cookies and punch that Florence always sent down with me. [Maybe he was smarter than I thought!]

One day Big Jim came to me and said he had heard Larry playing a harmonica the night before. He was amazed and so was I. When I next ran across Larry, I asked him to come to the chapel services earlier, before the cookies, and suggested that he could help me with the music. He showed up at the next one, a bit late, and got into a chair at the back. A man was playing his guitar and we were singing with him. I nodded to Larry and his big hands went to his mouth and a note or two came out, but someone in front turned quickly to see where the sound was coming from. Larry's face got red, he stopped playing and squirmed in his seat. "Larry, please play for us as we need you to help us." So Larry became a regular, playing by ear, not bad, and blending with whatever was being played.

Entering the track kitchen a few days later, I moved over to a big table where Larry was having his lunch with his boss and several other trainers. I spoke to all of them with my hand on Larry's shoulder. "Hey, guys, Larry can play the harmonica! Can you? I can't!" Larry sat tall with a smile. I wondered if Larry had ever heard that he could excel in anything.

One night, Larry remained behind to help me move

chairs back into my tack room. He stood there looking at me and blurted, "Ol' Man, I felt awful bad when my 'muvver' died." The Lord had now really given me the chance to speak to Larry one on one!

I put my hand around his shoulders and led him to sit beside me on my cot. "I felt awfully bad when my mother died, too. But Larry, did you know that when you feel bad, Jesus feels bad right along with you?" Telling him about Jesus showing compassion for Mary and Martha when their brother died, and in the Sermon on the Mount saying that those who mourn would be comforted, I put my arm around him and said, "Larry, if Jesus lives in your heart, you never have to be lonely!" We closed with prayer and Larry went out with both a smile and tears in his eyes.

That fall we were together again at Beulah Park. Favorite hymns were being called out by number and one turned out to be "Jesus Loves Me, This I Know." Larry was sitting beside Florence, whom he called, "Mom," and he was our only music that evening. I started out the singing but Larry was not playing. Instead he was singing loudly, "Jesus loves me, this I know, For the Bible tells me so..." My eyes filled with tears as I realized that Larry was the first person on the track [and the last one] that I had tried to avoid! God does know what He is doing!

On the opposite end of the intellectual spectrum was a horse owner from Cincinnati who came often to walk his horses. He was psychiatrist with a large practice in the Greater Cincinnati area. He told me one day when we were talking about education, that the year he got his degree, he was the youngest doctoral candidate in the nation. I noticed, but it seemed that nobody else did, that he often walked his horse behind Larry, doing the same thing! Opposite ends of the spectrum in IQ, but equals in walking hot horses!

CHAPTER 5

Reaching Out For Christ

**"She will give birth to a son, and you are to give him
the name Jesus, because He will save His people
from their sins"**

[Matthew, Matthew 1:21]

He was a fighter. He'd run to an argument, hoping there would be a fight, just so he could get involved. In fact, the stewards had once ruled him off the track for hitting a security guard. That's a no-no. He had been let back on with a cautionary lecture. Somehow, Big Jim and I hit it off. He became a regular at the track chapel services, helpful in every way. He loved to sing, although as the Track Superintendent Jimmy Henson said one night, "I've never heard such a bunch of bad singers in my life!" After a while, Big Jim would run away from an argument. Trackers got to talking about the change in him. In fact, if I were being looked for, people would seek out Big Jim to find out where I was. In spite of being a one-time fighter, he was bashful. One night after a service, he came up to me with an open hymn book, turned to the old hymn, "I Am Satisfied With Jesus." He stuck it in front of me and blurted out, "Chaplain. This says it for me!" Then he blushed, turned and went back into the crowd.

Knowing he was embarrassed, I just gave him a big grin, but the next morning he came into my office. "Jim, was your showing me that special hymn your way of telling me you had accepted Jesus as your Savior?"

"It sure was, Chaplain!" Some time later, he came to me to ask me to pray for his mother, who was in the hospital in Dayton, OH. We prayed right there and then, and I told him I was going to be in that area in a couple of days and I would visit her.

I got to the hospital, found her room and introduced myself as Big Jim's chaplain at the racetrack. She began to cry. "All my other children go to church with me, but Big Jim went his own way and now he's all but lost out there at the track! He'll never find Jesus there!" She cried for the son she was sure would never find the Lord. When I told her he had accepted Christ as Savior and Lord under my ministry, she nearly fainted! When the tracks were closed and Big Jim had a chance to get home, he faithfully attended church with his mother.

If someone did not show up or was even late, Jim would be the one to tell me, "Chaplain, Johnny's sick this morning!" or, "Chaplain, Pops hasn't shown up today!" And I would be off to see if I could help. He became my ears and eyes to help me.

* * * * * *

Bill King was a beginning trainer and pony man at Thistledown Racetrack in Cleveland during my first months as a track chaplain. He accepted the Lord as his Savior during a one-on-one conversation. A few days later, he came to me and informed me, "Chaplain, I think the Lord wants me to preach! Can you get me a church to preach in?" That seemed kind of sudden, but who am I to discourage what someone feels is leading from the Lord? So I told him I thought I knew a church with an evening service that would let him try his wings. A few days later, I told him it was all arranged. He would be the speaker on Sunday evening, a couple of weeks later.

"Great, Chaplain! Now, what should I preach about?"

I had to laugh to myself, but I leaned across the table in the track kitchen and replied, "Bill, you could talk about Peter, or you could talk about Paul, but if you talk about Bill King, you are an authority. Tell them what He means to you and what He has done for you, and you will be heard!"

The morning after his first preaching experience, he found me before daylight in the kitchen and excitedly told me, "Chaplain, it was wonderful!" I couldn't wait until Sunday evening, so I got up early and knocked on all the doors of my apartment complex. I told everybody there would be a Sunday morning Church Service in our apartment! There were about twenty-five people there, and there were three decisions for Christ and a healing!" The evening service at the church did not hold the excitement of the one in his apartment!

* * * * * *

Sonny was doubly addicted to both drugs and alcohol. He was a pony man and exercise boy. I went home during a picnic for the trackers one dark Tuesday. [A "dark" day is a day without racing: it has nothing to do with the weather.] I had stayed long enough to eat and take photos for the Ohio edition of the Racing Digest before I left. When I got back the next day, Big Jim was looking for me. "Chaplain, Sonny needs help! He got drunk at the picnic yesterday and beat up his wife! She's kicked him out and he looks terrible!" I went looking for Sonny in all the crowd of trackers busy at their morning tasks. I finally saw him, walking dejectedly, head down, looking as if his world had come to an end. Stepping out in his path, I extended my right hand, palm up, and let him walk into it.

"Sonny, I'm here to help, if you will accept it."

He grabbed me by both arms and with tears, exclaimed, "Chaplain, I've never needed help so bad in my life!" We went back to my tackroom/office and we sat and talked. He knew he needed Jesus, and during our counseling, took Christ as his Lord, but he was not ready yet to admit that he was an alcoholic. That took several more days of counseling. I went and talked with his wife at their trailer, and she let him come home. The tragedy was that she had married an alcoholic non-believer, and he was so changed that she could not accept him as a Christian. She left him this time and Sonny was heartbroken. He needed constant Christian companionship, so I took him up to Anderson Hills and introduced him to Pastor Glen Ray. His church took him in, and he was baptized, and well received. They cared for him on Sundays and I discipled him during the week.

Sonny was functionally illiterate. But he learned to read that summer by spending a lot of time with the "Good News" New Testament that RTCA supplied the trackers. It was a joy to see him grow!

On the last Sunday of December that year, Sonny drove up from Cincinnati and got to our house just before we left for a Sunday morning speaking engagement in a church about 100 miles west of Grove City. We took him with us. He'd come because he was scared. New Years Eve was coming in a couple of days. "Chaplain, I can't remember a New Years Eve that I didn't get drunk. What am I going to do this year?"

I called Anderson Hills and found that they were having a watch-night service on New Years Eve. He had no idea that Christians did that, but he went, enjoyed Christian worship at midnight, and stayed sober for the first time. Sonny remained sober. It's been nearly twenty-five years.

I had to be away from the track one evening when a Chapel service was scheduled. I had engaged a former jock's room valet, who was a lay preacher in his church, to cover for me, and had given Big Jim the key to my chapel trailer so he could open up. My speaker never showed up. The next morning, the track was abuzz with the news that Sonny had led the service the night before! As it was told to me, after waiting a few minutes past the hour, Sonny had nervously said, "If Chaplain Evans was here, we would sing." So they got out the hymnbooks and selected several to sing. No preacher showed up.

Then Sonny said, "If Chaplain Evans was here, he would lead us in prayer." So he led in prayer.

After another look out the door to see if the fill-in speaker was in sight, he said, "Well if Chaplain Evans was here, he'd read some scripture." Then Sonny struggled and read something from his New Testament.

Another look out the door, and, "If Chaplain Evans was here, I guess he'd say something about now!" And Sonny led in thoughts from his scripture, then closed in prayer. When I heard the story, I was elated! Better to have Sonny lead in his own simple way than to have someone else come in to lead!

The change in Sonny did not go unnoticed. From grooms to management there were expressions of pleasure, and God was given the credit!

* * * * * *

6:00 P.M. one afternoon, I was bushed. My game knee was hurting and I was tired, so I left the paddock area between the clubhouse and the grandstand in a misty rain, and headed for my tackroom/office at least a half-mile away.

I had reached the end of the far turn, walking by the rail, with hundreds of cars in the parking lot on my left, when a very audible voice said, "Stop!" I stopped, looked at the cars to see if anyone was there, and found that I was alone. So I started walking again. "STOP!" came the voice again.

I turned around. No one was following me and no one seemed to be among the cars. "Anybody there?" I yelled, feeling rather foolish. No one answered. "OK, Lord, if I should stop, I'll stop, but I sure see no reason to!" Just then the starting gate bell went off as the horses left the gate over at the three-quarter chute, half a mile away. Leaning on the rail, I dumbly watched the horses, until right in front of me, a horse went down, plowing up a wall of wet sandy dirt in front of it. Clarence Diel was the jockey, and he managed to roll under the inner rail, then lay immobile. Now I knew why God had told me to stop! I swung under the rail, ran across the track and slipped under the inner rail to Clarence. "Are you all right, Clarence!"

"Chaplain, how did you get here?" he replied in utter amazement.

"Never mind that, are you hurt bad?"

"I don't know, Chaplain. I can't seem to breathe good."

I laid hands on him and prayed for him right there, as it took the track ambulance a minute or so to get there. I went back to the track doctor's office, where I found him sitting up. Seems he'd had the wind knocked out of him by an errant hoof as the field of horses went over him. We thanked God.

On Labor Day, there was a turf race on the inner track. I wanted to get a good picture of Tom Baker, the track photographer and a friend of mine, shooting the finish in front of the tote board. Having permission from the stewards to climb an empty judge's stand just beyond the wire, I took the photo, but saw a flash of white jockey pants just as the shutter closed. I came down as quickly as I could and ran to the inner rail and hedge of the turf track, to find that

Clarence's horse had gone over the rail, and there was Clarence, laying on the ground again. "Are you looking after me special, Chaplain?" he asked.

"Well no, but God seems to be! He's had me in the right place twice in the last month, just to be able to pray for you!" Again, he was only banged up and still able to ride.

Later in September, Clarence went to Thistledown to ride. My assistant, Chaplain Sharp, was standing near the paddock talking to the ambulance driver when he suddenly said, "Get in, Chaplain! Horse down by the sixteenth pole!"

The ambulance pulled up to the jockey, lying in the track, and Chaplain Sharp jumped out and said, "I'm the Chaplain. Are you hurt?" It was Clarence. He started laughing. Every time he went down, there was a chaplain there at once. His response was a joyous laughter! God was looking out for him!

* * * * * *

Sam was a pony man. He was an alcoholic, but the track seems to be a place where both horses and people tolerate alcoholics, at least to a degree. I got him into a service once at River Downs, when he stopped by the door to talk. Once inside, he asked for a hymn that I said I didn't know. "I do!" he said and taught it to me. I never lived that one down! One night Sam and a blacksmith [actually a farrier] were in a local Grove City bar together, and Sam was ribbing the blacksmith about the fact that his pony was past due for new shoes.

The blacksmith responded with, "Well, I've got my tools out in the truck. I'm ready now!" Sam walked back to the track, saddled "Ole Buck" and rode him into the bar. There he was shod, I presume with somebody at the door checking for the police. Finally, Sam rode him back to the track, and a very nervous bar owner breathed a sigh of relief. He could have lost his license had he been caught with a horse in the bar!

On one of my return trips to Beulah Park, as a trainer for new chaplains, I saw Sam. He was in the last stages of alcoholism. His arms were like pipe-stems, his body seemingly nothing but bones, but with a little potbelly. "Sam," I exclaimed, "You look like death warmed over! Do you know what is happening? You can't keep on living like this! The next thing will be bleeding from your mouth as varicose veins in your neck break!" I did pray with him right there, and it must have made an impression on him. I saw him a few years later, surprised to see that he was alive, and that he had regained weight and strength.

"I quit drinking, Chaplain! I'm living with my sister in North Carolina now, and I'm making my living by small motor repair. I go to church with her, too!"

For years, Sam has kept in touch with me by an annual phone call and a card at Christmas.

* * * * * *

In my first summer at River Downs, in 1976, Steve Cauthen turned sixteen and started riding. He rocketed to the leading jockey position almost at once. His mother was a trainer at the track with a string of horses, and his father was there as a blacksmith. Meeting him one morning in my rounds, I stopped him to have a short talk. It had to be short, as he had more horses to ride before the track closed at 10:30 A.M. "Steve, you are going to be a great jockey soon, and if I could, I'd like to give you some 'old man' advice.'" He grinned and gave me the go-ahead.

"You are very fortunate to have your parents close by and be able to live at home. Some of the jockeys are thousands of miles from home, young, and living rather high if they can. Look at Tony G. up at Thistle. He is said to have a $1,200 bar bill every week at the Holiday Inn across the street from the track. Some day he will have to stop racing, and he'll wish he had invested that money instead. Look over there. See that former jockey? He has to walk a horse before breakfast in order to eat! Let your parents help you with your money. Don't drive a Mercedes or something, just because you can afford it. Save, scrimp, and when you stop racing, you'll be able to do anything you want! You'll have the funds!"

He thanked me very politely, which was one of his trademarks, especially noted in England, where he spent several years of his career. Little did I know how accurate my prediction was, for in 1977 he raced all over the country, and hired a financial advisor. News came through his family that he had recently purchased a Kentucky horse farm.

In 1978, Steve rode Affirmed to the Triple Crown, winning the Kentucky Derby, the Preakness and the Belmont. While a bunch of horses have won two of the Big Three races, it has been twenty-five years since Steve rode Affirmed to victory in all three. Funny Cide won the hearts of the people in 2003, but at the Belmont Funny Cide was overtaken in the stretch by both Empire Maker and Ten Most Wanted, who had both sat out the Preakness. It's a tough grind to do all three. Affirmed's chief foe in 1978 was Alydar. In the combined distance of these three great races won by Affirmed under Steve Cauthen, Affirmed's total combined lead was only three-quarters of a length! In the stretch at the Belmont, the lead kept changing, as the two horses ran beside each other. Suddenly, as they neared the wire, Steve switched hands with the whip and hit Affirmed on the left hip instead of the right one. That is not an easy trick. An old jockey had told Steve about it when he was just a boy, and for years, Steve practiced changing hands, sitting astride a bale of straw in his father's barn. To control the horse, one must have a firm grip on the reins; that must not change when the right hand comes up to take the reins and the whip is passed to the left hand. Horses are creatures of habit, and Affirmed was used to feeling the whip on his right hip. When suddenly he felt it on the left hip, he was startled enough to put on the extra effort that put him ahead by a nose.

I have used that race as the basis of a sermon several times, for I really believe, without knocking Alydar's jockey, that if Steve had been riding Alydar, Alydar would have won the Triple Crown that year. In the end, Alydar proved to be the better sire, for a good number of his progeny have gone on to be top horses, while Affirmed's get [offspring] have nearly always proved disappointing.

My use of it as a sermon is the comparison with the Four Spiritual Laws illustration of a circle depicting our lives, with a chair in the center. If we put Jesus into that chair to run our lives, instead of ourselves being there, we lead a Christ oriented life. I invite my audiences to put Jesus in the saddle of our lives and turn the reins over to Him. With Jesus in control, we'll be able to have the lead at the far turn and not break down in the stretch!

* * * * * *

Mr. Ted just generated respect. He was a black man of some years, who was Mr. Ted to everyone, including all those of his color. He came to the services at Beulah Park, where I first met him. He came with a trainer, who was his close personal friend. In talking with them at their barn one day, I found that they were going to ship to Green Mountain Racetrack in Vermont when Beulah ended its spring racing days. They had been together for several years, and they told me that River Downs was too hot for them: they were heading for New England together. He had gotten some horse leg medicine in his eyes and had a hard time seeing. One night at a Chapel service, Florence handed him a hymnbook and put her hand on his shoulder when she did so. At the next Chapel service, he stood up to tell everyone that he had hesitated to take the book because of his eyes, but when he opened it, he could read again! Ted said to me, "That wife of yours, Chaplain, she in yo' corner!"

I was very surprised to find Mr. Ted at River Downs when I got there. "Mr. Ted! You told me you and Barney were going to Green Mountain! How come you're here?"

"You're my man, Chaplain. I decided to go where you go!"

We traveled a bit together that summer, up on the hill to do shopping and occasionally to eat together. I learned a lot about the black community through him. One time he'd had a young white man as a friend and they went into a restaurant to eat. When their orders came, Ted noticed that the waitress stayed in a door looking back, and that the cook had also shown his head. His white friend announced playfully that Ted's plate looked better than his own did and switched plates. When he did, Ted saw the waitress put her hand to her mouth with a shocked look. As his friend started to eat, Ted grabbed his hand to stop him and got them out of there. His food had been tampered with to make him sick, by all the circumstantial evidence.

Mr. Ted did not carry loose change in his pockets; it made them wear out according to him. He carried his change in his ears! He knew just what coins would fit over one another and he could carry up to $3.00 worth of quarters tucked into his two ears.

Ted always wore a fresh, white shirt every morning. I found his secret one-day when he wanted me to take him up the hill to a dry-cleaner. He took in a load of dirty shirts and came out with about twenty, cleaned and pressed white shirts! No groom I ever knew dressed like that!

He told me a story one-day that came from a black preacher. It seems that in the black community, it was the custom to sneak up on someone at Christmas, and surprise them with a "Merry Christmas." The one who was surprised had to respond with a gift of a coin or candy. If you failed to surprise your target, no gift.

"Satan was sneakin' up on God, who was walking about heaven deep in thought. He managed to get close and surprised Him with a 'Merry Christmas, God!' God never looked around; He knew who it was. He just responded with, 'You can have Louisiana, Georgia and Alabama!'" The preacher continued with, "You know, it's been Hell down there ever since!"

* * * * * *

Born October 1, 1899, Howard King was our connection with the "Old West." Trackers liked to gather around him in the kitchen or in his tackroom and get him to talk about his past. It was in the 1860s that his grandfather moved from Mexico, Missouri to Lockhart, Texas to try his hand at cotton farming. He brought with him his eight sons and two daughters. The boys all decided that cotton farming was hard work, but they enjoyed training horses. This was the day of the mustang in Texas, and ranchers had a variety of different mixtures of horse bloods. When grandfather died, the boys all went to work – on horseback. The oldest, George, became a key man on the trail. While all the boys drove cattle and horses up the Chisholm Trail from Texas to Nebraska, George made the trip eleven times with longhorns and five times with horse herds. He knew the trail, the waterholes and the Indians and was paid extra for his knowledge.

Being a cowman myself, I was very interested in his description of the cattle drives. Most of their drives had 1,500 to 2,000 head of longhorns. If there were more, they tried to spread them out. The longhorn breed was especially adapted for the long drives, as their horns made them stay apart from each other, and air could circulate through the herd. This kept them cooler. Our present English or European breeds of cattle would get too hot in a long drive, due to more fat and shorter horns.

Howard told me, "There was none of this John Wayne stuff, shooting and hollering. Why, those steers actually gained weight on the way to Dodge!"

Once the King brothers took a herd of horses all the way from Texas to Florida, swimming the Mississippi on the way!

Howard used to sit at the feet of his father and uncles and soak up the stories of the cattle and horse drives. He was too young to enter the army in WWI, but he and his father broke horses for the government, horses for both the Cavalry and workhorses to pull the caissons. After the war, he and a brother trained rodeo-bucking horses. The trick was to find the right horse and build its ego. By grabbing the top rail of the corral and getting off, he let the horse think it had thrown him. His horses were among the cream of the crop in the 20s and 30s. He spoke of Barrelhead, Spider, Glass Eye and Midnight, all famous in their day.

Bucking horses in the ring all have a bucking strap, which is a strap from the saddle, that is cinched as far back as possible. One of his prize bucking horses got loose one night and disappeared. Howard laughed as he told of meeting a young lady riding that particular horse about a year later. He asked her if she knew she was riding a famous bucking-horse, which he named. She was indignant! The horse was well mannered and a perfect ladies horse! He convinced her to let him put a bucking strap on and demonstrate. The horse went into his bucking routine. When he took the strap off, he was again a ladies horse!

Howard rode his track pony to exercise his thoroughbreds every day, but his family worried about him. In the summer of 1979, as he was nearing his 80th birthday, he called me over to his barn one morning. "Chaplain, now that I'm almost 80, my family has insisted that I get a younger man to work with me. I want you to meet John, from Kansas. He's only 75!"

I ministered to Howard, but it was only a year or so later, after he finally retired and went to Texas to live with his son, that he accepted the Lord in a definite way. His son Jim reported to me that before he died, he talked to his family about my ministry to him on the racetracks.

* * * * * *

The rail by the entry chutes was a place to stand and converse with trainers and owners who came out to watch their horses in morning exercise. One morning at Beulah Park a young man and woman of jockey size stood there as I came up. I introduced myself as the Chaplain, but was brought up short by their shocked looks. "Are you a born-again Christian?" she blurted.

"If I wasn't, I wouldn't be here!" I shot back with a smile. It seemed that they were Ron and Brenda Copeland, Christians, and Ron had been a quarter-horse jockey who wanted to break into racing thoroughbreds. They became close friends and helpers in my ministry.

Ron applied for a jockey's license, but the stewards said he had too much experience and refused to license him as an apprentice. Since an apprentice has a weight advantage, Ron thought he should appeal to the Ohio Racing Commission. While the appeal was going through the proper channels of time and red tape, Ron had to eke out a living for the two of them by exercising horses in the morning. Finally, the Racing Commission ruled in his favor. In the Fall meet that year, two days shy of the end of the meet, Ron was the leading rider. One of his mounts that day was Bayside Bill, who broke a leg at the eighth pole. In the resulting fall, Ron lacerated a knee so badly that a tendon was exposed. By the end of the day, Ron was no longer the leading rider.

A visiting reporter asked him if he was bitter. "Not at all!" said Ron. "I thank the Lord for the success I had at Beulah Park. I got a chance to ride for some top horsemen, a chance to show people what I could do, and I'm deeply thankful!"

Ron was exceptionally strong. In fact, when you see the jockeys in the jock's room in various stages of undress, most of them look like a little Hercules. Ron worked out at a Florida gym lifting weights one winter while riding at Tampa Bay Downs. The gym manager wanted Ron to stay in Florida for a while to wait for the Florida Weightlifting Championships, as he figured Ron would easily take the Florida state title in the 110 pound weight class. Ron declined and came to Beulah Park to ride because "you can't eat trophies!"

* * * * * *

To be born in Ireland on St. Patrick's Day is a cause of celebration to an Irishman. Such a man was "Irish" MacLaughlin, with special pride in being Irish and a brogue that set him apart. Irish won our hearts with his stories when questioned about his life. He had gone to England when he started into his teens and was a good steeplechase jockey. Wanting to expand his abilities to the States, he signed onto a freighter headed for America. The freighter was lost at sea but he was rescued and entered the USA and went to the tracks where he immediately became a jockey. He told me once how many bones he had broken both in England and here. However I cannot remember the exact number. His body and his walk showed the effects of the rough life and broken bones. He "retired" from being a jockey to become a horse owner and trainer. In Irish's earlier years had worked with some wealthy owners and expensive horses.

His home and small stable were located just south of Grove City and he raced mainly from Beulah Park, shipping to River Downs or Thistledown if he had a horse that fit a race and was ready. He was well known as a specialist with horses with behavior problems and several other trainers would get Irish to go out in the morning to exercise horses that the regular exercise riders did not like. One morning he had just entered the track at the three-quarter chute and started down the backstretch when a young horse upended him. He told me he landed on his head and kept bouncing along. "When ya goin' to fall, Dummy," he said to himself. He sprained his neck badly but did not go to a doctor; he just wrapped a towel tightly around his neck and kept going. Liberal applications of horse liniment helped, but he worked in pain. Nights were difficult for him as the pain often kept him from sleeping well.

Irish and his wife Doris were always at the Chapel services at Beulah Park. He loved to sing the hymns and his favorite was "The Old Rugged Cross." During the time it took for his neck to heal Doris bought him a second-hand piano. At night when he could not sleep he would sit at the piano and try to play by ear. One night, without ever having had a piano lesson, he sat down at the piano in the rec room Chapel Service and played "The Old Rugged Cross" with both hands and all ten fingers!

* * * * * *

Jockey Pat Day never raced at my Ohio tracks but is a close friend. The reason he never raced in Ohio can best be explained by comparing racetracks to baseball. Baseball has the major leagues, minor leagues [or farm teams owned by a major league] divided into A, double A and triple A teams. Most players are sent to the minors when signed up and improve their skills there until called up to a better A team or the home team in the majors. Horses are similarly rated. The majors in horse racing are the big tracks like Belmont,

Saratoga, Hollywood Park, Santa Anita and a few others. Churchill is in the majors until after the Kentucky Derby when it reverts to something like Triple A. My tracks in Ohio would probably compare to double A most of the time, attracting better horses at some big races with better purses. Steve Cauthen started in Ohio but never came back as his skills were needed on better horses at the bigger tracks.

Pat Day raced at bigger tracks than those in Ohio but we met through Race Track Chaplaincy of America. Pat became a Christian in a hotel room experience that transformed his life. As he tells it, it probably saved his life as well, for he was deep into drugs and alcohol at that time. He became a witness for Christ wherever he went, helping our chaplains at every track where he raced. One chaplain told me that Pat Day preached and gave his testimony at his chapel service the night he raced there [a well known jockey does a lot of flying to reach tracks where a trainer makes it worth his while to ride for a big race day.] Several trackers went forward at Pat's invitation to receive Christ as their Savior, but several more sought out the chaplain the next day to tell him they had hesitated the night before but now wanted him to help them accept Christ, too!

Pat Day has won the Eclipse award for jockeys eight times. In 2002 at Saratoga, he broke the record for the most purse money ever won by the horses ridden by one jockey. Pat has been a great help to RTCA and has served as National Vice President and as our industry representative. His autographed picture of us standing together, which is on top of my computer, looks like David and Goliath!

* * * * * *

A slender young man came by my chapel trailer one summer at River Downs. His name was Ted and he hailed from Michigan. Just discharged from the Army, he came to the racetrack looking for work, where he started as a hot-walker. Talkative, it did not take much to draw him out about his experiences, but only to a certain point. He was on the abortive flight to the Iranian desert in April of 1980 where he was to be one of the rescuers of our embassy captives. I marveled at his youth to be on such a mission, but I guess the Army considered him ready. That was the disastrous event where two essential helicopters collided at the rendezvous site and the rescue team had to be flown home. He had no idea where the planes were heading until well into the flight to Iran, after having been roused from sleep in the dark and told to get ready for a mission.

He also told me he had been badly hurt while at Fort Bragg where he jumped off the roof of the biggest building there. Seems he had been on angel dust and thought he could fly. He had a history of drug usage and alcohol even before he went into the service. Still, somehow, he stayed relatively close to me all during the meet and on to Beulah Park that fall. I did not understand why at the time but I knew he was testing me. He would ask for a ride and then fail to show up on time. There were many little aggravations that built up and I think he was trying to see if he could get me angry. I stayed calm and collected to see how it played out. He was always at my services. His mother was remarried that summer and he came to me because he had nothing to wear to the wedding except his work clothes. Out of my batch of clothes that were given me, I outfitted him with a suit, shirt and tie, even a pair of shoes. Fit was approximate but they were clean and he was pleased.

As the season wound down at Beulah Park in early December, I had him put his luggage in my van right after our last chapel service and waited to take him to the bus station. Before I started my van I turned to Ted and said, "Ted, you've been with me all summer and fall, but I don't know where you are in relationship with Jesus. You have heard invitations to accept Christ as Savior at all the services, but before you leave, I want to know where you stand."

He stared straight ahead through the windshield in the darkness and finally told me what had troubled him all along. "Chaplain, I was raised in a Christian home and grew up in the church. My father did not go to church and eventually left Mom and three of us kids to fend for ourselves. Mom played the organ and we kids sat on the front seat with her when she wasn't playing. I idolized the pastor and he helped me in growing up without a father. I was active in the youth group and I was baptized by immersion when I was in my early teens. Mom decided she should get a divorce from my father after many years of being alone. One Sunday morning the pastor asked Mom to stop playing the prelude music and come to the front seat with us. He then told us that he and others in the church thought that it was inappropriate for her to play the organ in church and be getting a divorce!"

By this time Ted was shaking and tears were running down his face. His own father and now his minister had betrayed him! Now I knew why he had been testing me! He wanted to know if I would let him down like his father and minister! "I left the church that day and started drinking and trying drugs. I kept on when I was in the military, but I've almost stopped since I jumped from the roof and almost killed myself at Fort Bragg." I was crying now as well.

I put my arm around his shoulders and pulled him to me. He sobbed on my chest. I began to pray, and I covered a lot of "waterfront" as I did. First, I asked that the minister be convicted of his sin in driving Ted and his family away from the church family they needed, and I prayed that that minister would seek forgiveness from God and learn about the love of Christ. I prayed for Ted and his future and asked that the Holy Spirit would guide him from there on and that God would bless his life and lead him into a good job. I prayed for Ted to have the strength to live free from those things that would hurt him, and to remember his early commitment to Christ before his betrayals. We both had to wipe our faces after the prayer. I took him to the bus station. I never saw him again.

* * * * * *

As I walked the barns and shed-rows each day to greet people and talk if they had time or wanted to see me, there was one young fellow who evaded me. His name was Jim and he was a groom. If I came upon him when he was holding a horse, he would immediately call to a fellow groom to come hold the horse; he had to go elsewhere. I never got beyond introducing myself. I was quite aware of his problems with drugs and drink, and he did not want me around. One early evening during the next meet, I was walking back to my chapel trailer when Jim caught up to me and said, "Good evening, Chaplain!"

I was so utterly amazed that Jim would give me greetings that I stammered in my response as I asked him how he was doing. "A whole lot better than last year!" he responded.

"Tell me what happened, Jim."

"Well, last year I was on every drug that came my way, drinking hard, and my language was mostly swear words. M-f was my favorite term. But it's all different now!"

With a smile, I asked him what had made the difference.

"Well, I was climbing a power pole."

"You had to be high on something to do that!"

"I sure was! I got to the top and was hit by 30,000 volts. A lot of people have been killed by less than that. It hit my arm here," as he showed me his forearm with a three-inch circle burned down almost to the bone. It was mostly healed but pretty ugly. "I sizzled and sparked, and I hate the sound of that big bug-zapper over there on the pole. Before I was tossed to the ground I did two things. I said, 'Oh, God! And

I thought of you.' "

By this time we had reached my trailer and we went in. My eyes were wet because of his last statement. He did not "go forward" as is required in some churches nor did he use the "formula" of asking for salvation that is so often used. But Jim had been divinely changed in that instant before he hit the ground. We prayed together and he left. I had a feeling of joy and humbleness.

He came back the next evening. As we sat and talked in the trailer, he said, "Chaplain, I didn't tell you the whole story last night. You see the voltage in that electrical charge evidently sealed off much of my stomach. I can't even eat a whole hamburger before I'm full. I've already lost ten pounds and the doctor says I'm going to keep on wasting away until I'm gone! And I'm only twenty-one!" He had tears in his eyes.

It may seem to be the wrong thing to have done, but I laughed heartily and put my hands on his shoulders. "Jim, you can't tell me that God saved your life up there on that power-pole cross just to let you fade and die! God did it to show you His power and to let you know you had a life to live for Him!" Then I prayed in joy that God had indeed saved him and that he had work for him to do, that he could eat enough to get strong and live in joy instead of fear of early death.

Jim had lost his job when he was out on injury but when he came back he was put on someone's badge list so he could be on the track. Every day he would get a list of ship-ins [horses coming in that day to race] and stand in the guard shack until they pulled in. Sometimes they brought their own help, but more often than not the trainers hoped to pick up a hanger-on to help. Jim was there first, often getting a horse in an early race and one in a late race so he could do two. He did so well that he got more horses than he could handle and got his girl friend to help. He did better than he ever had working as a groom for a stable. His spirit was contagious. The trainers began to ask for him. He had one of the best work ethics on the track.

Most of the River Downs horsemen went to either Beulah Park in the fall or Latonia in Kentucky, which ran all winter. Jim went to Latonia and continued his hard working ways. I was at Latonia early the next spring to visit the chaplain down there when someone reached around from behind me and nearly squeezed the breath out of me with a bear hug. As he released me, I turned and here was Jim with a huge grin on his face. "Pretty strong, huh?" God had answered my prayers.

* * * * * *

Ron Ennis was a groom. He was a small man and not very talkative but he was a poet. His education was not extensive but he had been brought by Christian parents and what he was taught stuck in his mind. He wrote poems on most everything: paper bags, overnights and such scraps of paper as he could find. Here are some of his poems, just as he spelled and wrote them. Forgive the errors; the words came from his heart.

> The Feeling of Christmas!
> It's that time of year
> When Christmas is near
> And all of the people is full of good cheer
> While shopping for gifts and presents galore
> To celebrate birth of God's only boy
> God gave us his son on this Christmas day
> In hopes that we all would follow his way
> So this Christmas morn with your family all
>   near
> And filled with good spirit and all Christmas

cheer
Remember one thing on this Christmas day
It's <u>never</u> to late to bow down and pray.

My Dad 4-28-84
I'll tell you a story of a man I once knew
He was so beutiful and real loving too
He gave us his love and raised us all right
Through all of the hard times
Both day and the night
He cheered us all up when looseing his sight
And we never knew he was going that night
But Lord Jesus Christ was right by his side
And said to my father your kids will servive
So now you all know that beautiful man
And I hope and I pray I'm as much of a man
– as My Dad

<u>The</u> Winter at Latonia!
When you make it from the fall to the spring
You just can't wait for the robins to sing
You're really lucky that you're alive
Cause <u>GOD </u>only knows how you had to
    servive
You went through the rain and went through
    the snow
And worked long days at zero below
But at the end it's well worth while
Cause then you'll know that your <u>Christ's</u>
    child

Just for you Chaplain
We all go to church yes me and most friends
And we hear the good words that <u>OUR</u>
    Chaplain sends

And when I think to myself what a fine man
    he is
Cause deep in his heart to him we're his kids
So thank you Norm Evans and lovely wife
    too
For all of the joy that we got from you.
3-1-84

I have maybe twenty of his poems, simple yet full of
faith and heartfelt expression. He could not talk but his
poetry said it for him. I cherish the poems that I have.

* * * * * *

When news of the pending arrival of a chaplain came to
Beulah Park, the track photographer, Andy Anderson, heard
about it in the track kitchen. "He'll never make it! We'll get
rid of him!" was his immediate response to the news. Andy
was born in 1902 and had worked uninterruptedly at Beulah
Park since it opened around 1925. He was an institution at
Beulah and had known more "greats" than anyone I'd ever
know. Everyone on the track knew Andy and practically all
of them had been in front of his Hasselblad camera at one
time or another. Since I was also a photographer of sorts I
gravitated to him.

His domain was the Winner's Circle where he photographed every race at the finish and then the posed picture
with the winning horse, jockey up, along with the owner,
trainer, groom and assorted friends. The result was a color
photo of the finish at the top of an eight by ten and the posed
photo below. I talked to Andy a lot in the Winner's Circle as
well as the track kitchen where he ate his lunch. He was
wary of me at first but warmed up when I did not get in his
way as he went about his business.

One noon in the kitchen he told me something of his life.

His first wife had died of cancer. She had been devout and Andy had prayed mightily for her, but to no avail. When she died Andy lost any faith he had and started drinking quite heavily for a time. Eventually he remarried and stopped the heavy drinking. He put a question to me. "Chaplain, I can picture Jesus on earth but so help me, I can't fathom God. Would you come to the Winner's Circle between the first and second race today and explain God to me?"

I was there at the right time and when he had gotten all the information he needed from the program and the tote board, we sat down on two folding chairs in a corner. I started with the scripture from Colossians 1: 15-20.

> "He is the image of the invisible God, the firstborn over all creation. For by Him all things were created: things in heaven and on earth, visible and invisible, whether thrones or powers or rulers or authorities; all things were created by Him and for Him. He is before all things, and in Him all things hold together. And he is the head of the body, the church; He is the beginning and the firstborn from among the dead, so that in everything He might have the supremacy. For God was pleased to have all His fullness dwell in Him, and through Him to reconcile to Himself all things, whether things on earth or things in heaven, by making peace through His blood, shed on the cross."

Pointing out that Christ was the image of the unseen God, and that God wanted all of Himself to be in Christ, God had sent Jesus to us so we could know what God was like. I told Andy to hold up his index finger and look at it at arm's length. The finger was in focus but the horizon was blurred. Then I asked him to focus on the horizon and now the finger was blurred. "See, Andy, God gave us a focusing point! Now, through Christ, we can see God! Your photos are sharp because you know exactly where to focus. Focus on Jesus and you'll understand God!"

We sat there and I showed Andy some other scriptures and then we prayed together. I tried to drop by the Winner's Circle every day as he continued to have questions and he began to pray with me. Because of his age, some of the younger officials who lacked respect for their elders teased him. One day Andy came to me sputtering. "So-and-so just accused me of talking to myself as I was driving into the parking lot today! I wasn't talking to myself; I was praying!" Another time he mentioned to me that, "I was thinking of what we talked about yesterday as I went down to the "Praying Circle…" I didn't correct the slip of the tongue; because the "Praying Circle" is the "Winner's Circle!"

* * * * * *

In the fall of 1986, RTCA asked me to go immediately to Belmont and Aqueduct in New York City two or three days a week for a "couple of months" as Interim Chaplain to save our ministry there. A Hispanic chaplain had left and management and horsemen had requested an Anglo chaplain who could speak Spanish. We had to swallow hard to accept this obvious prejudice, for RTCA has Hispanic chaplains among our very best. But since they were paying the bills, we tried to meet their requirements. In the meantime, there was some thought among management that a social worker might meet their needs. So I was to fill the gap until we could find a Spanish speaking Anglo and persuade everybody that a Chaplaincy program was exactly what everybody needed.

At that time I was the pastor of Castorland Baptist

Church in NY's North Country, as well as serving RTCA part time as Chaplain at Large. After clearing things with the church, I headed for New York City.

On arrival at the track, I first checked in with Security to get my badge. Then I had to find the Chaplain's office, the office of the HBPA and NYRA [New York Racing association] to tell them I was on board and start getting acquainted. The first job I followed up was with a native of Mexico who spoke no English. His name was Gabriel Barbano and he was the hinge point of a great change. Gabriel was in the hospital with knee surgery. By pointing and a few rudimentary words, plus a lot of smiling, we communicated. When I prayed with him, he knew I was his chaplain.

As the days and weeks went on, we developed a good friendship. I took him to follow-up visits and read all his instructions for him, took him to fill prescriptions, and visited him every day that I was there. We went to Friendly's restaurant one evening for supper. He looked over the menu for a while and asked, pointing to one of the meal photographs, "What is?" We were both laughing as I moo'd like a cow or clucked like a hen, but we understood each other.

Gabriel had been left behind when the Woody Stevens stable went to Florida that fall. In theory, he was to go back to work for Woody on his return in the spring. I was concerned about him, as the time for my "couple of months" of interim Chaplaincy came closer and closer to the end.

Horsemen had been repeatedly asking me when they were to get a fulltime chaplain. All I could say was that RTCA was working hard at it. One noon I called Carol Marino of San Mateo, CA [our executive secretary at the time] to ask about progress. She told me that a candidate had appeared in CA who was an ordained minister, spoke Spanish, had formerly handled and raced thoroughbreds and was interested in the position. The only problem was that after three interviews with three groups or individuals no one could make up their minds. She was even thinking of flying him out to NY to see me! I asked her about his background and she said he had taught school in Malone, NY.

I exclaimed, "I was in Malone yesterday at a ministers meeting!" Now Malone is almost as far from NYC as you can get in the state. It's way up on the St. Lawrence River, our border with Canada, at least 500 miles from NYC. I got his telephone number and called him that night. His answers to my questions were slow in coming, as if he was being careful to get them just right.

Finally, he asked, "Just what kind of a man is RTCA looking for, anyway?"

"Well," I answered, "They got me and I'm kind of a character. I own a yoke of oxen!"

"Oh, the man across the street where I lived in Malone had oxen!"

"Was his name Saxton?"

"Yes."

My mind was boggled. What are the chances [racetrackers would say "odds"] of my calling from NYC to CA to talk to a man I had never met, and finding out that his previous neighbor in Malone was a friend of mine? I call such things as this not coincidences but Godincidences!

The next morning I called my friend in Malone and asked him about the man in question. "Norm, I don't want to say anything about him."

"I think you should anyway, since he is a candidate for one of the most prestigious Chaplaincy appointments in the country, Belmont and Aqueduct in NYC and Saratoga near Albany."

"Alright. He bought my brother's farm across the street from me. While he was there he sold the barn windows and doors, ripped up the house and then turned it back to the bank when he left. The bank even had to put money into the farm before they could sell it again!"

That was enough for me, so RTCA had no prospect to fit the qualifications given to us.

It was now December and my travel time was becoming longer. I couldn't even get home one night in a storm. As my ninth week arrived, I notified RTCA and began closing up my work at the NYC tracks. I was concerned about Gabriel. Since we could not communicate on details because of the language problem, I asked a young Hispanic named Tony to help me. Tony had been assigned to me by security to work out a Florida court order for community service. We went together to Gabriel's tack room. Tony was to ask Gabriel if his green card and immigration status were all in order, if his tackroom was safely his for the rest of the winter, did he have enough funds to get along and was he sure of a job when Woody came back from Florida. They talked quite a while and we were satisfied that all was well. "Now Tony, I'm going to pray for Gabriel, and you, and you will translate what I say so Gabriel will finally know what I am saying."

Tony was a little shaken as I doubt if he had done too much praying, but he warmed up to the praying as I went on. We were in a three-way huddle with our arms around each other. After the prayer I said goodbye to Gabriel and we went out. As we walked, Tony said to me, "Gabriel wants you to stay and be his Chaplain!"

"But I can't speak Spanish!" was my stunned response.

"Yes, but he knows you love him!"

I was astonished, but a revelation came to me. I went immediately to the offices of the HBPA and NYRA and told them what had just happened.

"We've had trouble finding an Anglo who speaks Spanish and who would be willing to quit his present job to become a racetrack chaplain. BUT, we can get you an Anglo who will learn Spanish and who will love his people!"

Both groups bought the idea. Gabriel had been the catalyst to solve the whole problem! I called RTCA and told them. With rejoicing, we welcomed Chaplain James Watson to the NYC tracks and I made a few trips down to introduce him and supervise. We also set up a Metropolitan New York Council of RTCA to support him in every way. In that summer, Jim had gone to Erie Racetrack near Erie, PA, which was like a strictly minor league track, had been moved on to Thistledown racetrack in Cleveland that fall, and was now in the Major Leagues! He learned Spanish and preaches in both languages and loves his people and they love him. At this writing, Jim has been there seventeen years, ably supported by his wife, Becky. All because of Gabriel Barbano!

CHAPTER 6

Chapel Services At The Racetrack

"Let us not give up meeting together, as some are in the habit of doing, but let us encourage one another – and all the more as you see the Day approaching."

[Paul, Hebrews 10:25]

"I've never been in church before, if this is church." The young man stating this was looking around at the pool table, on which the preacher rested one hip while he preached, and at the bank of soft drink and food dispensers at one side of the room. He was telling this to Pops, who had children and grandchildren on the track.

"If this is the first time, why did you come?" asked Pops gently with a smile.

"Well, I got into trouble with the Grove City police and when the chaplain heard about it, he came to me and told me that whether I was right or wrong, he would go with me and stand with me when I had to appear before the judge."

Chapel services at the racetracks are, well different from our regular church services. One never knows what music will be available, what interruptions will occur or whether one's planned message will be appropriate or a question from a tracker will send one off on an entirely different track.

Location may be different at each track. At Thistledown, the HBPA had their office over the track kitchen. A lounge area was part of the floor plan. Here, after lunch and before the first race, I held my services. Sometimes a flood of horsemen came in on business. One day two trackers were near to accepting Christ as Savior when a contractor came in to put up new window shades. I looked around, saw the restrooms and said, "C'mon!" The three of us went into the men's room and there it was that they will always remember as the place where they prayed to have Jesus come into their hearts.

Attendance at Thistledown grew from three at the first service to a respectful twenty-five or more, depending on duties assigned by their trainers or claims that a horse in the first race might make upon them. We held services at different times at different tracks to merge our schedule with what worked best there. At Beulah Park, services were held in the evening in the rec room off the security office. My own office was also in that building. We have had more than fifty at a time there. In fact, for four weeks running one spring, I could not use my planned message there. There were testimonies, requests for prayer, good news to report and spontaneous stories of God working in trackers' lives. We tried to have some special music at Beulah Park. Often youth choirs or groups from different churches would come. The trackers always welcomed them and gave them a new view of racetrack people.

One night at Beulah Park will always stand out in my memory. I had been at the starting gate at the three-quarter pole that afternoon when the last race went off. A jockey was jolted from his horse as the gates opened and the horses bumped together in their initial jumps. I saw him, ten feet out from the gate, being bruised and kicked by the hooves of at least two horses. I had dashed out and knelt by his side. He was facedown, with his forehead resting on his wrist, semiconscious and in pain. As the ambulance pulled up I laid a hand on his head and prayed with my mouth close to his ear. There was concern in our hearts as the ambulance left, for he was a well-liked young man.

News had gotten out via a few trackers to ministers in the Columbus area that things were happening in our chapel services at the track. Outsiders could always get by the security guard at the gate by telling him they were coming to my service. The guard shack was so close that they were just waved to a nearby parking spot and the guard could see them enter. One night I arrived with Florence to find a strange minister with the biggest Bible I've ever seen a preacher carry. I walked over to him and as he introduced himself, he nervously jerked the big Bible up over his chest like a shield. I could tell that he was not sure if he should even be in a place like this!

Early on in the service that night we had had special prayer for this jockey. Later, as we were singing praises in the service, the jock's agent opened the door and waited for an opportunity to speak. I stopped the singing and he announced loudly that the jockey had no broken bones and would be exercising horses in the morning. There was a loud cheering from the over fifty people present and I led in a prayer of praise and thanksgiving. The youth choir from the Grove City Baptist church sang and were well received. I introduced the guest preacher who had come. One of the trackers shouted out, "Hey Chaplain, why don't you let him say something? I joined the crowd in laughter and told the minister to go ahead.

He stood up with the huge Bible automatically coming

up to nearly cover his chest. "Well, I'm glad to see that the gospel has spread everywhere, even to the racetrack!"

I jumped up, pointed my right arm at him and interrupted him with a rather belligerent, "Watch that 'even' stuff brother!" The trackers laughed as the preacher turned a bit red. "Just what kind of people did you expect to find here tonight?" I asked him.

"Well, I guess I expected to find a bunch of, well, ruffians!"

"And what did you find?

"I found a group of Christians worshipping God."

I laughed then and informed the congregation that we had a wonderful opportunity to discuss the reality of people's expectations versus the reality of what was actually taking place. "Trackers, have you been to church? How were you treated?" What a response we had! The youth choir and a few church people had a chance to see how they looked from the outside.

Besides the many responses from the trackers that night, I told them about a couple who had come to me the year before at another track, telling me what had happened to them. A church bus had picked up onto their small son and he enjoyed church and Sunday School. He wanted his parents to come with him next Sunday. They thought it over and decided it had been a long time since they had been in church, so the next Sunday they put more horses on the walking machine than usual and were out on the track real early with the rest of the horses. They got to church. They felt the pull of Christ Jesus on their hearts. They were there the next Sunday. The minister gave the invitation; they looked at each other, joined hands and went forward. The minister was very pleased to see them come, but in a whisper, asked them where they were from. When they whispered back that they were training horses out at the racetrack, the minister exclaimed loudly, "Then you can't belong to THIS church!" Tears had run down my cheeks when they told me. They did not try another church.

A female horsewoman had come to me with a question. "Chaplain, I've been going to a church down the road from my home for a while and I enjoy it very much, but I am afraid someone is going to ask me what I do. What should I tell them? I'm afraid they will tell me not to come if I tell them I work with horses on the racetrack every day!"

I told her gently to tell the truth, and she might add that there was a chaplain at the track that they might like to check out; that he was there day and night and held regular services there. It was near the end of a meet and I never found out what happened. I pity the church if they told her not to come.

I spoke in churches some eighty to ninety times a year on Sundays and often I told them what we looked like from the outside. It seems as if we are saying, one way or another, usually by our unconscious attitudes, that "Jesus loves you, and I will too when you become like me!" But they hesitate to become like us because of their impressions of our attitudes.

Much was learned at that service in the discussion that night. Everyone left hugging each other in Christian love for frankness had mellowed all.

I always had to be adaptable to whatever happened in a service. One night at River Downs, where we met in the outer part of the racing secretary's office, two middle-aged drunks wandered into the service. I welcomed them and had them sit on a bench in front of me. Their interruptions and actions led one of the trackers to go to security. A security officer showed up quickly. I spoke to him saying, "I really don't want these men removed, officer. I'll listen to them if they will listen to me!" The guard immediately sat on the bench between the drunks and helped them find the right pages in the hymnal as we sang.

I asked for prayer requests before I led in the evening

prayer. One of the drunken men spoke up immediately. "Schaplain, would you pray for the Schinschinati Judishiary? They need help!"

"Certainly. The Bible tells us to pray for those in authority over us!" And I prayed for the Cincinnati Judiciary.

There were always kids in the tracker congregation and I usually involved them in the message. That night the same drunk was impressed at this and he interrupted with, "Schaplain, that's great to talk to the little ones like that!"

I grinned back at him and told him that Jesus called the children unto Him, and He once said we all must become as little children to make heaven. Then I added for everyone's benefit, "My philosophy is to treat children as adults and adults as children. Everyone has to understand the message and the kids like to be treated as somebody important by an adult." It was a good service.

The most memorable service I ever had was in front of my tack room in the parking area. I could not make my regular night so I held it the next night. That meant I could not use the secretary's office. I had some chairs which the Track Director of Operations, Horace Wade, had provided for me out of his own pocket, and I moved these out onto the blacktop. I had saved two parking spaces with chairs so we would have room.

There were about twenty-five people there, trainers, exercise people, grooms and jockey agents. I had prepared what I thought was a good, appropriate message, but I could not use it. We had sung, prayed and gotten to the place of the message. I stood up, found my scripture and started to read. Except I could not. No sound came out. I tried three times. Same result. By that time I had figured out that God had something else in mind. I closed my Bible and spoke to the group. "Do any of you have questions for me or a scripture you want explained?" To my amazement there were questions and discussions that lasted for over forty-five minutes!

The astonishing thing was that all the trackers participated in the answers. After rolling the questions around they would look to me for summing up. I used more scripture that night in answering questions than I would have in a month of preaching! In discussing the questions, people often referred to a denomination that they were connected to at one time. The slight differences in interpretation were evident. There were Methodist, Roman Catholic, Lutheran, Free Methodist, Baptist and Pentecostal views, plus some from no denomination at all. Finally as things were beginning to slow down, one of the trainers said, "Chaplain, Rudy says his church, Yvonne says her church, John says his church. Just what is a church, anyway?"

I started to answer but the Catholic girl beat me, saying, "A church is people!" Pee-Wee, an ex-jock from years before, sat up straight in his chair, eyes as big as the proverbial saucers, and exclaimed, "Then we're a church!" The hair stood up on the back of my neck with awe, as I watched everybody there turn and look at each other with a whole new understanding. They were a church, probably never again to meet in the same exact configuration of folk they were at that moment, but a church of God! It was awesome to see them and I silently thanked God that he stopped me from preaching that night!

The special musician one night at Beulah Park was a black soloist named Alice Willis, who was both beautiful and accomplished. I have never heard her sing without getting tears in my eyes. She had tapes for most of them, but sometimes sang without music. There were over fifty folk present that night but there was a bit of disturbance from a sixteen-year-old Commanche apprentice jockey who was set on having a high old time and showing off. At last I got up from my chair near the front and walked back down the aisle toward my office. The jock knew he should be reprimanded and sort of cringed as I went by, sneaking him a grin as I did. In my office I picked up a tambourine and returned, slipping the tambourine into the jock's lap as I went by him. When Alice finished the song she was singing, I asked her if she would go back two tapes and repeat one that had a real good beat to it. Then I called the jock to come forward and help her. Now he was bashful and had to be urged, but we got him up beside Alice and I told him to beat the rhythm with the tambourine. He got into it and both got a great hand of applause at the end. After the service, the jock came to me and said, "That was great, Chaplain! When is the next service?"

One visitor that night was Tim Findlay, who was soon to start the Christian Harness Horse Association, which is now international with almost a thousand members. Tim was amazed that evening. He exclaimed to me, "I acted like that boy and I got kicked out of church for it! You made him part of the service! Wow!"

In my rounds of the track I had a chance to talk with a trainer. We were alone and he confessed to me that in his youth he thought God was calling him, but he ran from the call. He was nearing the end of his active training days and had a wonderful head of curly gray hair. He was an impressive man and to top it all off had a voice like Walter Cronkite. But he would not promise to come to a service. One evening at Beulah, I found him sitting in a chair by the door as I came in. "Hey, I'm glad you decided to come tonight!"

"No. I've got a horse coming in so I'm just watching the gate."

"I hope you get to stay for part of the service anyway. Enjoy it while you're here!"

There were six or seven rows of chairs. As we sang and had the service, I noticed that my reluctant trainer kept moving up a row every few minutes. Near the end, he sat right behind me and he reached over and tapped me on the shoulder. With mouth to my ear he whispered, "Let me close the service!"

I thought fast. I had no idea what he was going to say. Then I figured that if he messed it up I could mend it again. "OK."

"Folks, Bill has asked to close the service. Please listen to him." He stood in front of them, one of their own, and proceeded to tell how he ran from God as a young man, but was going back to God. He talked for ten minutes, quoting scripture fairly accurately for one who had been away from it so long. He then gave an invitation to accept Christ as Savior as well as I could have, all in that rich bass voice. All I could do as he finished was to lead in prayer, asking for the raising of hands of those who accepted Christ at Bill's invitation. I could hardly talk as hands went up.

Bill had run from God all his life, but God would not allow him to come to the end of life without using him! Christ, the Hound of Heaven [from the poem by Francis Thompson,] brought him home!

In one of my trips as a Chaplain at Large [some called me a large chaplain], I was at a brand new track opening in Birmingham, AL, training a new chaplain. This had to be twenty years after RTCA was started and things were certainly different than when I had begun ministries at the Ohio tracks back in 1976. Horse people were there from all over the country as this brand new track opened. Trackers who had been ministered to by our other chaplains were welcoming the new chaplain by the droves. The welcome mat was out! While I was with the chaplain, a Christian jockey came up with an exciting report. He had been given permission to hold a short service and time of prayer in the jock's room every night before the evening racing. He could hardly contain himself as he told of fifty-four jockeys, valets and track officials in attendance at the first meeting!

The Horsemen's Beneficent and Protection Association [HBPA] is THE organization looking after Horsemen's interests in thoroughbred racing in this country. But local politics in Birmingham had set up another organization with an office on the track and forced the HBPA to set up off-track. I took the new chaplain to see the HBPA representative at their office. At that time, the HBPA had a national president who was rather anti-RTCA, and was growing in disfavor among many of the horsemen. The rep. for the HBPA, in response to my question, told me she was having a rough time signing up horsemen, and a lot of it was from dislike of the national president. I asked her if she would sit in proxy for all the HBPA as I prayed for them. She did, and I can remember praying that God would do something to soften the attitude of this president and to get RTCA and the HBPA back on a closer relationship. I picked up a horsemen's newspaper the next week and read that this national president had resigned his office, sold all his horses and left racing! God does not fool around!

The racetrack chaplain truly ministers to everyone there and they are there from all over the world! I was friend to all and their usual response was to come to a chapel service. We always had a mixture of Protestants and Catholics. In fact, I found that there were more kinds of Catholics than I had ever known before! Plus, at different times I have ministered to Jews [some were regulars], Buddhists [a jock from Thailand], Hindus, and Moslems, both American and Arab. It was a joy to be able to minister and bring God's Word to our own little United Nations!

It might be hard for some ministers to handle the interruptions and changing situations involved in a racetrack ministry, but I have decided that if you can minister on the racetrack, you can minister anywhere!

CHAPTER 7

Planting The Seed by Every Means

Then Jesus asked, "What is the kingdom of God like? What shall I compare it to? It is like a mustard seed, which a man took and planted in his garden. It grew, became a tree, and the birds of the air perched in its branches."

[Jesus, Luke 13:18-19]

I had the opportunity to write a column of track news and a devotional in the Racing Digest, a small paper with state editions. As a photographer with my own darkroom in Ohio, many of my photos were published in that paper, which is no longer in existence. My devotionals were like mustard seeds, written with the prayer that they might grow in horsemen's hearts. Before that I put out a sheet when I could to be passed out at the tracks. Without a secretary this was hard to keep up. I came out of the racing secretary's office where they had just printed my first issue. It was on legal size, colored paper, just like the track overnights. In fact it was off the same mimeo and out of the same stock as the regular overnights.

An overnight is a legal size sheet of paper, done by the racing secretary and his staff, listing the horses running the next day in each race. The trainer's name is there and the jockey he has selected to ride his horse. It is "required reading" for horsemen.

As I came out with my first edition in the crook of my arm that afternoon, a horseman hollered to me, "Hey Chaplain, could I have one of those overnights?" With a laugh, my paper became the "Chaplain's Overnight." There was always a "mustard seed" of a devotional in them. A lot of trackers collected all of them.

I must include here some racetrack language that might not be understood by non-racetrack folk. A "claiming" horse is a horse that runs under a price. It is listed in the program and form. If a registered trainer puts his or her name as being good for the money listed on the form into a special box before the race goes off, and that money is on file in his track account, when the race is over the horse is his, alive or dead. If more than one trainer puts in a claim, the racing secretary settles it by drawing names. I heard about five trainers that claimed one horse that actually broke a leg in the race and had to be put down. Four of the five wanted to share the price equally, but the fifth demanded a draw. He won the dead horse and lost his claiming price!

The claiming price can vary from $1500 and up in Ohio to $30,000 or more at major tracks. The whole idea is to find a race where a particular horse may win, even if it's out in the sticks somewhere. Some folk are so fond of their horses that they race them up a class or two to keep them from being claimed. Some will get rid of a horse by putting it in a cheaper claiming race. The idea of claiming a horse is that you hope you can do better with it than someone else.

Next up are "allowance" horses. They do not run for a price but run in higher purse races than claimers.

"Stakes" horses run in the highest purse races like the special races you see on TV. They are the elite of the breed and the smallest percentage of the total.

Following are devotional "mustard seeds" from my writings.

* * * * * *

WHERE ARE YOU SHIPPING TO?

The meet at River Downs is nearing its end. Where are you going to ship to? Do you have stalls at Beulah Park, Thistledown or where? Questions are in the air as meets close and meets open. Horsemen are on the move, "traveling light," picking up and setting down – but not for long. It's a way of life that horsemen are used to, but little understood outside the industry.

Did you ever stop to think that Jesus also moved from place to place like a tracker? Born in a stable in Bethlehem, fleeing to Egypt to escape death from Herod, back to Nazareth, pilgrimage to Jerusalem, forty days in the desert alone and three years of wandering with the disciples in Palestine.

He knew what it was to be lonely [like many trackers whether they admit it or not]. He knew insecurity and being hungry. He knew what it was to be criticized and rejected by people who would not understand Him. He knew what it was to be "let down" by close friends. He traveled light, but "Light" traveled with him.

Light can travel with you, too. Jesus is the "light of the world." He is Light, and He is Life. "I am the way, the truth and the life," He said. "There is no other way unto the

Father but by Me." [John 14:6]

Sometimes people refuse help or friendship from people who "just don't understand." But Jesus understands, and He knows the hardships, the insecurities and the loneliness of your way of life. He lived it. He earned the right to be your Savior, your Lord. He paid with His life, dying on the Cross for all of us.

So, as you come and go in the changing meets, just tell Jesus you want to move with Him. He'll light your way, and your life.

* * * * * *

GOD AND MAN AND HORSE

Few people outside the many-faceted horse industry understand the bond between horse and Man. To be sure, poetry and prose have been composed for centuries concerning the war horse, the faithful work horse, the "noble" wild horse and so on, but few understand what keeps many folks on the racing circuit.

When you think of "trackers" a whole spectrum of people come into view. Some are making it big and living well. Or they did last year, or the year before! Some are going broke and hope "next year" will compensate for all the bad years. And some are getting by - almost. When you add the hours and the uncertainty, the mud and the dust, the heat and the cold, the tack rooms and the rest rooms, why do so many stay with the horses? The simple reasons, beyond all hopes of monetary gain and "next year", are the horses themselves. They respond to people.

Barring the occasional "bad actor" and making allowance for the thoroughbred's normally nervous nature, horses respond to love and care. And people respond to horses. Horse racing may be a business, but in no other business will workers love their production machinery and show it affection and care during non-working hours. Grooms often love "their" horses and show them to me with as much pride as if they owned them. Attachments can grow to the point that claiming becomes a personal tragedy. Horsemen talk to their horses as if the understood all they say [and who is to say where the line of understanding shall be drawn?] And to often-lonely horsemen, the nuzzling of a warm nose may fill an unspoken, unrecognized need. So they stay with the horses.

To be sure, human nature being what it is, some people are meaner, and some more affectionate to horses than others. Some horses respond to one groom or trainer and not to another. The strength of the bond between horse and groom may determine the running of the race. The horse senses confidence, hope and care, and within its limits may respond in proportion.

As the bond of affection can hold people and horses, so the Bond of Love should hold us to God. He loves us. He has given us all things that we might have abundance. And through Jesus Christ, He became one of us that He might show us the extent of that love by running the race with us. Jesus died for us and the claiming price He paid for us could have been no larger. The claiming price of His own lifeblood was paid for us, even though we made a bad break out of the gate, faltered in the backstretch, blew the far-turn and pulled up sore in the homestretch.

What is our response to a Love like that? Are we like the "bad actor" that lunges over the webbing to bite the hand that feeds us? Are we so nervous and non-trusting that we "cow-kick" the one who grooms us? Are we so ungrateful for our blessings that we take calculated aim at God and kick about the condition when it's our own fault that we're in it? Or do we recognize His love and love Him back with complete trust and abandon?

Next time a horse bites at you, ask God if you act like that. If so, ask forgiveness, receive it and proceed to change. Next time a horse "kisses" you, tell Jesus you love Him and want to serve Him. And as you pat the horse, know God is blessing you.

* * * * * *

THE WINNER'S CIRCLE

Every horseman strives and hopes to get to the Winner's Circle, and as often as possible! To be there is to show proof to all of talent, skill or judgment. To get to the Winner's Circle is to celebrate and to be congratulated.

A good number of times, I've had someone yell, "Hey! Chaplain! Come get in the Winner's Circle with me! My horse just won!" And I have shared in the pride of the Winner's Circle.

Who's in the photo? There is the jockey who rode with skill; the horse which went all out; the groom who was faithful and correct in handling the horse; the trainer whose skill, experience and judgment have just been proven; the owner who put up the money as an investment; and perhaps the exercise boy or girl or someone else who had something to do with the win. Everybody there had a part in the win – except me.

But I was invited by someone who had earned the right to be there. And that is the essence of the Gospel, the Good News of Jesus Christ.

Once in a while you or I may sometimes achieve the Winner's Circle in this life, but there is no way we may earn the right to stand in the spiritual Winner's Circle. The Bible says our righteousness is like worthless rags; in other words, as far as being good is concerned, we just can't go the route.

But Jesus earned the right to be there. By His life, His

death and by His resurrection, He proved He is the final Winner! And He says, "Come, stand with Me!"

It's great to get to the Winner's Circle and hear the crowds. But it does not even compare with being in the Winner's Circle with Jesus. Hear Him! Enter and celebrate!

* * * * * *

ROSIE RUIZ AND THE GOSPEL

At the end of more than twenty-six miles of strain, pain and agony, Bill Rogers ran between lines of cheering people to win, again, the world famous Boston Marathon in 1980. Years of training, self-punishment and self-discipline paid off! He had done what we are instructed to do by the Apostle Paul in I Corinthians 9: 23-27, controlling his body so he could run the race to win!

Not too far behind Bill Rogers came another figure. The crowds cheered lustily as the first woman crossed the finish line, smiling, and not very winded at all. Rosie Ruiz was crowned winner in the Women's Division. Later, there was confusion. Where had she been earlier in the race? No photos showed her. Witnesses claimed to have seen her emerge from the sidelines somewhere in the last half-mile or so and run only from there. Her title was taken away and the Boston Marathon had its first scandal.

An enterprising promoter soon had an event publicized, which was to be called the "Rosie Ruiz Marathon." Before lawyers had it canceled, there was to be a lengthy course laid out with a very wide finish line at the end. Hundreds were to line up at the finish line while one contestant ran the race. At the very end, everybody would step over the line together and all would be proclaimed winners of "The Rosie Ruiz Marathon." Sounds anti-American, doesn't it? We are brought up to "play the game," "to put out one hundred percent," to "play by the rules!"

Yet, while Rosie was wrong, and the Rosie Ruiz Marathon was to be a big joke, if you look deep, it was Gospel!

Jesus ran the race for us. We can only "step over the line." We cannot win salvation or heaven by winning a race. We can only accept it. To the thief on the cross who repented moments before he died, Jesus said, "This day you shall be with me in Paradise!" The thief did not "win" the race, he stepped over the line like a Rosie Ruiz/

Jesus told a parable in Matthew 20: 1-16 about workers hired late in the afternoon being paid the same amount as those hired at dawn. If that were to be done today, there would be labor problems for sure! But the symbolic wage in the parable is salvation. Again, it is the Rosie Ruiz Marathon! Salvation is free! You cannot earn it! You don't have to be "good enough" or even sober enough to win salvation, for Jesus has earned it and He wants to give it to us if we will but step over the line!

What about "running as if to win" as Paul tells us? That's the race that comes after salvation, not before. Because He loves us, because He has made me a winner with Him, I shall "run the race that is set before me" [Hebrews 12: 1,] "driving hard for the finish" [Philippians 3: 14,] and "compelled by the love of Christ" [II Corinthians 5: 14.] We run the race for Him, after we accept His salvation, simply in response to a love as great as His.

And running for Jesus can be summed up in loving God and loving others. That's the race for you to put out one hundred percent!

* * * * * *

THE MEANING OF THE CROSS

Many of the things we do on the racetrack are done with or through the partnership of someone else. No one person does everything that has to be done with a horse. A trainer trains, a groom grooms, a jockey rides. If I wished to own a horse, I'd find a trainer [after I'd found the money] and get him to claim a horse for me. Whether we do something right or wrong, we share and identify with each other. In the Winner's Circle the jockey, groom, trainer and owner share in the victory celebration. On the other hand, if we were to agree to do something wrong, against the laws and rules, we would go before the stewards together.

Perhaps this is a strange preface to a devotional message on the meaning of the Cross of Christ, but it might help to illustrate what Paul the Apostle meant in Galatians 2: 19-20.

"I have been put to death with Christ on His Cross, so that it is no longer I who live, but it is Christ who lives in me. This life that I live now, I live by faith in the Son of God, who loved me and gave His life for me."

When Paul wrote "I have been put to death with Christ on His Cross," it was many years after His death on the Cross and we are many centuries beyond that. Yet, if we believe that Christ died for our sins, and if we identify ourselves with Him, time falls away. We died with Him.

The Crucifix shows Christ hanging dead on the cross. When we see that it should always remind us that, "I died on that Cross with Jesus, for it was my sins that He died for, and indeed have killed me." Paul had been writing in earlier verses that the law could not put us right with God – that only faith in Christ could. He acted for us in dying on the cross. Believing that, we died too!

But by faith, Christ now lives in me! The empty Cross says that Jesus did not stay dead on the Cross! He rose from the dead and now lives in me! "It is no longer I who live, but it is Christ who lives in me!"

Both the Crucifix and the Empty Cross speak to our belief. Sometimes our lives don't say the same thing. Look at the Crucifix! Say to Jesus, "I died with you!" Look at the Empty Cross! Say, "Christ now lives in me!" And then let Him live His life in you.

Someday the Heavenly Steward, God the Father, will have to rule on our partnership. Jesus paid the claim. Have you accepted it, identified with Him and died on the Cross? Then let Christ live in you in Celebration!

* * * * * *

IN THE POST PARADE

I watched a Post Parade at Beulah Park the other day, where one horse and jockey, for whatever reason, came onto the track minus a lead pony. When the Parade made its turn at the upper end of the grandstand to come back by on its way to the gate at the three-quarter pole, the horse without the lead pony bolted into high gear and took off like it had just heard the bell! The rider was unable to slow the horse down and it was left to an outrider to haul him down after more than a quarter-mile sprint around the club- house turn. There was nothing new in this to a racetracker, but it got me to thinking about the way we sometimes run off in our desire to be independent.

II Corinthians 5:14 says, "For Christ's love controls us." In theory this horse was under control. The bridle was on his head, the bit was in his mouth, and the reins were in the hands of the jockey who was in the saddle. But taking the bit in his teeth, he made his move on his own without waiting for instructions.

We may have put Jesus Christ into the saddle of our lives, turned our reins over to Him, and be wearing His bridle. But even so, we sometimes take the bit in our teeth and run off with the Lord. In His love, He made us creatures of choice. His bit is gentle. He does not yank us up with a harsh curb bit, but allows us to still choose, wanting His love to be the controlling factor in our lives, not His power or His judgment. When we don't wait for His instructions we get into trouble of our own making! Just as the bolting horse blew his conditioning and lost his edge in the ensuing race, we end up losing the very things we wanted, or finding out that what we got when we ran off was not at all what we thought it would be!

Racetrackers are an independent breed! Some folks could make more money elsewhere but would rather be "independent" [if being a slave to a horse is independence!] However, independence is a misnomer for we are all dependent on each other in countless ways. No way can we be totally independent although we still cherish the idea of independence.

Only when we realize that in Jesus Christ we become really free, can we learn that complete submission to Him results in a life of joy and freedom. Paradox? Not at all. The class horse that waits for the hands of the jockey to signal his moves becomes the horse in the Winner's Circle and is celebrated!

How about you? We are in the Post Parade. Hebrews 12:1 says, "We are surrounded...by a great cloud of witnesses...Let us run with perseverance the race marked out for us." First of all, name Jesus as your rider. Make it known! It's time to print the Overnight! Then, out there in the Post Parade, allow the Hand of Discipline to take over. Imagine yourself "controlled by Christ's love." Wait for instructions. He promised us Power, but told us to wait. Then, when the gate is sprung and the starting bell goes off, look to Christ and run for Him! The Circle awaits.

"Let us fix our eyes on Jesus, the pioneer and perfecter

of our faith, who for the joy set before Him, endured the Cross, scorning the shame, and sat down at the right hand of the throne of God." [Hebrews 12: 2]

* * * * * *

SHIPPING OUT AND FINDING STALLS

The season is winding down for racing here and some stables have already left for warmer climes where snow does not cover the track, and the rest are preparing to ship. There are always some that are not sure just where they will race this winter.

As chaplain, I often ask people where they are shipping not only because not only am I interested in them, but also so I might steer them to another chaplain when I can. We are family on the racetrack and all the chaplains, east and west, north and south, are part of the family. Look up the chaplain when you ship and tell him where you've had stalls. We share you!

Speaking of stalls, some horsemen know they will have to vacate at the end of the meet, but don't know where they'll go because their stall applications where they had intended to go were not granted. That's a tough spot in which to be. Many have tried to use "pull" at some track to get in. Sometimes it works, but not always.

Almost as bad as not having stalls somewhere waiting for you is not having the shipping money to get to the stalls you do have! The last couple of weeks of the meet are tough on the guy or gal trying to pull off a last minute win or two in order to get on the road free and clear and have the gas money to get somewhere else. I'll never forget the long faces I saw in the Thistledown kitchen one morning a few years back when an early snowstorm cancelled the last week of racing. The big stables had already pulled out for the

Florida tracks; this was the last chance for the "little guy" and it was scratched!

We can talk about earthly races, but we'd better be ready for a Heavenly Meet. This meet on earth will end. Do you know where you'll ship to when you have to vacate your stall on earth?

Jesus told us there are many stalls in His Father's Shedrow and that He was going to prepare them for us. [John 14: 2] But. There is always a but. We have to get our stall applications in before the end of our earthly meet. Lots of time? You don't know. The meet may end suddenly for you and those things you've put off doing will not get done. You have to get those Heavenly Stall applications in! Don't wait! You'll not like the alternative to the Master's Shedrow and don't think you'll pick up stalls nearby. There are no ship-ins at the Heavenly Meet!

One thing about these stall applications is that if they are in on time you will never be turned down! Put in your applications now! The chaplain can help!

Don't worry about the shipping money, either. We don't need it and we can't take it with us. There may be pockets in a saddle pad, but not in a shroud!

Ship with peace, thankfulness and high hopes! Go with God and return in love! *Via con Dios!*

* * * * * *

LEAVE THE GATE!

Those of you who see me often on the tracks are used to seeing me with a camera around my neck. On those occasions when I don't have it with me, I usually wish I did for I'm trying to catch moments on the track that so often are both taken for granted and unrecorded.

One day at River Downs I was asked to take a picture of

an approaching track pony and the pony-girl rider. Afterwards, they told me I had photographed a track pony that had been purchased for $70,000!

"$70,000! Then it has to be a thoroughbred!"

"That's right. It's a thoroughbred."

"But why would anyone use a $70,000 thoroughbred for a track pony?" I asked in astonishment.

"Because he won't come out of the gate!"

It seemed that once this horse found that coming out of the gate meant he had to run, run, run, he decided he really didn't want to work that hard. Evidently he was smart enough to figure out that to get out of running, he'd refuse to break when the gates opened.

About the second time that the race was over before he could be budged from the starting gate, the stewards intervened on behalf of the bettors that could not read a racing form. He was banned from racing.

So the $70,000 thoroughbred got his wish. He no longer had to work down the stretch, heart pounding, lungs bursting – he's now a track pony, working longer hours perhaps but at a speed more to his liking.

Lots of people are like that horse. We refuse to "come out of the gate" and go through life plodding at an easy pace, not wanting to really exert ourselves for anyone, let alone ourselves. I realize that plodders do a lot of the world's accomplishments and I would never knock a plodder if that were all he could do. After all, there's nothing wrong in being a good track pony. [I've seen a few worth more that the horse beside them!] But if a horse has a $70,000 potential, then it's a crime to be only a track pony!

How about you? Are you working up to your potential? If you are a ten-talent person, coasting along using only one, that's a sin. If you have only one and are using it to the utmost, that's great!

II Corinthians 5; 14 says, "For Christ's love compels

us." [Alternate translation, "controls us."] His great love compels me to expend myself, to work down the stretch toward the finish using everything He gave me for His glory. Paul in Philippians says, "Leaving the past behind, I DRIVE toward the goal of the high calling of God in Jesus Christ! [Philippians 3: 13-14]

In I Corinthians 9: 24, Paul says, "Do you not know that in a race all the runners run but only one gets the prize. Run in such a way as to get the prize."

Are you running for Jesus using all He has given you, or are you stuck in the gate?

One more thing, you can't really run for Jesus until you've named Him as your rider, put Him into the saddle of your life and turned the reins of your life over to Him. Having done that, break out of the gate, and run the race of your life compelled by the love of Christ!

* * * * * *

BLOODLINES AND PEDIGREES

Bloodlines, pedigrees and families: put two horsemen together and we talk horses and breeding. In fact, every thoroughbred horse in the world can be traced back to three sires. When I was a dairy farmer I could talk Holstein pedigrees with the best of them. Successful horsemen plan breeding to match quality with quality hoping to produce the horse of the year, decade or century, but are satisfied to get a stakes winner. There is always the hope of breeding the "super-horse." To do so you breed the best bloodlines backed by performance. What would a mating between Genuine Risk and Spectacular Bid be worth?

Bloodlines are all important in the auction ring, the advertisements and to some extent, on the racetrack. They are less so on the track because just having the bloodline is not enough – the horse has to have heart and be a runner as well. This is where bloodlines backed by performance come in.

We too have a bloodline. Not that our personal pedigrees are all that great. It's pretty easy to find the black sheep and darkhorses in our genealogies and our past performances are seldom up to our potential. However, our pedigree is not locked-in to our blood ancestors for in Christ we have a new bloodline! We can become God's children, blood brothers with Christ Jesus and joint heirs with Him!

Romans 8: 16-17 says, "The Spirit Himself testifies with our spirit that we are God's children. Now if we are children, we are heirs – heirs of God and co-heirs with Christ."

In other words, when we accept Christ as our Savior and Lord and ask Him to take over our lives, we enter God's Shedrow and become His adopted children, saved by the Blood of Christ, and members of the Family of God! There is no better Bloodline.

If we carry His Bloodline, then performance should follow, not precede. Performance cannot earn His Blood. He gives us our salvation by His grace. But performance should follow! Jesus said, "If you love Me, keep My commandments."

James 2: 12, 18 states, "What good is it for someone to say, 'I have faith,' if his actions do not prove it?" and later, "I will show you my faith by my action!" What James is saying in relation to bloodlines and performance is, "I'll prove my Bloodline by my performance!"

Christ has given us a new Bloodline. Now we should let His Spirit control our lives so we can have a "past performance" worthy of Christ's Blood.

Horsemen often say, "Never give up on a thoroughbred." Know that God does not give up on you. No matter how many times you've failed to perform according to His Blood, He will help you try again. And His Bloodline will come through!

* * * * * *

OF KIDS AND COLTS AND ALL OUR HOPES

"Suffer the little children to come unto Me and forbid them not, for of such is the Kingdom of God. Verily I say unto you, whosoever shall not receive the Kingdom of God as a little child shall not enter therein." Mark 10: 14-15 [KJV]

What a potential exists in each child! What are our dreams of their future? Beauty, possibly a Miss America or a movie or singing star. Maybe a future President! [Maybe some people would like to be President, but not me!] Yet most of us would settle for much less than this as long there was love, happiness and the development of the child's talents and abilities. From a religious viewpoint this can only happen as the child grows up in God's love, or at least finds and accepts it sometime later in life. It's never too late, but oh the wasted years!

The same holds true every time a colt or filly is foaled. This is the one that will be the big winner! A Secretariat, a Forgo, a Seattle Slew, an Affirmed [or at least an Alydar!] What potential there is in every foal and how glowing the hopes as you watch it grow!

Yet what happens? Out of every year's crop of thoroughbred foals only two-percent become stake horses. Only two-percent! What of the dreams and hopes? What happened? Horsemen know. Dreams are crushed with a broken leg or hopes dashed with a yearling's accident. Training problems, sickness, bowed tendons, stone bruises, cracked sesamoids [a small bony cartilage around a joint] and maybe good health but no heart, and all your time and effort, money and dreams for that foal are gone. True it is that some survive to make their way and pay their bills, but they remain in the claiming circuit, never reaching the class you'd hoped they would show.

How about our children? You were once a child – how did you turn out? Was your potential reached? Are you a "stakes horse" in God's sight or have you slipped in class – along the way? Are you in the Winner's Circle with the Lord, or one of those "fallen by the wayside?

"Enter through the narrow gate; for wide is the gate and broad is the road that leads to destruction and many enter through it. But small is the gate and narrow the road that leads to life and only a few find it." [Matthew 7: 13-14]

The Good News is that if you come as a little child to Jesus, taking Him by faith into your heart and life, He will redeem your life. That's true even if you can be compared to a broken down old claimer on the ramp of the killer truck, the last step before becoming dog food!

But you have to look for the "narrow gate," not because it's hidden but because our eyes are usually on the broad, easy way. Not every jockey finds that "hole on the rail" but if you look for Jesus, He'll find you!

"Whosoever will may come," He says, and "I am the Way, the Truth and the Life... no one comes to the Father except through Me." [John 14: 6]

* * * * * *

CHAPTER 8

Molding Your Attitude

**"I have been crucified with Christ and I no longer live,
but Christ lives in me. The life I live in the body,
I live by faith in the Son of God, who loved me
and gave Himself for me."**

[Paul, Galatians 2: 20]

To be a racetrack chaplain, a minister or a Christian layman and to be effective in spreading the Gospel of Jesus Christ, may require a change in attitude or personality. Some would say that attitudes could change but not one's personality. My own response is a not very subtle, "Poppycock!" If that expression is so old as to be unintelligible I could change it to "Baloney!" [Which is just as old!]

I used to teach in the annual Chaplains' School that was held once a year in Ohio. It is taught now in conjunction with the annual meeting of RTCA to save travel money and time. I had watched racetrack chaplains come and go since

1970 and I always taught about attitudes and personalities needed in a chaplain. A chaplain needs to be a special kind of minister. In my travels, I often made the observation that this minister would make a good chaplain and that one would not. What we have learned about this would help all ministers and laymen as well as chaplains.

The racetrack is a special kind of training ground. One chaplain spoke at a chaplain's school with tears in his eyes. "I'd never known how to walk as a Christian before I went to the track!"

We cannot make a mold to make every chaplain alike, although I once remarked at an annual meeting that if we could clone about thirty of a particular chaplain and use them as we needed them, we'd be in good shape! But no two chaplains are alike. We are all different and that is good. But good chaplains [and I include ministers and layfolk in this word in this chapter] are alike in that they **live their love!**

You have to be able to meet people by the hundreds as well as individually. You **must** be a conversationalist. A conversationalist is not just one who likes to talk but one who draws out the conversations of others. A good conversationalist also knows when to keep still and listen, not to wait for a chance to start talking again but to **really** listen to what the other person is saying.

No chaplain should be hired by RTCA [opinion of Norm] unless they are **openly and actively friendly among strangers of every style, class, color or job.** Success as a racetrack chaplain has always depended more on the ability to meet people and draw them into conversation than on their preaching ability. RTCA's standards of acceptance are, however, weighted heavily on soundness of doctrine, as it should be.

Shyness and fear are rather natural. There is no sin in being shy or scared of approaching new people. The sin comes when we let that shyness or fear stop us from being friendly and approaching new people. The **PRACTICE** OF OPEN-FRIENDLINESS drives out shyness and fear. It is a growing process and takes place only as we do it in spite of shyness and fear. We all have to be willing to grow!

Extreme shyness or, for that matter, extreme gregariousness is unproductive. We should learn to be an "ambivert," able to really relate to people and to be self-reflective as well. It is a growing process and may not be easy for some. It wasn't for me. I would have been left-handed but was changed in an era when lefties were not wanted. I stammered so much that I even had trouble saying my own name until I was eighteen! I did not stammer when I was singing or mad but I reasoned that I could not do either all the time! I finally got over it by prayer and a whole lot of personal effort.

Even though there are those who say one cannot change, we have Scripture that says we can! II Corinthians 5: 17 says, "If anyone is in Christ, he is a new creation; the old has gone, the new has come!"

To be shy and fearful is not to have reached your potential in Christ. It seems that most never do, but in Christ, we learn new aspects of the Abundant Life, and being an ambivert is one part of the Abundance.

Shyness is often associated with a lack of self-confidence, which means you often hesitate when action [like smiling and introducing yourself] is essential Shyness is perceived as not being friendly. A chaplain **must** be seen as warm, loving and friendly!

Fear comes out of a lack of self-esteem. Fear of people makes one apprehensive and nervous about how you will be received. [I know. I had butterflies in my stomach for a long time when I approached a new track.] It makes you apt to be thin-skinned and stiff when you need to be flexible and adaptable. [It comes easier every time!]

I have found that small dogs bark more than big dogs. Nervous dogs bite.

A confident dog is a friendly dog. So much for old farmer wisdom and country philosophy!

A successful chaplain is **ASSERTIVELY FRIENDLY.** He walks the track/paddock/rail/ kitchen and offices. A minister can figure out his own places to be seen. Most laypeople have greater opportunities than ministers where they work or play.

More chaplains have fallen short in smiling, greeting people and walking the beat than in any other trait. Always introduce yourself to someone you don't know. Never walk on by because you don't know them. [Admittedly impractical in places like Times Square, but you get the idea.] Don't just greet them if they don't know you as chaplain, let them know who you are. Always be conversational. Find out who they are, etc. Don't walk away too quickly. It goes without saying, but needs to be said anyway, that you should not interrupt, bother or interfere with a work in progress. BUT don't ignore ANYONE, ANYTIME.

SMILE! If you are always frowning, you won't make it as a chaplain. But you can learn to smile! It feels good! It takes fewer muscles to smile than to frown so learn to conserve energy by smiling! Just do it! Smile! A frown is another defense of the insecure. Start smiling and it will become a habit. Not only you but also others will feel better!

If you smile because you love people that does not mean you smile at the wrong time. Tears, real tears will come when they ought to come and people will know that you love them.

If you would like to get a second opinion on smiling, see Dale Carnegie's "How to Win Friends and Influence People." It's a classic and a good refresher course if you have read it. Also, Robert Schuller's "Self Esteem, the New Reformation" would be of help both to you and to many racetrackers.

Please, never tell yourself or others that you are "just naturally shy" or a bit awed or even scared. That is only a stage in life if you are willing to grow and learn. After all, Jesus came to give us the Abundant Life.

If you are unwilling to try moving from being shy via the ambivert process, you may be out of place as a racetrack chaplain. Harsh words? Perhaps, but in spite of the fact that some happenings, problems and circumstances can be scary, defeating and fearsome, these are VITAL WORDS! Every successful ministry on the tracks has come with an outgoing and loving chaplain.

Still scared? OK. Remember that a brave man is a coward who did not run. Also that a mighty oak was once a little nut that stood its ground!

Some people stand out in a crowd. Some disappear in a crowd. The chaplain must stand out, but not like the proverbial sore thumb! The chaplain stands out in a positive way in his love friendliness and openness. The chaplain does not have to be flamboyant. Leave that for the TV guys and gals. Trouble goes with flamboyancy. Let your light, which is the Light of Christ, SHINE!

Recognition is very important. Again, we don't want to be flamboyant with pink pants and a top hat, but simply recognizable. Some chaplains go bareheaded, some wear special hats, some have a jacket, some are in shirtsleeves. Something about you needs to be recognizable both at a distance and close up so that someone can say, "There he is, over there." Or "I saw him going into barn 14 a few minutes ago." People will be looking for you. Be visible.

It might help to be very tall, but no one has a problem in finding our shortest, ex-jockey chaplains! Standing out in a crowd is a matter of personality. You CAN change from one who is not seen to one who is by continuing to become a "becomer," to enter into the process of becoming outgoing.

Madison Avenue might say we are actually in the merchandising business. In the church pulpit we may "have the floor" but not on the track. We are the wrapping, the presentation of the Love of Jesus. If we package it in a plain dull wrapper and do not show the wonderful effects of our product, people will not be drawn to the product we are merchandising. God's Love needs the best promotion we can give it.

On the other hand, people are constantly being led astray by cults because the wrapping is very friendly and inviting.

So far most of this chapter on the chaplain's attitudinal traits has been practical and experiential. However, Scripture and theology agree that bashfulness, hesitancy, shyness and introversion are not what Christ wants in His servants.

"I have been crucified with Christ and I no longer live, but Christ lives in me. The life I live in the body, I live by faith in the Son of God, who loved me and gave Himself for me." Galatians 2: 20

Another verse to consider is, "For you died, and your life is now hidden with Christ in God." Colossians 3: 3

Our "natural" inclination to shyness and fear are therefore no longer for Christ's servants, for having died in Christ, Christ's life is to show forth in our lives, not our own. We replace self-life with Christ-life. We let Christ replace our self-consciousness with Christ-consciousness.

We now live by faith. Christ is now our life. We lose self and live in Christ.

Christ IS our life.

"When Christ, who IS your life, appears, then you will also appear with Him in glory." Colossians 3: 4

To be self-conscious and to hesitate in our ministry of loving and being Christ"s "agents" is therefore sin, for we all fall short of what He expects of us. [Racetrackers understand the term "agent" better than "ambassador." See II Corinthians 5: 20.]

If this is sin, then all of us have problems with it and we all need to ask forgiveness for the times we have failed to show

Christ's life and love because of our shyness or hesitancy.

When we are shy, Christ is not having His way in us. We are not allowing Christ to use us to the fullest extent. After asking forgiveness, we need to pray for Christ to continue His work within us, to continue to change us, to continue the process of "new-personhood" [II Corinthians 5: 17] which we often resist. Resisting is "putting out the Spirit's fire," or "quenching the Spirit's fire" in the King James Version and, therefore, also sin.

Let God have His way! Let Him make His changes! You do not do it yourself, it is in letting Him do it to you!

"For it is God who makes you willing and gives you the energy to do what He wants." [Philippians 2: 13, Beck translation.]

For it is God who works in you to will and act according to His good purpose." [Philippians 2: 13]

With Christ-consciousness and with Christ-life within us fear is cast out and replaced with holy-boldness!

"For you did not receive a spirit that makes you a slave again to fear, but you received the Spirit of Sonship." [Romans 8: 15]

"...And so we should not be like cringing, fearful slaves, but we should be like God's very own children." [Romans 8:15 Living Bible]

Paul puts it plainly: "For God did not give us a spirit of timidity, but a Spirit of power, of love, and of self-discipline. So do not be ashamed to testify about our Lord." [II Timothy 1:7-8a]

Let shyness, bashfulness, fear and hesitancy give way to Christ working in you!

BE THE NEW PERSON CHRIST WANTS YOU TO BE!

CHAPTER 9

The Gospel in Horse Stories

**"Behold, I stand at the door and knock; if any one
hears My voice and opens the door,
I will come in to him."**

[John, Revelation 3: 20]

Jesus talked about sheep, which were common animals to
everyone at that time. Most everybody had a few sheep
and His parables and stories were understandable. We like
sheep in our Bible stories, but hardly anyone now knows
much about sheep. They're not very smart and they sure like
to get into trouble! Besides, the lanolin in their wool makes
them sticky!

I admit to a bit of prejudice here as I am a former dairy
farmer and love cows. As I mentioned in an earlier chapter, I
used cow stories in seminary to illustrate theological points.
While at seminary, I served a church in Camden, NJ, which
is a long way from the farm! I told the congregation that my

head was full of farm illustrations and could they take them? When they assured that I could still call on my reservoir of cow stories, I relaxed. One Sunday morning after church I was asked by one of the ladies if I felt all right. Assuring her that I felt fine, she still said she thought something was the matter.

"Why do you think I'm not feeling up to par?"

"Because you didn't tell a single cow story in your sermon this morning!" she responded. That brought a good round of laughter from the group gathered by the front door.

The racetrack was a place where I figured I should go easy on cow stories and talk horses. Nothing on a racetrack is a horse except the thoroughbred racehorses. A pony is the horse used to exercise the thoroughbred horses, but on the track he is not a horse but only a pony. Even the sawhorses used to keep horses off the rail area during morning exercising are not sawhorses but "saw-dogs." Absolutely nothing on the racetrack is a horse unless it is a thoroughbred!

Consequently, I looked for horse stories to enlarge my background of illustrations. I found one rather quickly. Darlene was a groom – and owned one horse of her own. In my rounds she proudly showed him to me. Here was a fine looking stallion with the slight dish to his face that pointed back to the Arab blood of one of the progenitors of the whole thoroughbred breed – the Barb. He was groomed to perfection. His hoofs were polished black. Out on a shank [leather lead rope with chain and a snap on the end], he looked at the racetrack and screamed a note of defiance, as if to say, "Let me out there!" His name was "Bonerack Ricky" and he had the best of everything - feed, grooming, vet care and exercise under Darlene's care.

He had evidently broken his maiden [won his first race] somewhere in Florida, but had failed to win a race since. In fact, his former owner for whom Darlene groomed got so disgusted with him that she sold him for dog-food to the folks who drove the killer truck. How Darlene loved that horse! When she found out that he was sold, she dickered with the buyers until she bought him back! Her boss said she could keep him in the string, but she was responsible for all expenses. Talk about Gospel! Bonerack was like me! I couldn't win a race for losing, either, and my fate was death! But Jesus paid the price and led me into His stable where I live like a Prince!

Darlene got Bonerack entered in a race by nagging the racing secretary. His job was to come up with a fairly even card of horses for a race, but what do you do with a chronic loser? The tote board does not show odds beyond one hundred to one, but someone calculated the odds of Bonerack winning as about one hundred and fifty to one. Some surprises were in store. He broke out of the gate with vigor, but was soon at the tail end of the pack. However, he was game! He gained all down the Backstretch and at the head of the far turn he made his move! His efforts were valiant and he continued to gain on all the horses! He also finished dead last, but he was still loved!

I saw myself in Bonerack. When I fall behind in the Backstretch, throw a shoe on the far turn and end up with a bowed tendon in the homestretch, I lay there in the mud whispering, "Lord, I goofed again!" He reaches down, picks me up, wipes me off and says, "Norm, I still love you!"

With tears in my eyes, I turned to Darlene and said, "What you did for Bonerack Ricky is what Jesus did for me!"

"What do you mean?"

"Well, I couldn't win a race either. Nothing I am or could be would earn it but Jesus loved me, just as I was! And out of His sheer love and love alone, Jesus paid the biggest claiming price ever – He laid down His life for me. He bought me when my fate was worse than Bonerack's."

"And when I came into His stable, Romans 8: 17 assures me that I am a 'joint-heir' with Christ, which means that I own all that He does, just like Bonerack has all that the best horse here has."

I took out my Living Bible New Testament from my back pocket, turned to Romans 4 and read to her about Abraham, the father of the Jewish people.

"Why do you suppose God picked him to be the first of His Chosen People?

Was it because he was so great? Was it because of his good deeds that God accepted Him? If so, then he would have something to boast about. But from God's point of view, Abraham had no basis at all for pride."

"Hey! Darlene, Abraham couldn't win a race either! But the next verse says Abraham believed God! He responded to God's love as Bonerack has to yours, and I have accepted Jesus as my Lord and Savior in response to the greatest love ever shown! And look Darlene, the next verse says;

"But didn't he earn his right to heaven by all the good things he did? No, for being saved is a gift. If a person could earn it by being good, then it wouldn'tbe free – but it is! It is given to those who do not work for it!

"Darlene, Jesus loves you! You may be a loser or even think you are a winner. But only Jesus can make you a winner, only He can transform your life. Bonerack is a winner because he has accepted your love; he's still a loser on the track. The real measure of success is not by worldly standards, but by eternal ones. We can only be a winner with Jesus!"

And Darlene accepted Jesus as her Savior and Lord.

I wrote up this story in a tract. I no longer remember how many printings or numbers of copies in total went out, across the country, to churches, to horsemen, or how many times it was reprinted in papers such as the "Cowboys for Christ" or in another chaplain's track news. I had someone translate the tract into Spanish and that went through multiple printings. Some got all the way to South America! For a couple of years every conversion to Christ on the track or in the churches came with the story of Bonerack Ricky as a part of the background message. A partly inebriated groom came up one night to tell me, "Chaplain, I know Bonerack; I know Darlene. I'm Bonerack, too."

I once received a long letter from a minister in Boise, Idaho. It seems that he worked with the little bush track at Boise when it was running. He told me that a Bonerack Ricky tract had shown up on his desk one morning. After reading it, he went to the hospital where a very depressed trainer lay uncommunicative on his bed. He read him the tract and left it on his bedside table. The next day the trainer was out of bed and walked with the minister asking questions. The minister thanked me for writing the tract and told me his trainer was gaining rapidly.

There is a postscript to the story of Bonerack. The last time he raced at Thistledown, a whole group of about seventy or eighty racetrackers was gathered near the paddock just in case Bonerack should win. They were going to swamp the Winner's Circle if he did and send me the win photo. It was a nice try on both the tracker's and Bonerack's efforts, but to no avail. Bonerack ran in his usual position.

Eventually, even Darlene had to bow under the pressure of supporting a losing horse. On a groom's salary it was all outgo and no income as long as Bonerack could not finish in the money. A horse trader from the west came through one day who thought Bonerack might be valuable to upgrade Indian ponies in a reservation herd. After two years of scraping the snow for grass in the winter and enjoying a harem, he was entered into a cheap race in Boise. Within two days, the "horsevan express" brought back the news that Bonerack Ricky had finally won a race!

When I first heard about Bonerack and had that eventful conversation with Darlene, I went to the track kitchen and told Big John Rutherford about Bonerack. I was excited!

Big John told me we should have a Bonerack Ricky Club and a button! That came to pass as well!

But Big John, in grasping the essence of the story said, "I'll give you another one, chaplain. It's the story of a horse named, 'Half A Man.' A young man, who later became a veterinarian, was grooming horses down near the gate. He came to me and asked if he could borrow $75. When I asked him why he told me he wanted to buy Half A Man back from the killer truck, and he was already loaded!"

"Well, I told him he was throwing his money away, but if he was set on it, I'd loan him the money. You see, chaplain, Half A Man's fetlocks were so weak that it looked as if he was walking on them. But the groom bought him and began to work on him. All of us old-timers gave him advice as to what to rub him with and he tried them all. That man sat in the stall for six to eight hours a day, rubbing that horse every moment he could squeeze in during the day and before work and evenings. Well sir, he began to improve! Then we all tried to invent some kind of brace that would help during exercise. Finally, by that fall, Half A Man was standing right and ready to run. No one who had seen him when he came off the killer truck could believe he was the same horse!"

"I told the groom who had worked so hard that he needed better competition than he would get at Thistledown. We got a trainer friend of mine at Detroit to take him, and he won $19,000 at that first meet and went on to be a steady money-winner!"

Without Jesus, I am only half a man. I have hurts that need to be rubbed and healed. Without the healing touch of God, I am only half a man. Healing may not be instantaneous; it may be a process, but with the Hands of God on me, my life in Him is open-ended! Half A Man is my namesake!

CHAPTER 10

A Missionary to the Churches

"...Peter and John replied...we cannot help speaking about what we have seen and heard."

[Luke, Acts 4: 19-20]

My position in Ohio differed from most chaplains in that I was the state missionary for the Ohio Baptist Convention. The agreement hashed out between RTCA and OBC was that I was to be free on Sundays to preach in the churches. Also my honorariums for this speaking were to be turned in each month with my expense account. The honorariums were then used to extend my expense account. It worked well, for speaking at a big church would let me also speak at a small church that hesitated to ask me to come. I often arranged to be at a small church for an evening service, or the other way around if I had to speak in the evening at a large church or association meeting. It worked well! The smallest group I met with was only five people including the preacher! Many times we drove up to five hundred miles on a Sunday with three speaking engagements. When we did that, Monday mornings kind of dragged.

One Monday I came into a barn and a trainer took one look at me and blurted, "Chaplain, you look like you were brought in hot and put away wet!"

As my reputation grew, my speaking engagements took up nearly every Sunday. Also, in February, when the tracks were nearly always closed, National Ministries of the American Baptist Churches, USA, had me speak in churches across the country for the America For Christ Offering. Sometimes there was a special request for me to speak somewhere, so National Ministries would set up a group of churches in the area or state where I would speak. Flight plans were made for me and often I rented a car to make connections. At Rock Springs, Wyoming , my seat-mate, who made this flight often, told me that about half the time the pilot had to buzz the field once to scare the antelope off the strip. No antelope there for me but how the jackrabbits scattered! Another interesting landing was during the winter in Kansas. It was a smaller, commuter plane and everything went well until he tried to get down. The wind at lower levels was so strong it tossed the plane right back up! After a couple of tries he literally dove the plane toward the field until he could level off and land.

My biggest danger on these extended speaking trips was the endless succession of church breakfasts, lunches and dinners! Many times an area minister had set up the church schedule and he had arranged for a meal at every place! If I tried to cut back on my intake some evenings, feeling I didn't need much food after a sumptuous lunch, it always failed. Some lady who had prepared her best recipe for the visiting missionary would note that I had taken none of it or only a little. Up she would pop, go get her casserole and come to my place, saying, "You've just got to try this!" Not to be outdone, other ladies would follow suit. I could just sit there and my plate would fill to overflowing! Overall, it was enjoyable – most of the time. Except for air travel. I just don't fit the seats in regular class airplanes, [they come in a maximum size of 46, and I am a size 52!] and while first class seats fit me, I could not afford them.

Once I did ride in first class and that was on a complimentary ticket. I had just finished a speaking tour in Arizona and stayed with a friend ready to fly out in the morning. Phoenix had had two one-hundred year rains in a bit over a week. The TV news advised people that evening to stay up that night to be certain they got flood warnings. About 9:00 P.M. it was announced that one end of the International Airport was under water, that the radar installation was surrounded by water and that the Interstate was about to be closed. My host made a couple of phone calls and we took off for the airport. I got a complimentary first class ticket on another airline since the other seats were full. This left at 2:00 A.M. and I dared not go to sleep for fear of missing my flight. A fifty-eight year-old flight captain [who was going to be forced to retire at age 59] had the seat next to me, deadheading to Des Moines, Iowa. We both introduced ourselves and talked about our respective occupations. As we leaned back to sleep in those wonderful first-class seats, I spoke up one last time. "Tell me, Captain, you don't have to answer this if you want to sleep, but have you seen things from the cockpit that you're not supposed to talk about? He snapped to attention and talked until we landed at Des Moines!

The story with the strongest attraction to me was when he talked about bringing a big passenger plane to Dayton, OH on a night with a very low ceiling of clouds. As he approached the Dayton International Airport, the tower said that at moment the ceiling was at 1,000 feet. As they led him beneath the cloud layer to land, his tower contact excitedly asked him if he had seen the UFO. He concentrated on getting his planeload of people safely on the ground and to the gates, but the UFO query had him puzzled. He decided to visit the tower himself and see if someone had been drinking on the job!

"What's this nonsense from you guys about UFOs?" he asked. One tower operator just pointed out the tower window at a huge round disk hovering just below the cloud level. It had been there for some time, he was told, going higher when the clouds rose and lower when they came down, always remaining in sight. It did disappear for a brief interlude when two jets from the Dayton Air Force Airport, which was right next door, were sent up to intercept it. Then it vanished into the cloudbank, only coming back below the cloud cover when the jets gave up the chase.

While the captain was examining the UFO from the airport tower, a controller came in, telling those around him that, "I had to come back! I went home but knew I just had to return and see what happens!" He was an Air Force tower controller and worked a few extra hours at the civilian base. The phone rang. It was from the Air Base and asked to speak with the airman controller who had just come back. Nobody could hear the caller, of course, but the airman said a bunch of "Yes, sirs" and "No, sirs", hung up the phone and announced, "Boys, I didn't see a thing. I've got to get back to the Base!"

The captain had seen lot of unexplained thing in the air. He could stay no longer in the tower as he had to make ready for another take-off. It was still there when he flew out.

It was extremely interesting, but I started a new day with no sleep. No one complained, but I was not up to par for a day or so.

I saw a lot of country and have preached in twenty-six states. If I wanted to provide more statistics, my files contain the name of all the churches I was in, but I'm not going to make the effort to dig them out [until this book is published!]

The racetrackers knew that I was a missionary to them from the churches, and in my presentations to churches, I was a missionary from the racetrack to the churches. Many attitudes were changed. A man caught up with me after one service. He was crying. He was a veterinarian who stopped taking calls to the track because he looked down on the trackers as "sinners." He then repented and told me he would follow Jesus. He would go back to the track to treat horses and talk to people for whom Christ died!

In Illinois, at the first church on a several day tour, the minister told the deacons before the Sunday morning service that he expected two people to come forward. He had talked with them that week. I had the opportunity to show my slides during the Sunday School period and then to preach later in the service. I gave the invitation and folks began coming forward. With the pastor and deacons working with them, the floor got crowded, so I went back to the pulpit and continued the singing and the invitation. There were eight new decisions for Christ!

As the pastor closed the service he asked that those who had come forward to go out onto the narthex and form a reception line for people to greet them. I was on the right side of the door and the eight lined up across from me. A dinner had been prepared in the lower floor, so people kept on going down a flight of stairs to a landing, then an abrupt turn down the second flight of stairs. A young man of about seventeen years of age stood last in line, next to a rail that protected a fall of at least sixteen feet down to the cement steps below. I saw him waver, then fall sideways directly over the rail! While at least eight to ten feet from him, I jumped across to grab him. Only his feet were above the rail when I reached him, but I grabbed them, hugging his ankles to my chest with both arms. He was that close to death!

The man next in line reached over the rail and grabbed

the young man's belt and we hauled him back up and laid him on the floor. He came to with no memory of falling. He'd not had breakfast that morning and presumably had low blood sugar. How close rejoicing could have turned to shock and grief! Satan tried to kill the joy, but I'm just glad the Lord had my eyes on the young man when it happened!

A River Downs trainer's mother went to a small church nearby. She arranged for me to speak one evening in her church. Florence was with me and I stopped at the track to see if I could pick up anyone to take to the service. Several wanted to come but couldn't, so I had picked up only one tracker, Pee-Wee, a former jockey.

It was a good service. When I returned Pee-Wee to the track, one of the grooms who had wanted to go with us, called out, "How was it, Pee-Wee?"

Pee-Wee stopped in his tracks and responded, "Man! You wouldn't believe it. He yell – he pound the pulpit! He preach like that to us, we be scared!"

We laughed hard, but that is how it came across to Pee-Wee.

Another memorable event took place in Austin, Texas. A lady from Texas had visited me at Beulah Park, wishing to talk with me about the status of racing in Texas. We sat down together in the horsemen's section of the grandstand so she could show me clippings and posters. Texas thoroughbred horsemen wanted pari-mutuel racing in Texas but their campaign was up against adverse campaigning. Neighboring states that had racing did not want Texas to open up, because that would take rich Texans [that's not to say they are all rich] away from their betting windows. A lot of money poured into Texas politics from racetracks out of state that did not want Texas to open their own tracks. The thing that shocked me and brought tears to my eyes was the outright slander of my people by several religious groups!

I saw cartoons depicting racetrackers as criminals. I saw

an article that purported the closing of the Kentucky breed-ing season in 1983 due to a venereal disease that was trans-ferred to the horses by humans! The truth was that a European import had brought the disease to Kentucky and that it was strictly a horse disease! I saw anti-racetrack liter-ature and lies from prominent churchmen that should have known better!

I am not advocating wholesale adoption of racetracks and pari-mutuel betting, but I am an advocate for the truth! The anti literature, while mostly false, could still have an effect on the average voter.

We sat, going over these lies together, for she had wanted to see a racetrack chaplaincy in action, and to get the reaction from a chaplain to racing's problems in Texas. We were in our own world there, and I started to pray for the situation when the gates opened at the three-quarter pole. Soon the roar of the crowd was so loud as the field approached the wire, that I had to cup a hand around her ear to finish the prayer!

She was an officer of the Texas Thoroughbred Breeders Association. An invitation soon followed asking me to speak in January at their 1984 Annual Meeting in Austin, Texas. At the hotel, I was assigned a room and had to carry my bag – no bellhop in sight. I got there, set my bag down and unlocked the door. Opening the door, I was struck by the sight of an open bag on the nearest bed with some femi-nine clothing spilled out from it, and the sound of the shower from the open door to the bathroom. I backed out as silently as I could! Lugging my bag back to the desk, I asked the clerk if he was trying to get me killed! After all, this was Texas! The next room I tried was OK, but I was still cautious! And I asked for and got a bellhop!

The program the next afternoon was rather auspicious! Ex Governor Connally, who was riding in the Kennedy car in November of 1963, and wounded when the President was assassinated, gave a speech just before my own. I was in great hopes that he could stay and hear me, but like most politicians, when he was through he left with his entourage.

When I rose to take the podium, I noted that they were probably surprised to see "Rev." before my name, but told them to prepare for a shock because I was a "Baptist" minister. I saw jaws drop for Texas Baptists were leading the attack against racetrack proposals. I told them about Race Track Chaplaincy of America and about our work. I told stories and told of changes on the racetracks where we were present. Just as I was getting ready to close, I had a Spirit-inspired thought.

I closed by stating, "Just as the Conquistadors had once landed on the shore of Texas and, planting a flag, claimed the land for their king or queen, I, in the sight of God and members of the Texas Thoroughbred Breeders Assn., hereby claim the future racetracks of Texas for Jesus Christ!"

There was rather stunned silence for a few moments, then a ripple of applause that soon became loud. God is true. Today, Texas has pari-mutuel racetracks, but by state law, they cannot run without a chaplain at the track!

CHAPTER 11

Rounding Up Loose Horses

"We all, like sheep, have gone astray, each of us has turned to his own way; and the Lord has laid on Him the iniquity of us all.

[The Prophet Isaiah, Isaiah 53: 6]

And a very, very loose translation for horsemen;

"We're all like loose horses!"

[Norm Evans]

"Loose horse!"
Closer now, another voice yelling, "Loose Horse!"
I stopped where I was to see what the fuss was about. After all, I had caught my own horses from the pasture many times. One would even come to me when I called him and lay his chin in my extended hand so I could lead him by his chin whiskers. But there was a special sense of urgency

153

in these yells. Maybe thoroughbreds were different.

A pair of strong hands grabbed me from behind and moved me sideways to the wall of the closest building. After I got there I was released and the voice of a trainer spoke to me, "Sorry about that, chaplain, but I figured it would be easier to move you out of the way first and explain later. When you hear 'loose horse!' get right out of the way! A loose horse will run crazy, scared and wild. They are likely to run right over a man trying to stop them and have even killed themselves running into barns and trucks! You get out of the way and let us horsemen take the chances!"

"Thanks! I really appreciate your warning! And I take advice pretty good," I responded with a smile.

Then came the Beulah Park meet. The main part of that section of barn area consisted of two long lines of barns and shedrows with the track kitchen anchoring one side, and the security building with the rec room and my office at the end of the other side. The main gate with a security guard was in the center of the road between them.

I was at the far end and far side of the last shedrow conversing with a trainer who was sitting beside his horse, putting on leg wraps. Then I heard a horse running. Remember, horses walk on the Backside because running gets the rest of the horses all stirred up. "Sounds like a loose horse coming from the track!" I immediately went down onto the road that ran all the way around the two lines of barns to see if I could spot the horse. It was coming straight for me! Fast!

Now, do I follow practical advice and get out of its way to let the horse hurt itself against a truck blocking its way; or do I act like an old farmer and try to stop the horse? I decided to try to stop it and get out of the way at the last moment, if I could! So I stood in its path with my arms spread wide and started talking to her, projecting in a calm voice that was at odds with my inner feelings. I picked a place just off the road to which I intended to fly, like Pete Rose going into third base. All the time I was trying to calm the oncoming horse, I kept glancing at the spot to make sure it hadn't moved! When the horse was about eight feet from me I prepared for my headlong flight, but at the last split-second I saw a change in her eyes and ears. Standing my ground, she stopped right at my chest. Taking her lead rope, I walked her around the backside of the barns where the pony person who had lost her caught up. What I had not expected was that each barn had a cluster of people in the big door on the track-end, who had come out to see what happened. As I came around the corner leading the horse, a cry went up that passed from barn to barn. "Hey! The chaplain caught that horse!"

My reputation was made. Soon the whole track knew, from security to management, that the chaplain had caught a loose horse! Being an old farmer that day sure helped! I have calmed many a mad or scared animal in my farming time.

A track service was coming up. I figured I better use the event in a message while the trackers still had a little awe at my success in catching the loose horse. I got up before them and said, "Does anyone here want to know about sheep?"

What a turnoff question to ask on a racetrack! As I expected, all heads shook "No-way" and faces were glum. I had talked with a farrier earlier who told me, as I gave him a special Racetracker's New Testament with racing horses on the cover, that someone had given his wife a Bible and she had tried to read it. One day she got disgusted and threw the Bible on the table, exclaiming, "I don't want to know anything about sheep!" That was a bit of a surprise to me at that time, for most churchfolk grew up on images and parables of Jesus the Good Shepherd and we as the people of His pasture! Lovely images, but horsemen talk horses and not much else.

So I shifted gears and told them maybe we could

substitute horses for sheep. I read, "All we like sheep have gone astray," and changed it to, "All we like horses have gone astray." "Nope," I said, "that sure doesn't sound right does it?" Again, heads shook "No!"

"Hey! How about, we're all like loose horses!" Now they all sat up ready to listen.

"There are three kinds of loose horses! First, there is the kind of loose horse that runs crazy, scared wild, and will trample the one who tries to help, or kill or injure itself running into a wall or truck. We've all seen horses like that." Heads nodded now. "We can be like that. There are a lot of ways to ruin our lives. Sin beckons to us all the time. We run away from the Lord who loves us, paid the price for us, and we live for ourselves." More nods. "In fact, Scripture tells us that the wages of sin is death. Just as some horses have to be put down after running loose, we stand to lose our spiritual lives if the ravages of sin don't kill us first. Make sure you never become that kind of loose horse. Let the Lord take your lead rope and bring you home!"

"The second kind of loose horse is like the one I caught!" There were smiles and chuckles now. "That horse was running just as crazy, scared wild like the first kind of loose horse. I know. I could see its eyes! But there was one difference. It really wanted to know the way home to the safety of its stall! While that horse did not know me, it finally decided to trust me because my voice was calming and I stood my ground without showing fear [not to say there wasn't a lot of inward fear in the last few yards!]" There were smiles of understanding now. "You know of Jesus who tells us of His Father's house, a heavenly home with lots of stalls. You know that He calls us to be His, to stop our senseless running away from Him. If, in your running, you really want to know the way home, and you hear the gentle voice of Jesus, go to Him!"

"The third kind of loose horse is like Ole Buck!" The

place erupted with laughter!

"You see, Ole Buck knows the way home, and we should be like Ole Buck, letting nothing stop or scare us on the way home!" Ole Buck was actually older than some of the trackers in my congregation that night! He was a track pony owned by Gayle Christman that worked all morning under Sam, the pony man. Most afternoons Sam and Ole Buck worked together taking horses to the paddock and returning them after the race. Sam would ride up to the track kitchen late in the morning when the horses stopped training, slip off Ole Buck, slap him on the rump and say, "Go home, Buck." Ole Buck would start out, plodding up the central road, avoiding manure trucks, feed trucks, people, cars and other horses while heading home. About six barns up he would turn in, go to the fifth stall on the left and wait. He was home! He knew the way home. Nothing scared him. He was at peace. "If you know the way home to Jesus, you'll have Peace as you go by the scary things in life!" As preachers will do, I spent about twenty minutes on a five-minute story, but it was in tracker's language and widely talked about on the track.

Not long after this service, I had the honor of teaching an adult Sunday School class in a large church. I told them of Jesus making parables about sheep, which were common in all of Israel, when Jesus spoke, and of seed and crops, which were all around them. I told them one of my cow stories, which were a specialty to me and did a pretty good job of interpolation of some Scriptures, and of my horse illustrations to horse people. I challenged them to think of something they could illustrate out of their own livelihoods. When asked they all spoke up to tell us what they did for a living, like truck driver, housewife, teacher, factory worker and other jobs. Then they put on their thinking caps. In five minutes nearly all had come up with a story more understandable to their unsaved neighbors than a sheep story would have been to them. Sometimes I think ministers who look up illustrations for sermons in seventy-five year-old books would be much more understandable and illuminating if they shut the books and drew from life around them! It's not hard if your eyes are open! Someone once told me we should have a "minister's eye," along with a "minister's heart" as we walk through life. Given the illustrations from life and stories that relate to you or the congregation, fewer people will fall asleep during church services! Vibrant stories that illustrate the meaning of Scriptures will stay with people!

Not too long after this, Mary Jane Wall, a free-lance writer for the Horseman's Journal, called me to set up an interview. She came to River Downs and followed me all day, observing my ministry there and spending time over lunch to go over things in depth. I told her about my sermon on loose horses. She wrote it up in her article, entitled, "Rounding Up Loose Horses." Later I read where she received a $100.00 first prize for the best article in the Horseman's Journal that year! Not only that, but on reading of my photography skills in the article, Horseman's Journal commissioned me to take pictures of older trackers – like seventy five and beyond. In an issue devoted to age related topics, I had an eight-page spread when it was published. I learned a universal truth when I told my subjects I was taking photos of older trackers. Every one insisted that old age was at least ten years beyond their age!

CHAPTER 12

Messages From The Track

"If we are out of our mind, it is for the sake of God; if we are in our right mind, it is for you. For Christ's love compels [controls] us, because we are convinced that one died for all, and therefore all died. And He died for all that those who live should no longer live for themselves, but for Him who died for them and was raised again. So from now on we regard no one from a worldly point of view. Though we once regarded Christ in this way, we do so no longer. Therefore, if anyone is in Christ, he is a new creation; the old has gone, the new has come! All this is from God, who reconciled us through Christ and gave us the ministry of reconciliation: that God was reconciling the world to Himself in Christ, not counting men's sins against them. And He has committed to us this ministry of reconciliation. We are therefore Christ's ambassadors, as though God was making His appeal through us. Be reconciled to God."

[Paul, II Corinthians 5: 13-20]

I had many visitors to my ministry on the racetracks. Church groups would often come on a Saturday morning in time not only to meet and talk with horsemen, but to watch a half hour or so of training on the track before the tractors started preparing the surface for the afternoon races. After lunch in the track kitchen, if they had time, they would go with me to the grandstand to watch a couple of races from the horsemen's section.

A visiting minister from California showed up one day watching the mob of horses going in different directions and at different speeds. I figured he was amazed that they weren't interfering with each other. Horses were coming and going through the quarter-pole chute and there could have been sixty to eighty horses using the track at any one time. I remarked casually that there was a traffic pattern out there, with no white lines. "If there is, please explain it; I'm having trouble trying to figure it out!"

"Well, these horses that are going backwards, that is to say, clockwise, are going by us within a few feet, staying on the inside of the outer rail. Notice that they just came on at the quarter-pole chute from the barn area. They start out walking and go no faster than a slow trot until they reach a point that the trainer has instructed the exercise rider to go to before he or she puts the horse into another lane. That could vary either side of half-a-mile or more.

"Then he turns into the track, just inside where he trotted out. In this lane the horse will 'gallop' slow held back by the reins, not allowed to run free. They are getting warmed up just like human athletes."

The preacher was nodding as he understood, then said, "Here comes a couple of horses going fast!"

I chuckled and replied that that was the 'breezing' lane. "After going a specified distance in galloping to get loosened up, they were allowed to 'breeze,' that is to go as fast as they wanted to go.

"After a specified distance set by the trainer in breezing mode, the horse would be eased to the inner rail where it had to 'work,' meaning it had to go as fast as the jockey wanted it to go. If you will look over on the backstretch, you can just see a jockey's head above the hedge. When they get here, you'll know what fast is!"

"Wow! the preacher exclaimed. "Now I see what you mean! There is a traffic pattern out there!"

"Of course, as they finish they have to work their way back out, slowing down in the breezing and galloping lanes until they can go out the chute where ready hands are usually there to take the horse, and perhaps to provide a fresh one. Sometimes a pony horse will take it back to the barn, where the yell will go out, 'Hot horse!' and a hot-walker will come out to cool it down by walking it. Then it gets a hosing down and a soap and water bath before going back to a freshly bedded box stall.

He asked a couple more questions, and then I told him if he could remember the pattern, he had good base for a sermon. "Thinking like a preacher, you see illustrations everywhere. For instance, II Corinthians 5: 14 says, 'Christ's love compels us.' One translation has the word, 'controls' us. Our horses are controlled by the bit and bridle and compelled by the jockey's short stick, or whip. But in our race of life we should be compelled and controlled strictly by the love of God!

"We all know that a horse should let the bit control it, but sometimes a horse will take the bit in its teeth and run off, in spite of what James said in James 3: 3. [The bridle with the bit steers and controls the horse.] I've had it happen to me with a western horse a time or two. Scary if you are in the wrong place!

"Compare these horses with a church congregation or a group of Christians. Going backwards is something a lot of folks do. If continued long enough, we know that ruin and grief, despair and problems result. Fortunately, most get turned around in life and start galloping for the Lord, but like these horses, they are held back by a lot of pressures. We are restrained by adherence to secret sins, bitter things of the past, sorrows, unforgiving natures, and love of money or obsessions that keep us from putting Christ first in our lives.

Finally, they get turned around. A lot of people are heading in the right direction at last, but severely hampered in their witness just as the horses are held back.

"Then there are the breezing horses and people like them. They get kind of proud at how much they are doing in the church, but still doing it at their own pace. They may even get to showing off by telling others what *they* are doing; getting rather showy about it. However they are setting their own pace and doing it their way!

The minister interrupted me to say, "Here come three horses in the breezing lane and going real fast!"

"Yes, the trainer of those three likes to send out his horses to breeze in company. The horses know each other and on their own are actually racing their stablemates. And we've got trouble shaping up with the outside horse! Notice its ears and eyes. Ears laid back, eyes rolling to the outside. It's going to bolt out of the group!" We watched it, and sure enough, it cut right out into the chute full of other horses and people. There a groom caught its bridle and a spare pony person took it back onto the track. There it was given some punishment, in hopes that it would think twice before taking the bit in its teeth and running off again. "Isn't that the way a lot of breezing Christians end up? They start out strong but their commitment is not totally to Christ and sooner or later will go their own way again. How many people, still alive, used to be our church workers, but are not present now? Our church rolls are full of them! They have decided that they have done enough, or taken up golf with business advancement, or bought a new boat and a camp on a distant lake. Their whole weekends are now spent away from church until the habit is set so that if the weather is too bad to go somewhere, they just stay at home. Just beware of someone who tells you how good a Christian they are in order to impress you!

"But look at the horses working the rail! They are tight against the inner rail, taking the shortest route possible, running at their utmost. The rider with the stick gives encouragement when it needs it, but he's talking to the horse as well, urging it on. I want to work the rail for Jesus, straining forward to the finish, compelled by the Love of Christ! How do I know when I've reached the finish line? Either I will be home with the Lord or He's come again! I don't have to worry; I can still serve him even when I am in bed in a hospital! My goal is to help more people into that inner lane, working the rail, both compelled and controlled by the Love of God in Christ!

"And there is much, much more to preach about in the verses following! Especially verse 17. 'Therefore, if anyone is in Christ, he is a new creation, the old has gone the new has come!' One translation I like says we are a 'fresh creation.' I like that because when we get through mucking a stall or currying a horse, we smell anything but fresh. I remember coming in from the cow barn one forenoon, smelling of a cow barn, to find Florence baking bread. Wow! What a fresh smell! I'd hang over her shoulder until she gave a fresh heel from the new loaf with some butter on it and I'd be a new man! If perfume manufacturers would make a scent that was like fresh bread just out the oven, it would revolutionize the whole industry! Men would just come trotting! Our witness to God however can smell kind of stale! People outside the church notice it and are not attracted. Some corrections are needed."

I was using this particular group of verses from II Corinthians at the track services for about three sermons.

The 20th verse says we are "ambassadors for Christ." I asked my people if they knew anything about the ambassador business. Response was negative. Here we are, most of us in work clothes, some with no time to wash up after doing all that has to done after a race, and some might have had horses in the last race. I told them that being an ambassador gave me the impression of dressing in striped trousers, cut away coats, overseas flights, locked attache cases, formal receptions and intrigue. That image certainly did not fit this old farmer! So I asked if they thought "We are agents for Christ" sounded OK. There was overwhelming acceptance to this, for the racetrack was full of agents!

For non-racetrackers, every jockey has an agent. He or she gets twenty-five percent of all that the jockey makes. Some agents have two jockeys. He earns that money by studying the races and conditions that are printed up by the racing secretary. Then the agent gets the overnight. Each trainer, on entering his horse in a race, has to name a rider. A popular rider might get named for two or three horses. The agent looks at these, knows every trainer and most every horse. If you see someone going back and forth, walking very fast in the barn area, know it's an agent. He finds the trainer he wants and tells him that the jock he named will undoutedtly ride another horse in that race [and if the agent has the leading jockey, he picks which horse he should ride]. But he contends that he has just the solution for him, that he has an up and coming jockey that the trainer ought to put on his horse. Maybe that jockey is still an apprentice with a weight advantage. Whatever the case, the agent is representing his jockey in the best light possible. If the trainer agrees, the agent will tell him that he will go to the racing secretary's office and make the change. Then he might tell the trainer that his allowance horse, or a high claimer would fit a race coming up in a week or so. That interests the trainer who had not had time to study the

Condition Book. He takes the book, studies it, and if he agrees, tells the agent to make that entry for him when he changes the rider on the more immediate race. He may even get some morning exercise on the book for his jockey, to get used to the horses he will be racing.

Then the agent is off on a trot to make the changes. He comes right back to the Backside to see more trainers to urge them to try his jockey, mentioning that so-and-so has just agreed to use him in another upcoming race. An agent is a non-stop sales representative for his jockey. They are busy, they earn their money, and they keep the jockey busy in the morning and line up races in the afternoon.

As agents of Christ, we are out there telling people what Jesus has done for us, and what He will do for all who sign Him up to ride in the saddle of their lives and trust the reins of Love to Him. We are His agents, God's representatives, to spread the news of His Love!

"The 19th verse says to tell people that, 'God was reconciling the world to Him through Christ, **not counting men's sins against them.'** That is kind of a switch from what Christians usually do. They know God forgives, but they still remember the sins of others. We are not to be 'sin wardens' to tell others how bad they are, but to tell of God's wonderful love and forgiveness!

"The racetrackers knew all about agents, and now they knew what it was to be an 'Agent of God!' "

CHAPTER 13

But How About All That Gambling?

**"'Then he said, 'this is what I'll do. I will tear down my
barns and build bigger ones, and there I will store all
my grain and my goods And I'll say to myself,
"You have plenty of good things laid up for many years.
Take life easy; eat, drink and be merry.
But God said to him 'You fool!'"**

[Jesus, Luke 12: 18-20]

One of the questions that church folks and pastors often
ask me is, "How about all that gambling? Can you
justify being around all that tainted money and being partly
supported by it?"

I usually tell them that if it's tainted, "Tain't enough!
And if you call it Satan's money, he's had it long enough; let
the Lord use it for His purpose now!"

Yes, there is gambling, but nobody ever asked that I be
kicked out of the church for gambling. I was a farmer for

twenty years, and there is no bigger gamble than that. I gambled with the weather all summer. Would the rain hold off for two days when I mowed a field of hay? Would we get enough rain for the crops to mature? Would the frost hold off in the fall? If I plant a cash crop, will the price at harvest be enough to cover the expenses of that crop? Would the price of milk hold up this winter to cover feed grain, hired help and taxes, and would there be anything left for us after the milk check was divided up to pay expenses?

All farming is a gamble and decisions have to be made each day whether or not to do something that is really based on odds. We don't call it that in farming, but it's true; the bigger the farm, the bigger the gamble. How much can we borrow against equity to get that new tractor, or put in a milking parlor? How many years will it take before that investment will pay off? Will it pay off, wondering about future prices?

I was once speaking in Detroit at a men's breakfast. I mentioned that to most church folks, the two-dollar window is gambling and sin, and fit for the Prodigal Son. To race-trackers, the stock market is too risky and fit for the Elder Brother. A lot of money is both won and lost in the stock market. To me, that is gambling in a sometimes-fickle market on a large scale!

The pastor had a phone call right after the breakfast. It was from a stockbroker who had just gotten back to his office. The minister chuckled as he told me the stockbroker wanted the pastor to bring me to his office. "I kind of figured you would hear from him. I think you got under his skin with that remark about the gambling in the stock market!"

At the office I was ushered to a nice chair and the broker started his defense. He told me, "I hate gambling! I want to set you straight on what I do. It takes a lot of study and when I recommend a stock, know that I personally have studied them out!

"For instance," he said turning to one of his many file cabinets, "let's look at utilities" He took out two identical copies of a list of utilities, handed me one and kept one for himself to read from. "You will notice that I have divided the utilities into thirds. The first are those utilities that have proved most worthy of investments. There is a middle third which might turn out well, and the bottom third are those that have not done well at all. So I direct you to the top third and suggest to clients to study the figures on earnings reported, size of dividends paid and total value of the company's worth. Is that gambling?"

"Umm. Sounds like you put a lot of time into this." He beamed. "But as I look at this, I can't help but think of a horseman studying the Racing Form. They do the same thing about dividing the field into thirds. They study for hours, crossing off the bottom third and the middle third, and then working on the past performances of the three or four horses in that race that have possibilities. He notes how long since the horse was raced, what track conditions were at that time, if there has been a change of trainers, which jockey is riding today and which jockey rode in the horse's last race. What was the time at a quarter, the half, the three-quarter mark and the finish? Has the horse been improving in speed? Did it fall off and behind in the stretch? Did it gain in the stretch? How long was the last race the horse ran compared to today? Did the horse race against any of its companions in the last race, that it will race today? Based on past performance, the decision is made and the bet placed. Then they watch the horse being saddled in the paddock and in the post-parade. If it starts to lather up, another wager is immediately placed on another horse, for the one picked is wasting strength in being nervous and sweating!

"A professional gambler may attend a race meet for a week and make only one bet! If he hasn't gotten what seems to him like a sure thing, he just does not bet. The favorite horse on the tote board only wins about a third of the time, so you can't go with the crowd. And I know all this and I don't even bet!

"It seems to me that betting on the horses with study and a little bit of instinct, is about the same as putting money into the stock market!" He was not very happy with my comparison. "Not only that, but entering the stock market on a whim or a friend's tip is like somebody betting on a hot tip at the track! If I had put two dollars to win on every horse that was given to me as a sure thing, I'd be way in the red. Racetrackers can get too high on their own horses!"

Even churches gamble a bit. Once I was introduced in a church that had given money up front to help start my ministry. It was announced with joy that the racetrack ministry was doing well, and they were glad they had had faith in me! When I got up to speak, I told them I was glad to be in a gambling church! They had gambled that my ministry would take off, and they did not even know my Past Performance. That statement was a shock to them but I clarified it to their satisfaction!

At one church a statement was made that the Bible was against gambling, but no proof text was offered. I was challenged, so when I came home, I looked in Young's Analytical Concordance. There is no direct reference to gambling. We might make a case for it, but it is not direct scripture. Some churches have no problem with gambling. Catholics often have bingo. There was a priest from Indiana who used to fly his own plane out to Grove City, Ohio at least once a week and spend the day at Beulah Park. I'm sure that many Protestants involve themselves in gambling, from casinos to racetracks. How about the constant office pools on the Kentucky Derby, or the Indy 500, or the Superbowl? The amount wagered on the Indy and professional sports makes horseracing look small! Check with Vegas for the odds and point differences.

Human beings need to emote! Would that it occurred in churches, but usually, except in Pentecostal or charismatic churches, we act sedate and dignified instead of praising the Lord with all of our being! Excitement, whether it be in a worship experience, an adventure or an amusement park ride, makes the blood run. Excitement is necessary to feel alive!

Beulah Park is right on the edge of the village. People walk to the grandstand from their homes. It is interesting to watch just after the first of the month when Social Security checks arrive. Two to four elderly women meet at the gate and go in together. I've watched them buy one program and pick out a horse because it had a nice name. Then they would each lay down a dollar or half-a-dollar on a two-dollar ticket, go to the rail and stand there pounding their handbags and yelling for the horse they had picked. They never bet beyond a few races but spent their allowance and went home. They would come out standing straighter, faces flushed and with grins on their faces. They always parted with the promise to meet again next month! They had been excited! It had done them good! They felt alive again!

One night I spoke in a church in Indianapolis. During the question time, a high school coach spoke up to say he knew of seventeen bookies in town that worked on high school sports betting alone, which amazed the congregation. One female college student was there and she floored me when she said, "I don't know about the right or wrong of betting, but it saved Mom and Dad's marriage!"

Talk about a bomb! There was a shocked silence until I stammered out, "Would you mind telling us how this helped?"

"Well, Mom was getting awfully stir-crazy because Dad was a farmer and never took time off for anything, including Mom. They went to a marriage counselor who told them that they had to do something together and soon, or they would have no marriage. They talked over what they might do together and decided to go to the horsetracks of Ohio or Illinois, because Indiana had no racing. They got excited together and it worked!"

"How is it going financially?" I asked.

"Mom used to let money slip right through her fingers, not budgeting or saving. Now she keeps a book of expenses versus winnings, and they are breaking even, figuring gas and motel costs, parking and a racing form. She budgets now at home, too."

"If they are breaking even and having enough excitement together to save their marriage," I stated, " they are doing above average!"

"Mom called me last night to read a romantic poem that Dad had written for her birthday, his first ever poem, and just for her!"

"This may be prying, but do you remember the poem?"

"Yes, it was, 'Roses are red, violets are blue, You're not bad for forty-two!' "

Another man told me if he went to a baseball game, he'd spend money for his ticket, his parking and program, plus he would probably have a hot dog, popcorn and a drink of some kind. All in all he would probably drop forty-dollars for the afternoon. Many recreational gamblers set themselves a limit of twenty to forty–dollars that they think they can spend on an afternoon at the track. When that amount is lost, they quit.

Grooms don't make much money when they first start working at a track. They are often carried away by the lure of the pari-mutuel windows, thinking they have a stake in their week's wages they can parlay into a lot more. Usually, within a few days they are completely broke and trying to borrow money for food. They learn quickly that they are headed for trouble if they spend much time at the windows. In the track kitchen at Belmont Park in New York City is a sign that reads, "Always eat your betting money; never bet your eating money!"

Addiction to gambling happens. It's bad. But in our culture we have food addicts, alcohol addicts, sex addicts, computer addicts, cell phone addicts, drug addicts and a lot of others. As far as gambling addicts are concerned, we sometimes direct them to Gambler's Anonymous, but on practically every track we have Alcohol Anonymous groups, for alcohol is a far greater menace to racetrackers than gambling. Active drug programs are also going on at the tracks and most chaplains have had special training to handle all sorts of addictions. We may have every problem on the hundred acre backside that there is on the outside, but not nearly so bad. The very presence of a chaplain on the track seems to make a big difference.

When I reflect on my childhood, I think of my mother bawling me out for losing some marbles. When I told her I had just learned to play marbles "for keeps," that was the end of that. Perhaps her guidance let me be on the track for nine years without placing a bet, but what would she have thought about my living in the midst of gambling on the racetracks, of all places?

Some churches cringe to think that the chaplaincy is supported by three main sources: church, denominational and individual giving, and from the organized horsemen and by track management itself. Church giving is a very small part of the giving because most congregations look askance at the betting. Both the horsemen's money and the track money come out of betting money after the state takes its portion, according to a negotiated formula. So, the money bet at the windows largely supports the chaplaincy.

In June of 1982, a pastor in the state of Washington wrote a letter to a chaplain from his church, who in turn sent the letter to our executive secretary. He sent the letter on to all the chaplains for their input. There were three objections, but the first concerns our using these racetrack funds.

It was, "Accepting finances from racetrack institutions," which of course is an objection based on aversion to gambling, something that church had decided was sin. Also implied in the other questions was that we should not be there with racetrackers.

Here is a partial list of responses. The first is from a Florida chaplain "Christ said in Matthew 28: 19, 'Go, then, to all peoples everywhere.' Part of everywhere is the race-track. Because the track is a sub-culture within our culture, and is privately owned, not everyone has the privilege of witnessing there. With a chaplain on the track, the Great Commission can still be carried out. The local church just cannot reach the people with a sustained type of ministry, which is required. How can you reach someone if you reject them and put them down? Christ sat with the 'wine bibbers', prostitutes and dishonest tax collectors; how else could He have reached them!

"I had no problems when I looked at Jesus and the needs on the track. There are many verses, which have helped me but the passage I use most is Matthew 9: 10-13;

> 'As Jesus went on from there, he saw a man named Matthew sitting at the tax collector's booth. "Follow Me," He told him, and Matthew got up and followed Him. While Jesus was having dinner at Matthew's house, many tax collectors and 'sinners' came and ate with Him and His disciples. When the Pharisees saw this, they asked His disciples, 'Why does your teacher eat with tax collectors and 'sinners'?' On hearing this, Jesus said, "It is not the healthy who need a doctor, but the sick. But go and learn what this means. I desire mercy, not sacrifice. For I have come, not to call the righteous, but sinners.'

"I don't defend my stand, I simply explain it. Personally, I don't think Jesus asked who furnished the meal or where it came from; He saw a need and met it. The first question in my mind if we have to depend on the Lord's people is, 'could we ever support this ministry?' "

From New Jersey came this. "...My approach is: ...The Lord is working through the RTCA, and He will supply the support and the supporters... I look for the day when the RTCA can make it without any help from the racing industry. But for the time being, since we are not yet accepted by the men of our 'Christian brethren' as bona fide evangelists and ministers of the Gospel of Christ, we need to take second best, i.e. we need the support of the industry. This is God's way of getting the work done now...[I hope] that the church will finally be rid of its hang-ups. Until then, I will rejoice and praise God for the way His work goes on."

Another letter came from Kentucky. "Those who live their lives sheltered from the world find it easy to be judgmental and paint everything black or white. Life is not simple, nor are the answers to life's problems. Jesus tells the religious people, 'If you love them that love you, what reward have you? If you greet your brethren only, what do you do more than others? Do not even the publicans so? ...' Jesus' own marching orders are: 'to preach the Gospel to the poor, heal the broken hearted, preach deliverance to the captive [many here are locked in a position that is difficult to escape], recovering sight to the [spiritually] blind and freedom to the disadvantaged.' [Luke 4: 18]... If God's people will not support the evangelization and Christianization of racetracks, then God will raise up Christian and/or non-Christian people or organizations to finance His word. For a ministry to be so spiritually sound and which has been supported so sparsely by local churches, is either an indictment on them or deserves a heavenly applause to those who do support us."

The last letter I will quote came from my own typewriter when I was in Ohio. "I sure hate to get into a proof-text debate with someone whose mind is already made up. It's like trying to smooth and level cement after it is poured and before trowling but waiting until the next morning to do it! By that time it has 'set'! Jesus would have a tough time with a Board of Deacons with questions like these. They would ask Him why He associated with sinners, gamblers, tax collectors, thieves and streetwalkers. I would like to know how many of them have any money in stocks, bonds or pork-belly futures, buy or sell insurance, have a business or have ever been a farmer? If the churches that are holding back would give enough, then we would not have to take racetrack money. Would they hold people out of heaven because they [God's people] stole from God? [Malachi 3: 8] Praise be to God that His Word will go forth in spite of His people! Esther 5:13-14 tells that God will not be thwarted in His purpose if His anointed fail. Does your Bible say, 'Believe on the Lord Jesus Christ, don't take money from a sinner, don't work toward a common goal with anyone who is not in perfect agreement with you [including which note Gabriel will play on his trumpet when Christ returns], and you will be saved.' Funny, I can't locate that verse right now, but there is a much shorter version, spoken by Jesus, in John 3: 16. They might look it up."

There were more letters than these, but they covered much the same ground as those quoted here. I'm not trying to make a case for gambling, but rather to look at it in a different light. Where there are people, there should be a ministry.

CHAPTER 14

The Greatest Jewish Jockey

"Jesus sent two of His disciples, saying to them, 'Go to the village ahead of you, and just as you enter it, you will find a colt tied there, which has never been ridden. Untie it and bring it here. If anyone asks you, "Why are you doing this?" tell him, "The Lord needs it and will send it back here shortly."'

[Jesus, Mark 11: 1-3]

"He's got a good hand!"
So might a jockey's agent speak about a new apprentice. Often, you can see that their hands are a bit larger than you would expect of a small person, although like a puppy, they sometimes grow to fit the hands as it grows harder and harder to make the weight. The hands hold the reins from the bridle and have to be strong so that the grip will not be lost. However, it goes much further that that.

Almost undefinable is the touch of the hand and it's effect on a horse. It can be a calming, relaxing hand, or a fearful hand. I once asked a Hungarian jockey why he thought a certain South American jockey won so many races. After thinking it over for a while, he replied that he thought the jockey in question terrified most of the horses he rode.

I'm very glad that his kind is in the very small percentage of total jockeys. When a jockey takes his mount out of the paddock, you may see him or her pat the horse on the neck to keep it calm. It's often repeated at the starting gate when you see a horse getting nervous about entering its given gate. My own hands have calmed a good number of horses [and a lot of cows!]

"The Touch of the Master's Hand" is a well known poem by an unknown author about an old violin at an auction that was ready to be knocked down pretty cheap, when an old violinist took it in his hands and played it. Then the bidding resumed, at a much different level! The Touch of the Hand of Jesus, our Master, on a human, like the Master's hand on the old violin, is like what Jesus showed when He laid His Hands on an unbroken colt. Never ridden, it submitted to His touch! Never ridden, it submitted to having robes thrown over it for Jesus to sit on! Never ridden, it let Jesus on its back with no fuss. Never ridden, it walked over robes and garments laid down as a path for it to carry Jesus through the gates of Jerusalem! Never ridden, it walked down an aisle of shouting people waving palm branches!

All these things are no-nos when training a colt! I would have let the colt see what was put on top of him before throwing it up. Strange motions in its peripheral vision would have most colts shying away and rolling their eyes! But Jesus laid His Hand on the colt, and the Hand of the Master made it trust! As far as walking over robes scattered in its way, I have never owned a horse that would walk over a burlap bag on the ground or not shy away from a bag or paper on the side of the path! But Jesus laid His Hand on the colt, and the hand of the Master made it trust! Waving palm branches or people shouting from each side of the road is enough to scare even an old horse, but Jesus laid His Hand on the colt, and the Hand of the Master made it trust!

In 1976, I was asked to take part in an outdoor drama commemorating our Central New York history in our Bicentennial Year. I was to represent a traveling circuit rider. Someone had brought in a quarter horse for me to ride. It was a beautiful horse but I had to enter the arena through a spillover crowd, mostly children, sitting on the grass, and it narrowed the entrance to the path. The horse got up to the funnel of people and stopped dead, rolling its eyes and quivered like a coiled spring ready to let loose! I was supposed to urge it through but I also knew that if I used a heel signal to urge it, I would be tossed and we'd have a runaway horse! So I just wiggled the reins while talking to him and putting my hand on him. Anyone in the crowd who knew horses that day was holding their breath. One lady told me afterwards that I had done the right thing. "If you had given him one little kick with a heel, he would have exploded right there and people would have been in danger! We could see the horse trembling!" After about three minutes of embarrassing silence, the horse relaxed and walked into the drama. Whew! Horses have tossed me before but I sure hated to have it happen before hundreds of people! I thank God that it did not happen! I don't bounce back on my feet like I used to, and I was wearing my "preachin' clothes!"

What a jockey Jesus would have made! He had the Hands!

Someone will be sure to object to my analogy here because the colt was a donkey and not a horse. But the principle remains true. It had never been ridden and still was subject to the fears of its cousin, the horse. Jesus chose a donkey to ride into Jerusalem because it was so prophesied, and by custom; a king coming in peace rode a donkey. A king coming as a conqueror would ride a war-horse. In either case it would be an un-gelded male.

In preaching this Palm Sunday text, I always use the analogy I referred to in a previous chapter. When Jesus puts His Hands on us, we are changed, and forever want to do His Will. Let Jesus ride in the saddle of your life, giving up the reins with which you've been trying to steer your life. Let Him continue to use His Hand on you to quiet your fears of giving up power, to encourage you to love others and to give the Holy Spirit a chance to show the world that you belong to Jesus!

There have been a lot of Jewish jockeys in the racing world. Some have come to my services on the track. They had good hands, but not the hands of Jesus, the greatest Jewish Jockey of all time!

The trainer of all animals knows the value of a gentle hand and a soft voice. My oxen knew my voice and my hand. They would come running whenever I called and quiet right down when my hand touched them. Together, my hands and voice were reassuring to them. I've had them on the road in heavy town traffic, and they walked with one ear turned back to hear me, and one ear turned forward to take in the strange noises they were hearing for the first time! If anything became threatening, a touch of the hand took care of the fear.

Strange it is that we humans are just learning the value of "the healing touch." Society allows someone else to enter our "personal space" only when given permission. Some folk are resistant to being touched. But our hands can be the Hands of Jesus to quiet, calm, reassure and show His love.

I was once assigned to a large hospital as a chaplain. A seminary professor monitored our "cases." One was a man who was dying, filled with hate and unresponsive in general. I sat beside him and took his hand in mine. I prayed for him. Next time I came to visit, he opened up to me about the object of his hatred. Again, I put one hand on his forehead and held his hand with the other and prayed. By the fourth visit, he had accepted Christ as his Savior, forgiven the person he hated and wanted out of the hospital. When my professor read the progress reports, his eyes filled with tears. "You can do something I cannot!" he said. "I just can't touch anybody! I would have had to make my prayers from the foot of the bed!" What problems that phobia caused him through his years! He could not touch another person beyond the shaking of hands! Never married, never sharing happiness or sorrow, he had cut himself off from the healing touch!

One final word about my patient. Five years later I got a letter from his daughter in another state. She told me he had had five more years of life, happy and contented. He wanted her to write to me at his passing, thanking both me and the Lord for touching his life!

Another thing, it works both ways. Touch and be touched! Heal and be healed! Receiving a hug works wonders as well as giving one! After all, we are humans together, made in the Image of God, made to give and receive the healing touch!

CHAPTER 15

Christian Presence

**"You did not choose Me, but I chose you to go and bear
fruit – fruit that will last."**

[Jesus, John 15; 16]

"Fruit that will last" This is one weakness of the
church. Our fruit should taste good or it will be
rejected. Our witness should taste good, to attract those to
whom we witness, or it will be rejected. I firmly believe that
the church has turned away more people than have been
saved. I say this after years of talking with horsepeople.

I used to own an old, overgrown farm on Muller Hill in
Georgetown, NY. My son has it now. It's a natural nature
preserve. Wild apples grow in profusion, providing much
deer and turkey food.

I know that Jesus was talking about grapes when he told us
to bear fruit that will last. The only trouble is that I know nothing beyond the basics of grape growing. So I'm going to talk
about apples. I'm sure He would go along with me on this.

I used to hunt deer on this property. They would use the apples that dropped freely from the trees and it was a central feeding area in the midst of a large area of public forest. I like apples, too. When hunting, I'd always check out the fruit. Usually, I would select one that looked great, but at the first bite, I would usually spit out the morsel, throw the apple as far as I could and start looking for a sweeter apple to take the sour taste out of my mouth! When I found the right tree by continuing to sample, I'd eat one and load my pockets with others from that tree. Satisfied, I could get to the task at hand.

In case you are the inquisitive type, you just might be interested in why there are apple trees there in the old pasture. Johnny Appleseed never came near us. You may be surprised, but the answer is cows. They were fed the "pressings" left over from making cider in the years gone by. All the seeds were in the mash of pressings. I don't think I have to go further to explain the process, but the seeds had their own organic fertilizer.

Our fruit, our fruit that will last, is sweet and long lasting. If our fruit, and we all bear some kind of fruit, is as bad tasting as most crabapples, it turns people away. Our fruit is our witness for Christ. How does it taste to people who are outside the church? If you ministered outside the church, like a racetrack chaplain, you might be in for a surprise.

I have found that folks outside the church think of Christians in several different ways. First, is that we are "Do Gooders." Second, is that we are like "A Cop Sitting in the Median." Thirdly, they may think of us as "Sin Wardens." Fourthly, they may think of us as "Lapel Grabbers." And they may think of Christians as "Squabblers." They have these ideas because they have observed us in action or inaction.

Take "Do Gooders" for example. To me, a do gooder is someone with high ideals but no knowledge of what they are doing, throwing a monkey wrench into the wheels of progress. I once overheard a racetrack official, before the days of widespread acceptance of the RTCA, refer to us as those "Do Gooders!" I have one example of what I consider a "Do Gooder" act.

During WW II, those at home tried to do all they could to help the "war effort." The idea was that if civilians could learn and practice first aid, for instance, they might be able to replace someone who was fit for the Services but tied to an essential job. One young matron took a class in artificial respiration. This was the old Boy Scout method of straddling a person lying face down, and pushing down and letting up the ribcage as you bent over, to the rhythm of "Out goes the bad air, in comes the good." Definitely not the new kissing method in use today! This matron was walking home from her class when she saw a man lying on his face at the edge of the road. She immediately ran to him, dropped her handbag, and started with the artificial respiration she had just learned. She thought, "what a God given opportunity to serve!" She got into position over him and started in. "Out goes the bad air, in comes the good," over and over. Finally the man rolled up and said, " I don't know what you are doing lady, but I'm holding a light for the man in the sewer!"

I most certainly do not want to be thought of as a "Do Gooder!"

Most of us have driven on a modern, four-lane highway. Did you ever notice how traffic would be rolling along at sixty-five or up, when suddenly traffic slows to fifty- seven? When you get around a curve you see a trooper car sitting in the median. Traffic has slowed when he is in sight, but a little beyond goes back to speed. The trooper has served a purpose of getting people to take notice of their speedometers, at least for a mile or two!

The same holds true for the Christian witness in that theme. Some people stop swearing when we walk by, or try to act innocent if something they were doing might be thought of as wrong. If all our Christian witness does is make people feel guilty for the time we are near them, then our fruit does <u>not</u> last and we are guilty of not making the right kind of fruit! Our fruit should be so attractive that those outside the church would want to come in and find Jesus!

If you read James Michener's book, "Hawaii," you may recall that the early Christian missionaries to Hawaii taught their converts to be "Sin Wardens," acting as tattle-tails to inform the missionaries of the misdeeds or failures of others. You do not build a loving and caring heart by always condemning or disapproving people who live or act differently. Some of the trackers told me after I had been there for a while that they had expected me to lecture them every time I saw them with a beer, or cussed in my hearing! No! I did not scold them but treated them with love and was nonjudgmental! If they were sinning in any way, they knew it. I didn't have to tell them. My witness was always positive, not negative, and with love overriding their faults, amazing things happened.

As a Christian, or maybe not a Christian, have you ever been stopped and confronted, perhaps even had your lapels grabbed by someone and the sudden question asked, "Have you been saved?" It is an embarrassing moment, even if you love the Lord and approve of the motives. While it may work sometimes, lots of people have been approached in this abrupt manner and are turned off to our fruit of witness. There are better ways to introduce folk to Jesus that will remain sweet and long lasting in their lives. Some Christians may criticize my methods, but I don't think that our fruit is good and lasting if it is embarrassing to the person who tastes it.

Some folks think of Christians as "Squabblers," always involved in "church fights." We are often thought of as contentious people that want to change <u>them!</u> How do you think they ever got that idea! What goes on inside the church in widely known about outside the church. People often respond, "I've got trouble enough of my own; I don't need that!" Maybe our fruit tree needs a bit of pruning!

My own realization of what Christian presence really meant came as a shock to me! I'd heard the term of course, but like most Christians, I had a rather hazy and incomplete understanding of the term.

One summer on the track, my bad knee got so painful that I had to walk with crutches. I was told that I had to keep off of my feet for a while. It was really bad. Only a new knee years later took care of the problem. While I rested at home for a few weeks, I continued to go down to River Downs once a week for our chapel service. We had a bed in the back of our van, and Florence would drive while I lay on the bed. When we got to the track, I went immediately into the track kitchen on my crutches to meet any trackers who might be there. From there I would go into the Racing Secretary's section and make an announcement over the public address system of the impending service. Then I limped over to Hobson's Tack Shop in a nearby trailer to talk with Mrs. Hobson, who always knew who was happy and who was hurting. While I was there, trainer and pony-man Gayle Christman came in. I greeted him warmly and asked how things were going with him and his horses, and especially how his father was.

When I hobbled out of the tack shop I went through the end of a barn where Irv Tannenbaum had his horses. His main groom was a redheaded girl. As I greeted her, she said, "I sure wished you were here last Friday!"

Concerned, I asked her what had happened that day. Her response was "Oh, not much. I just got mad at the boss. And I don't get mad when you're around!"

"You don't?"

"No, everything seems to be better for me when you are here, and I never get upset!"

I was dumbfounded as I made my way from her shedrow to the Racing Secretary's outer office where the service was to be held. Not long after I arrived, Mrs. Hobson closed the Tack Shop and came in for the service.

"Chaplain, Gayle said something after you left that I think you ought to hear. He told me that he was glad to see you back, because when he was ponying horses every morning, and saw you, his whole day went better!"

It was like getting hit in the stomach. My mouth dropped open in astonishment.

What was happening here? Then I realized that there was more to "Christian Presence" than I had dreamed of! Was my being among my racetrack people, with love for all, fruit that would last?

Then I thought of a wooden sign out by the horsemen's entrance. It was a good sign when it was put up. It was made of plywood painted white with good black letters, spelling out, "JESUS LOVES." But years had gone by since someone had hurriedly nailed it up, probably afraid that he might meet one of those "trackers!" Now the plywood was beginning to peel apart, and the paint, once so nice, was curling off. It was a hot, dry summer when I photographed the sign. All the highway's border vegetation was dead. The only green showing was a nice poison ivy vine, growing up the power pole that supported the sign and framing the decaying sign! Is our witness for Christ like that sign? Is our witness like sour fruit that will not last? [It might even be laced with poison!] The person who placed the sign possibly thought that horsemen coming in their entrance would be convicted of their great sin of working on the racetrack! That person presumably was sitting at home, satisfied that his sign was a lasting influence on those sinners out there on the track. But it was not done in love!

In the meantime I was spending most of my week throughout the meet living there with my trackers, night and day, helping them, loving them and living the Gospel. That brought fruit that has lasted!

Christian Presence might be easier for a layman than a pastor. The person who goes to work is usually with other people most of the time. Christian Presence and long lasting fruit can come easily since the fellow workers can watch us all the time. Are they attracted by our loving ways with them? You don't have to carry a big Bible to let them know you are a Christian; it should bubble out of your personality!

As I found out with the wild apples, all fruit is not sweet. Our witness, perhaps unbeknownst to us, may not be as sweet as we thought it was. If it has gotten that way, your life has to be turned over to Jesus, so that He really can live in us and through us!

There is an old poem that starts out, "I am my neighbor's Bible." There is truth in it that needs to be ingrained into our existence!

> **I am my neighbor's Bible. He reads me when we meet.**
> **Today he reads me in the home: tomorrow in the street.**
> **He may be a relative or a friend, or slight acquaintance be.**
> **He may not even know my name, yet he is reading me.**
> **Author unknown**

In my travels and experiences, I have met many, many people who had been turned away from Jesus, or the church, by a careless or intentional remark, or a raised eyebrow, or a word snapped in irritation by a Christian of the church, maybe even the pastor! People are wounded in their spirit by these things, and turn away from the Lord. When I introduce myself to trackers, you can usually tell which one a Christian has wounded. Many tell me later what happened. I have shed tears of sorrow several times to hear how the good, long lasting Fruit of Jesus Christ was corrupted. We drive people away sometimes without even realizing what we did!

Some Christians even go to church with long-lived resentments smoldering away deep inside them. I broke and trained a yoke of oxen, and have observed several other oxmen at work. The "near" ox [you walk on the left side of the yoke, and the left ox is the near one] is always the best behaved and eager one of the two. His brother, the "off" ox is on his right and his master on his left. Nothing to fear out there!

The off ox has the big wide scary world out there on his right and he can seldom see his master! That is why he gets upset and nervous, especially when he is young. He is separated from his master! No wonder he acts up once in a while!

If anyone, layman or pastor, has come between you and God and prevented you from tasting the sweet, long lasting fruit of the Love of Christ, you are like the off ox! Someone has gotten between you and God! You became the off ox! Try not to ever let anyone get between you and God! And Christian, never get between God and anybody else except as a clear, sweet door into God's Presence!

Sometimes I feel that I ought to stand in proxy to be forgiven for all those Christians, who by their sour fruit, have come between God and the person they drove away! If I could, those sour Christians would not know and would continue producing their sour fruit. But to all those, who, on reading this, would seek out sweet, long lasting fruit, and meet Jesus face to face, my joy would be complete!

And don't forget that Jesus forgave you your sins, and having been forgiven for you're off ox antics, you can now joyfully forgive the near ox that got in your way!

CHAPTER 16

Advent On The Track

**"Arise, shine, for your light has come,
and the Glory of the Lord rises upon you!"**

[The Lord, Isaiah 60:1]

"They rode their animals as fast as they dared. The journey was long, so they had to pace speed with endurance. Still, the beasts lost weight and probably pulled up sore at the finish.

The riders fared little better. They were sore themselves, and because they had to carry most of their food and water, they too were on light feed. At times, they stopped to loosen girt straps and check the feet of their steeds; at night they cared for their mounts before they cared for themselves.

Were they crazy? Most of the world would have said so if they had known, but their race across the desert was unknown – until near the end when they stopped to ask directions.

Were they foolish? Who else would risk life and limb to

cross a desert, following stars and interpretations of stars to get to a strange land, to bring gifts to someone they did not know, had never seen, and who in fact was only just born?

They must have been both crazy and foolish, for they ended their long race before a baby whose birth had been in a stable!

A stable! In the palace at Jerusalem, where rich foods, golden dishes and soft couches were the standard of living, a stable was a place only servants would visit. One would not even think of a stable if it could be helped. It was no place at all for a King, much less a divine King, impossible for the incarnation of God Himself! Crazy! Foolish!

But history says they were Wise Men. Nothing mattered but finding their Savior! It mattered not that would find Him in a stable.

Time passes – memory dims. Ask in the churches, ask in the courthouse, and ask the man in the street – "Where is the King, the Savior Messiah?"

Would anyone answer, "You'll find Him on the Backside, in a stable?" The odds are against it. But He's there.

Jesus goes where He is needed. To people who know no need, it's foolish to even think of a Savior. To people who feel superior to others, it's crazy to believe a Savior would even walk in a stable, let alone be born there!

But He's needed in the stables, and He's on the Backside. When the mud is deep and you're soaked through, He's there. When your feet hurt and the horses still need to be walked, He's there. When you celebrate a win, He's there. When you can muck a stall but have trouble cleaning up your life, He's there. In a stable. He's not ashamed of it. He was born there.

And you're not crazy, not foolish but wise if you walk with Him there. Sure it's a rough place, that's why He came. He's needed. He came to smooth out rough places, to walk with people who would admit their need.

Some called Him crazy. Some called Him foolish. Because He would not fit the pattern set by those who wanted the race to be run their way, He died on a cross, as a criminal, to the jeers of those who said no King could come from a stable.

Would you have bet on Him when He was dying on the Cross? Bleeding from the crown of thorns and the nails in His hands and feet? Raw and bloody from the cuts and welts of the knotted whip? Pierced in the side with a spear? No, not even a chronic loser would bet on such a long shot!

But He won! He lives, He stands in The Eternal Winner's Circle, asking us to stand with Him! Now, who is crazy, who is foolish and who is wise?

Jesus is still in the stable, and the wise, the people with needs and who know it, will walk with Him!"

I wrote the above as a Christmas letter in 1977, at the end of my second year on the tracks. I remember telling Florence that I was going to write our letter [personal news followed this] and sitting there trying to get started. All of a sudden, I started to write as fast as I could until it was finished! As I retype it here, I felt the same thrill that I had the evening that I wrote it! There is a big temptation [as a preacher] to expound on it, but I think it should stand by itself.

Christmas, 1976

"Jesus was born in a stable. Mary and Joseph were simple folk, and the place selected for His Incarnation was a simple place. The Christmas Cards show it as clean and soft, illuminated by starlight and halo-glow. The animals are pictured as peaceful and calm, awed by the scene before them.

But stables then and now are also places of roughness for man and beast. Places that require constant work to keep clean – and clean is a relative term. Dust from hay and bedding settles on beams, rafters and boards. Manure dries and becomes part of the walls. Cobwebs lace the corners overhead, sagging with collected dust. Stablehands are not always sweet and calm. Animals can kick and bite.

The stable that greeted Jesus that night knew both the sweetness of fresh hay and the acridness of manure. It had heard the gentleness of loving words to a dumb, but knowing beast of burden, as well as the cursing of a drover as he harnessed an ugly and unforgetting animal, galled and scared with leather and load.

Jesus came to a stable – He came to a world – where the smells of sweat and labor, anger and disappointment, often overpower those of joy and love, of peace and gentleness. He came – to change the commonplace into the extraordinary, to change blasphemy to praise – to convert weakness into strength, to place confidence where anxiety had been in charge, to bring forgiveness and wipe away the guilt of sin, to set peace and love in hearts where anger, hatred and mistrust had ruled. He came – God in man – to show us what he was like.

To show us, He was born in a stable – and died on a rough and brutal cross.

The world forgets the stable. Except for the once-a-year Christmas creche, and that prettied right out of reality. Even in Bethlehem, the traditional manger where Jesus was laid is now overlaid with marble, inset with a silver star, illuminated with jeweled lamps whose light flashes from facets of diamonds and bands of gold.

The stable could not be left simple. The world could not stand the real stable. Most of the world cannot stand the real Jesus.

There is still a stable. Thousands of people will sleep in stables tonight. Many more will work there in the morning. Forgotten people. Shunned by many, rejected and neglected, but people for whom Christ lived and died and rose again! The Good News of the Gospel is for them as well as for those who would like to forget the stables"

Christmas on the track depends on racing dates and the particular track. I do know that at Christmas time in New Jersey, many churches provide gifts for the chaplain to give out. Every gift has a Gospel, a Bible or a New Testament with the gift! It is well organized, thanks to a former chaplain who got the churches on board. It is now so big that the chaplain has a crew helping him. They have a big service and dinner as well.

In Ohio, when I was there, we had to celebrate Christmas near Thanksgiving time because Beulah Park was usually closed by early December, while River Downs and Thistledown were also dark at Christmas time. We had a special Advent service, complete with special music and lots to eat. Local churches usually supplied the food, and we tried to have something as a small gift for everyone.

It was a time of saying temporary good-byes to most of those at the services, for they were shipping out to another racetrack, even going home for a break. It was always a time of much prayer, hugging and "See you in early spring!"

After the tracks were closed, there were still local horsemen and horse farms to minister to, and to try and catch up on the paperwork and year-end reports. Then came January and a New Year of racing.

Eastertime on my tracks was usually spent at Beulah Park. Thistledown by this time in '77 had a chaplain to work out a program. River Downs was usually dark. Again we had a special service with music from some local choirs and, of course, plenty of food!

There are always a goodly number of trackers that are Catholic. They have no labels and most take part in our ministry. One year in New Jersey, Chaplain Homer Tricules thought of Ash Wednesday as having a lot of meaning to Catholics and Protestants alike, although most Protestants do not give out ashes. He decided he would, had a small table reserved for him in the track kitchen, got some ashes from his fireplace, announced that ashes would be given the next day, put on his robe and went to the kitchen at 6:00 A.M. The response was tremendous! Many received Christ as Savior that long day as they confessed they had sinned and wanted forgiveness!

Some of our chaplains have even arranged outdoor Easter sunrise services at daybreak, with wooden crosses for a backdrop. All chaplains are free to ask management for help or to come up with creative ways of celebrating the Resurrection of Jesus Christ. Something that will change hearts and lives; and hearts and lives are changed!

CHAPTER 17

Samaritans Among Us

**"But you will receive power when the Holy Spirit
comes on you; and you will be my witnesses in
Jerusalem, and in all Judea and Samaria,
and to the ends of the earth."**

[Jesus, Acts 1: 8]

We are to be witnesses to the whole world. To do so,
Jesus says to start at home, our Jerusalem. Then we go
into a wider area of our people. Then comes Samaria.
"Samaria! We don't truck with those folks, Lord!" You see,
the Jews despised the Samaritans, and all were Jews in the
group around Him when He made this last Word before His
ascension into the clouds. Without going into the historical
background of this very extreme prejudice, know that the
Bible has a long history of what developed into one of the
worst ethnic feuds ever. Jesus talking with a woman of
Samaria at the Well of Jacob between Mt. Ebal and Mt.
Gerazim was an event that would be both shocking and

unheard of among the Jewish people. Read the story in John 4.

They were different. Unorthodox. Not like us. Florence and I went early one Sunday morning to a country church near a town in Indiana. Forgetting that Indiana did not use Eastern Savings Time, we arrived an hour early, plus my usual half-hour to "settle" myself after a long drive. The minister came out to talk to us before he got dressed for church. He told us that I was the last of five missionary speakers in a series, and that evening they were to meet to decide what their church could do in mission in their locality. Already, there had been some talk about visiting every family in the area. The minister was concerned, for he told me that a few of his people had come to him privately to give him advice. "Look, Pastor, I went to school with some of these folks. There is no use visiting this family or that family. I know what they are like!" "Pastor, you haven't been here very long, but if you knew how they lived and acted, you would stay away from there!"

When we went in to see the church there was a huge banner across the front of the church, behind the pastor, which read, "ACROSS THE STREET; ACROSS THE WORLD!" I immediately went back to the car and began to meditate. I changed my sermon entirely, used a different text, and told them that Jesus ministered to Samaritans and outcasts. We had to be like Jesus and minister to the Samaritans/misfits that lived among us. They heard me. A large group of members came forward at the invitation to go where God sent them, even if it was to someone they didn't like!

Samaria, the region you avoided, where people that you hated lived, is not way off there somewhere! Samaria has come to Jerusalem! Racetracks in a town or city are seen by a lot of professing Christians as wicked places and wicked people because of the gambling basis of racing. [Some still sneak in at race time!] They don't seem to get the point that

"The Woman At The Well," a Samaritan, would have been the last person in the world that you would have expected to accept the teachings of a Jewish Savior! Yet she was the first Samaritan to follow Jesus, and she brought a whole village back with her to hear and believe the Good News that was Jesus Christ!

We read and hear sermons on "The Good Samaritan," found in Luke 10: 27-37, but seem to ignore the meaning to ourselves.

Not very far from Columbus, Ohio, I spoke one Sunday evening about the ministry on the racetrack. After the benediction, the pastor asked me if knew of any way to stop the noise from a country dirt track close to the church. He told me that the cars began revving up at 11:00 A.M. as church services were starting. It was a great irritant to the whole congregation. "Um, have you ever thought of going out there and starting your own mission? This church has the best opportunity to reach those people!" I don't think he liked my suggestion. It's easier to minister to Samaritans somewhere else than in your own Jerusalem!

The startling thing to me was that the last person I would expect seemed to come to acceptance of Jesus first. Salty Roberts, our RTCA founder, was such a man. He came one time to visit me at Beulah Park. We went out to visit the starting gate crew between races. To my surprise, the starter and Salty were good friends. They had been "drinkin' buddies" in the old days of Salty's life. Salty was on fire for the Lord. The starter turned to his crew as we left, shook his head and exclaimed, "Boys, if it can happen to Salty, it can happen to anybody! We used to go fishing together down in Florida. Salty would drink so much that when we came back, I would drag the fish in one hand and Salty in the other! He was the last man in the world I would have thought to find 'religion!'"

When I first began my ministry at Thistledown in January of 1976, Salty called me from Florida to ask me how things were going. He asked who was coming out to the daytime service I was holding in the HBPA sitting room, and my response led him to exclaim, "Big John Rutherford! He's the last person in the world I would have expected!"

One day a girl groom named Darlene came to the service, and Big John leaned over and whispered, "She's the last person in the world I would have expected to come here!"

Another man named John came in later, and afterwards, Darlene called me aside to say, "He's the last person in the world I would have expected to come!"

Big Max was one of the first converts at Coulter Racetrack in Florida, under Chaplain Cliff Holsema, a great man of God who is now helping to oversee us from Heaven. Big Max was a near giant of an African American. Chaplain Holsema told me that Big Max was "the last person in the world that he would have expected to come!" One time Cliff told me he was working with a groom, talking about accepting Jesus as his Savior, when Big Max came into the room unexpectedly, and immediately knelt in front of a chair and began praying for the man's salvation. He stayed there praying until his prayers were answered!

The first Sunday morning after Big Max accepted the Lord, he decided to go to church. Walking out the gate, he looked up and down the highway and spotted a church. This was a white, Southern Baptist Church, but Big Max just walked in and sat down. What he did not know was that some time before, Black advocates had it in the paper that they were coming to this church on a given Sunday with TV and the press. The congregation was so distressed at the publicity and actions, that the church did not open that Sunday. But Big Max did not know that and just came in and mingled with fellow believers in Christ. Six months later, at the invitation to join that church at the end of the sermon, Big Max went forward. As he arrived at the front, the minister spoke out, "Max! Why have you waited so long?"

With his deep bass voice Max replied, "I just wanted to make sure that you folks could love me!"

Everybody in the big congregation spontaneously got up out of the pews and came to the front and took turns hugging him. That was the end of the service as they milled around him. This "last man in the world," a racetracker/Samaritan, was loved! At least that church learned first hand that a witness to Samaritans could be a wonderful thing!

In my ministry on tracks and in churches, I have always seen this happening! "The last one you would expect" is often the first to respond to love and the Message of Jesus! There is no way that anyone should be ignored in any ministry, no matter how tough, how seemingly incorrigible, how low on the totem pole, how inconceivable it might appear that anyone could reach that person! If you know of someone you don't like, or who does not like you, start praying for that person. Do it silently every time you see, hear or read about that person. The Lord might even alter your feelings about that person [or Heaven forbid, alter the way you think about yourself! That's the danger of praying for someone you don't like; your prayers are often answered sooner than you think!]

Someone you can't stand at work? Try it. Do you ever avoid someone, try it. Are there kids or grownups in school that irk you, try it. Is there someone in your school class that has no friends, try it and be a friend to them. Try it, you'll like it! It even works for those you try not to sit beside in church!

A speaker from England spoke at a convention that I attended. He told of a church in England that decided on a campaign to woo people to Christ that were considered poor prospects. The minister picked the local bookie [the minister failed] and one man chose his next door neighbor. This man was disliked by all the kids and dogs in the neighborhood, plus most of his neighbors. Every time a child walked on his lawn, he was there to yell and throw stones at their dogs. He complained to the neighbors if grass blew onto his side of the line, or if the neighbor's fall leaves blew onto his lawn. He was mean and cantankerous toward everybody, not even responding civilly to a friendly greeting from the sidewalk. This is the person that our man selected to try to win for Christ. Certainly, he was the "last man anyone would expect" to be led to Christ!

Stumped by his problem our Christian man, who had taken on this seemingly impossible task, studied his neighbor. He had a pigeon cote out behind his house where he seemed to spend quite a bit of time several times a day. So our friend used his binoculars to check out the pigeons. Then he spent quite a few hours in the public library looking up pigeons and reading pigeon fancier's magazines. Thus fortified with a bit of knowledge, he walked on the sidewalk in front of the neighbor's house. The neighbor just happened to be up on a ladder, painting his house. This did not seem like the opportune moment to start a conversation, but he called out anyway, "How are your Blue Racers, neighbor?

The man turned on the ladder and answered back, "Are you interested in pigeons? Come on out back and I'll show them to you!" He came down from his ladder and put away his paint pail and brush, and together they went to the pigeon cote.

From that beginning they became better acquainted, and eventually the neighbor attended church with his new friend. Later, the neighbor rededicated his life to Christ, made a complete change in his attitudes toward others, and became a good neighbor.

This is what can happen when you really try to love "the last person you would expect." Who knows? Maybe someone once thought you were "the last person in the world" who would ever find salvation! And if you still haven't, there is nothing to hold you back from doing it now! Paul says in II Corinthians 6: 2, "Now is the day of salvation!"

CHAPTER 18

Running The Race

**"Therefore, since we are surrounded by so great a cloud
of witnesses, let us throw off everything that hinders
and the sin that so easily entangles, and let us run with
perseverance the race marked out for us."**

[Paul, Hebrews 12: 1]

We are all in a race. We need to "run with perseverance," [see above] but not all of us have the same
"race marked out for us." I Corinthians 9: 24-25 states, "Do
you not know that in a race all the runners run, but only one
gets the prize? Run in such a way as to get the prize.
Everybody who competes in the games goes into strict training. They do it to get a crown of laurel that will not last; but
we do it to get a crown that will last forever." [Paul]

There are a couple of people who ran a race and did not
win, but received accolades anyway. They were close to me
and their runs were a different kind of race.

Sidney [a former jockey] and his wife Ellen Kay Swartz

live in Indiana, not far from the border with Ohio. Sid had wrecked his career once with alcohol and drugs, but had found his way out mostly through the help of God and prayer, and Alcoholics Anonymous. Sid had raced for nine years and was twice named leading jockey at a Beulah Park meet. He told me that he had been an alcoholic ever since high school and had often ridden while under the influence. He was ruled off the track for some infraction brought on by being drunk and only then sought help for his problem. Ellen Kay had abused alcohol but had not been an alcoholic. She went with her husband on both a healing and spiritual journey.

They had heard of my work and came to River Downs one day to check out the ministry. I had no office that summer as the room was needed for more office space, so I spent all of my time in the barns, shedrows, kitchen and offices, sleeping that year in a borrowed travel trailer off track. They listened, followed and often I let them speak to trackers in need of help. I remember mucking out a stall so a groom could talk with them. Just like back home on the farm! One trainer elected to go to detox for drug abuse after talking with them. Sid and Ellen Kay had a small horse farm and used their home and the horses to help people recover. In fact they had AA, Al-Anon and Al-Teen meetings in their home. They were also overseers of a Mental Health Program through Adams Co. and several hospitals. They also guided weekend sessions in a hospital annex.

When I told the Swartzes that I was going to try to get a trailer for an office the next year, Ellen Kay started thinking. She had been jogging to gain strength needed in breaking horses. A rider or exercise person needs great leg muscle conditioning as they ride standing in the stirrups and crouched over the horse's shoulder instead of the back. The horse runs better with the weight forward over its shoulders instead of on the back. Then too, the horse pulls against the bit and the arms are constantly moving, and are no help in keeping your position on the horse. There was a thirteen-mile mini-marathon coming up in Bluffton, IN and she had once run twelve miles. "If I can run twelve miles I ought to be able to do thirteen," she told herself. She started getting pledges from neighbors, friends, and fellow church members, telling them she was raising funds for a chapel trailer for the Ohio chaplain. Even the local newspaper picked up the story and wrote up a big news item with a picture of both Ellen Kay and Sid with one of their own home-grown horses.

On the day of the race Ellen Kay was coming down with the flu. Her husband kept taking her temperature and advising her to "scratch" her entry. She however said she had to run because so many people were backing her! Finally she was at the starting line with a fever of 100 degrees, and an air temperature of 92 degrees! Her training and bodily conditioning sure helped her, for people were dropping out of the race all along the route from the heat. At the twelve mile mark, she felt like she was burning up, so when she approached the line of water cup holders, she yelled, " Throw the water on me!" Most all of the volunteers threw water on her! She kept on to the finish line, losing two toenails, and collapsed with flu cramps and chills three minutes after she finished!

But she ran "with perseverance the race that was marked out for her!" She wanted to do something for the Lord, and she did! At a well attended chapel service at Beulah Park one autumn evening, a tracker told me right after the closing prayer to seat everyone again for a special announcement. Sid and Ellen Kay were there and had wanted to give me an envelope quietly after the service, but someone who knew what she had done wanted everyone to know! Ellen Kay came forward and presented me with $768.91 from her thirteen-mile run! When I heard Sid tell what she went through to raise money for a chapel trailer, I cried. Tears were every-where, both in joy for her effort and a bit of shame for our own efforts.

No, she was far from winning the race, but she did win for Jesus Christ! We take better care of our horse's bodies in feed, nutrition, care and training than most of us take care of our bodies. A lot of folks condition their horses for the race, but puff all the way to the paddock with them. And we usually neglect our spiritual training. If we are to run "with perseverance the race that is marked out for us," we had better be in shape for the Race in God's Condition Book. We do not want to be "scratched at the paddock or gate" after calling others!

Ellen Kay had what horsemen call "heart." It's the will to keep going no matter what! Being tired, hurting, or in stress from any source, makes little difference if you have the heart to keep going. Sometimes a race is lost, but the runner is still cheered. It happened to Ellen Kay, and it happened to a six year-old boy named Chris.

Chris was a preschooler at the River Downs track with his parents. Like other "track kids" before him, he was everywhere, often helpful, often underfoot, often missing when he was wanted and always full of questions.

Having had a redheaded son for a firstborn, his red hair and freckles caught my eye when I first saw him. Add a missing front tooth, bare feet, a ready smile and a lot of mischief and you have the picture.

While track kids can and do get into trouble, [like off-track kids] there was one difference that year. We had eight weeks of Bible School in the Chapel Trailer. Chris was usually there and usually in and out whenever anything else was going on. His most frequent questions were about the available cookie supply, but he soaked up a lot of learning on other topics.

Someone told Chris that there would be a seven-eighths

mile foot race on the turf on Labor Day. As an annual event on the last day of the racing meet at River Downs, there was always a foot race and a trainer's race, where trainers rode horses in a quarter mile sprint. Chris asked his father about running and his dad gave his permission, but told him he'd better start training just like the horses had to train before a race. He started out by running barefoot races in the barn area just before dark, and soon was running barefoot on the turf course after the last race was over.

When the runners lined up for the start of the Labor Day race, there were the "little" kids as well as the "big guys," jocks, grooms, high school and ex-high school athletes and adults of both muscular and rapid abilities. The ragged line of runners under the wire was soon strung out along the rail, with the men in front. The first dropout was before the club-house turn, with about a third of the field, including adults, falling out before the far turn.

The early grandstand crowd, with the help of the track announcer on the big public address system, cheered as two young men, well ahead of the rest, ran a match race of their own. With win, place and show all settled and the race officially over, the roar of the crowd began again. About a dozen younger runners in a group were just rounding the far turn with a six year-old boy, smaller than any of them, out in front!

With nearly a furlong to go, Chris was running like a bear was after him, but the bear was gaining. Chris wobbled. His face was white with the strain. And the crowd was roaring! I knelt on the turf with my camera and joined the already finished runners and the crowd in yelling, "Come on, Chris! Keep running!"

The roar and the yells reached him and he kept running, looking a bit dazed. The older and taller boys in the pack closed in on him about 150 feet from the wire and it looked like Chris would be caught. But suddenly, he put on an unbelieveable burst of speed, those six year-old short legs pumping so fast they looked like he had three legs! In a blur of little bare feet, he shot across the line and collapsed on the turf beside me. The crowd was on its feet when Chris was stood up and other runners walked him. He lost the main race, but the crowd gave him a standing ovation. He won the "race marked out for him!"

Too often in life's situations, we stop too soon. It's the Race of Life. Depression, discouragement, worry, low self-image, problems and sins make us say, "It's no use!" Then we pull ourselves up and drop out. Somebody else has already won? We have no chance! People are fond of pointing out that "the big guys" take it all and the "little guys" get nothing. But the Bible says something different!

In John 26:23, Jesus answered Peter's question when he asked about John, his fellow disciple. Jesus had told Peter what his job was to be, and Peter asked his Lord, "How about him?"

Jesus answered with, "What is that to you?" In other words, "Don't look at the other guy; run your own race!"

Let's run our races like Ellen Kay and little Chris, but one thing needs to be understood. We don't gain salvation by running our race. This is what we do for Jesus in thankfulness that He ran His Race for us, died for us to forgive us our sins, and rose from the grave with the promise that we too could have Eternal Life with Him!

"We love Him because He first loved us!" John 4:19

CHAPTER 19

Talking To The Animals

God blessed them and said to them, "Be fruitful and increase in number, fill the earth and subdue it. Rule over the fish of the sea and the birds of the air and over every living creature that moves on the ground."

[God, Genesis 1: 28]

I talk to animals. How much they understand me, or what I think I get back when they communicate with me is a matter of opinion, but I have always talked with animals. From a German Shepherd companion when I was two years old to cows and horses, I talk with them all. I describe talking to a "loose horse" in Chapter 11, and I always spoke comforting words to the horses I was near on the track. I usually seemed to get through.

"Biters" are horses that stand in wait to lunge out over the webbing of a stall and bite the shoulder of the groom or hotwalker going by with another horse. A horse's teeth are formidable weapons. I know of one disfigured youth that was caught by a biter. The upper teeth locked in over the cheekbone and the lower teeth under the jaw. The right side of his face was ripped off. Surgery put him back together, but no plastic surgery could be afforded.

Many years ago at the New York State Fair in Syracuse, NY, a well-known breeder of draft horses was killed in the show ring by a huge stallion. He was literally torn limb from limb before the shocked crowd. The heroine of the day was this breeder's daughter, who jumped from the sidelines and calmed the stallion with voice and actions, and led him out of the show ring building to his stall! She was the only one who knew the stallion and everybody else had scattered when the killing took place. The newspapers and radio all carried the story across the country.

Almost every horse barn has a biter. Beulah Park had a real bad one. Just about every person who worked in that barn had the left top shoulder of their jackets torn out. They walked the horses clockwise, which exposed that shoulder to the horse. He tried to bite every time anybody came near. I knew that both ends of a horse were dangerous, but that with caution, you did not have to be afraid of them! When I walked in front of his stall, about six inches beyond his expected reach, he came out over the webbing, ears back, eyes flashing hate and his mouth wide open with teeth bared. I just stood there and scolded him as if he could understand my every word!

"You big bully! You ought to be ashamed of yourself! Here you are getting the best feed any horse could get! Somebody got you here because they had great expectations of you, and cared for you so that you could some day pose in the Winner's Circle! And you repay kindness with biting the hand that feeds you! You ought to be ashamed!" By this time the biter would usually turn around, put his head down in a far corner of the box stall and sulk! "And the next time I come by, you better behave yourself!"

Horsemen walking by would look at me as if I was a bit off my rocker, but after a couple of scoldings, just a word from me as I approached his stall and he would behave like a gentleman horse should!

A group from a church was visiting me one day bringing about twenty-five folks, mostly junior high boys, and twice as many as I wanted. I had told them to keep the group small. The ground rule was that they were to stay with me and not run or do any fooling around! I had them near the end of a shedrow talking to a trainer when I noticed a group of boys acting up out in the middle of the road between the ends of two shedrows. At the same time I noticed a mare walking up to the end of the other shedrow. She got to the end where she had to make a turn and stopped dead still. Mr. Church, her owner, trainer, groom and hotwalker all in one, had her on a long rope and was walking well behind her, "the way they used to do it." As she eyed the boys, I spoke to them loudly but calmly. "Boys, stand perfectly still. Don't even move an arm! The horse across from you is scared of your group actions. Don't move!" Then aiming my voice to the mare, I talked to her. She knew I was talking especially to her for she turned her eyes to me, then back and forth between the group and me.

"It's alright, they won't hurt you and don't be scared of them. Just keep on coming around the bend. It's OK. I'm sorry we scared you, you are a beautiful mare and we wouldn't hurt you for the world." I kept the calming tone in my voice and kept on in the same line until she relaxed and proceeded around the shedrow. I relaxed as well. Mr. Church gave me a wink as he went by and we talked later in the track kitchen.

"You did exactly what was needed for my mare! You know how to talk to animals!" Mr. Church was close to eighty years old or beyond. He had traveled the country with a pickup truck hauling a horse or two all his life. There was hardly a track in the nation where he had not raced, besides racing in Canada, Mexico and Cuba.

Horses communicate with each other as well. He told me that once when he retired a thoroughbred; he just started using him as a track pony. "Old Sarge, having been a runner, knew just what was needed in training for the races. He also had been ponied his entire career and knew just exactly what a good track pony should do! When I took a young horse out to train, Old Sarge would do the work; I just sat there on his back! He'd use his teeth and body to school the young one, and he must have some inner talk as well, because when he laid his ears back and just looked at another horse, it would immediately cooperate!"

Elmer Cowan owned and trained my favorite horse. Happy Monday was a gentle horse and maybe lacked a little of the fire that is in some horses. He had to be retired the next year because he would have reached eighteen, when all racehorses by law have to stop racing. Anyway, Happy Monday loved to race! He seemed always eager to go to the paddock and get out there and run. There was only one little flaw in his personality. He was called " The Bettor's Favorite," because he was pretty certain to return money if bet to "Place." He always broke well and ran hard until he had outdistanced the pack, but he always got up to the leader and then hung right beside him and about a head back! The only times he had won in his long career was when a lead horse faltered just before the wire and Happy Monday's momentum carried him to the finish by himself! I had a picture of myself with Happy Monday in my wallet for many years.

Since I was the chaplain, horsemen asked me to do what they thought a chaplain should do, including praying for a horse. One night in my first season, Slim Allen woke me up with tears in his eyes. "Chaplain, would you come with me? One of the horses I groom is awful sick and I don't want her to die!" The trainer had a veterinarian look at her that afternoon but she was shivering with blankets on her when I got to her stall. Both of us prayed for her, Slim in tears all the time. I stopped to pray and lay my hands on her every day until she came got well.

In another barn, a very valuable stakes horse was sick, covered with two blankets and with a heat lamp over her stall. The horsemen were all concerned and I was directed to her stall. I passed through her barn every day and looked in on her. Several others were also praying for her. When no one was around, I would usually stand there and talk to her from outside her stall before I prayed. [No one except those who work with a horse are allowed to touch it or go into a stall unless they give permission.] She improved enough to be moved, but the owner lived in Columbus and took her to his own barn. The talk in the kitchen was that she had won enough money for him so that she should have been flown to Florida where it was warm, rather than stay where it was cold! Eventually, word came back to us that she had died. The owner's wife had died a couple of weeks before and he was mourning. He slacked on his work feeling sorry for himself, and had turned the mare into his paddock one cold day and had left her there all day! She never got over that shock. The racetrack buzzed with resentment over her treatment!

One day I was near a gate to the track and someone walking their horse to the paddock to be saddled and made ready for the next race, called to me and asked, "Chaplain, would you bless my horse for me?" Since several people that I knew well had horses in that race, I figured that that I couldn't pray for one person's horse to win over another's. So I walked up to the horse, put my hand on its hip and pronounced, "May it do its best and come back sound!"

Since the horsemen near by thought that was good, it became my standard "blessing" when I was asked. One time there were other horsemen near by that were in a conversation with me, when a married couple interrupted to ask that I bless their horse. "May it do its best and come back sound!" I said with my hand on the horse. After they had gone out of sight a horseman remarked, "That's one prayer of yours that won't be answered, Chaplain. That horse isn't sound now! They entered it in a low claiming race, hoping to get rid of it!"

"Maybe that's why they looked at me so strangely when I said it!"

A Catholic trainer used to ask me to bless his horses and then with a loud laugh, inform those around him, "Naw, don't do it! You Protestants don't know the difference between a Blessing and The Last Rites!" This was usually a lead in to the very, very old joke, which I have literally heard hundreds of times. I hesitate to tell it, the odds being that you've heard it before.

A Protestant minister went to watch the races one day, presumably to get material for a sermon on "sin." He was surprised to see a Catholic priest out by the paddock, blessing a horse in each race. To his amazement, he saw that the blessed horses always won. Seeing how much money was made on winning tickets, added to the fact that he was rather poorly paid as a pastor, he succumbed to temptation and bet all of his money on the horse the priest had just blessed! The horse dropped dead in the final stretch. Very distressed, he sought out the priest and asked him how come the last horse died while all the other horses he blessed won! The priest replied, "That's the trouble with you Protestants; you don't know the difference between a Blessing and The Last Rites!"

This trainer was a friend and interested in my young yoke of oxen I was training on a roadway just back of his barn. One day he called out, "Do they know the difference between 'Gee' and 'Haw?' " I said nothing but directed them into a figure eight with just the gee and haw commands. Then I turned them toward him and walked them up until a final "Whoa," stopped them close enough to reach out and lick his face! "Chaplain," he said very impressed, "If you can train animals like that, you ought to be training horses!"

"Nope, conflict of interest."

A few months later an alcoholic tracker was dying in the hospital. I got a call from the hospital at 4:00 A.M. and went right up to see him in intensive care. We talked for a while, then he asked Jesus to come into his heart and forgive him of his sins. Then I asked him if his aunt in Cincinnati who had raised him was not Catholic. She was, and I then asked him if having The Last Rites said for him would not comfort her. Getting his assent, I then telephoned the hospital's Catholic Chaplain. When he arrived, he was rather surprised to find a Protestant pastor asking him for the service. He thought a minute and after thanking me for calling him, said, "Look, why don't you help me in reading the words of the sacrament?" We stood beside his bed and read it together. Later I took his belongings to his aunt and told her that he had The Last Rites before he died. She was very thankful.

When I got back to the track I looked up the Catholic trainer and told him that this Protestant did know the difference between a Blessing and The Last Rites just in case his horses needed either one!

In the spring of 1983, I wrote a story on Ole Buck, the horse that figured prominently in my message in Chapter 11. Gayle and Ole Buck got a full-page photo in the Racing Digest.

"Professional Pony Horse Old Buck Is Still Going Strong At Age 26

A recent issue of the Finger Lakes edition of the Racing Digest featured a 22-year-old pony named Ole Buck, who has returned to Finger Lakes with his owner, Howard Reilly. Ohio wants the world to know that Reilly's Ole Buck was named after his older brother, Ole Buck, who is still going strong and is now 26 years old!

Gayle Christman is the proud owner, and both Gayle and Ole Buck have been in the racing business for 21 years. Gayle actually began exercising horses when he was 14. He got his first license, and Buck, when he was sixteen. Most of the time, Buck was a professional pony, not just a stable pony. Although Gayle has always had a few thoroughbreds in the running, ponying has always been a top priority.

I met Buck when I first came to the track in 1976. At that time someone else in Gayle's shedrow was riding Ole Buck, but Ole buck was a central figure in one of my sermons on the track.

[Then follows a description of my catching a loose horse and using it as told in Chapter 11]

However, rumor has it that Buck has his weak points as well. There are those who insist that Ole Buck has a drinking habit. He never bought his own, but would accept anything that was offered, be it a glass, mug or bottle. The same people insist that Buck had been seen hobnobbing with assorted blacksmiths and others from the racing fraternity in at least one Grove City bar. Rumor also has it that Ole Buck even back-slid the very same night he walked into a track service in Jordan Hall to illustrate the sermon featuring him.

At 26, Buck can teach a lot of us who fight arthritis. Buck gets a bute pill every day, but still wakes up sore all over. But throw the saddle on him, take ten steps towards the track and he begins to prance. He tells his rider that he is ready! He's too excited to think about arthritis!"

A little over a year later, Buck was laid to rest. Gayle's sister-in-law, Adelaide Christman, wrote:

"Ole Buck's Epitaph"

"Gee, God, I've been around a long time; twenty-seven years to be exact. Twenty-two of those years were spent at various race-tracks ponying thoroughbreds. I've handled all kinds - good – bad – mean – gentle – nuts – runaways – you name it and I've done it. I've worked the best of the ponies into the ground and walked away laughing.

I could always find my stall or Gayle if necessary, and I knew those tracks like I knew the inside of my feed tub.

Arthritis finally got to me several years ago but it never stopped me. I took my bute and kept on going, loving every minute of it. In fact, I thrived on my work and wouldn't have wanted it any other way.

Sure, it was nice once in a while to come home and be lazy and graze in the fields, but the tracks were my real home. When there was a job to be done I did it with all my heart and gloried in it.

I developed some problems last week and the vet worked with me, but even he couldn't help. My time was running out and I

knew it. Thankfully, I was put down peacefully and quickly.

'Up Here' the tracks will always have a
good cushion – sunshine every day – the turf
green and soft underhoof – the sweet smell
of good hay and feed and a clean stall. At
this track I'll pony forever, stepping lightly
with my head up and proud. One thing I do
remember above all is that 'I was loved.'
Thanks, Gayle, for sticking with me for so
many years and their memories. I loved you
too. – Buck"

While dogs were banned from the Ohio tracks because
of the danger of a loose dog scaring the horses, lots of other
creatures were there. Some horses had a goat for a companion. The horse would "tend" the goat like a mother and
forget about its own nervousness. Sometimes a small pony
would be in a stall with a horse for the same reason. I've
seen raccoons on a leash and once a pet ferret. Cats were
abundant. Often-times there would be a rooster, usually of
the game type, and sometimes very beautiful with their long
tail feathers and neck plumes when sitting on a wheelbarrow
or scratching in the dust.

However, the most impressive bird that I saw was a duck
with personality!

I wrote the following for the May, 1982 issue of the
Racing Digest.

REQUIEM FOR PETE

The swallows came back to Capistrano,
the buzzards returned to Hinkley, the Florida-
wintering trackers came back to Ohio, but
"Pete," faithful companion and loyal guard-
duck, did not come back to Beulah.

His beginnings are somewhat of a mystery, but consensus has it that Pete showed up at River Downs, fully feathered, in the summer of 1976. During his six years of racing, he served several stables, but since the fall of 1978, Pete worked for Fred Watkins and his Angels [his all-girl crew.]

At the beginning, Pete showed signs of superdom that often brought him special attention. I recall photographing him in 1977 at River Downs in his own special plastic swimming pool, which his grooms cleaned and renewed daily.

He was mourned prematurely in May of 1978, when everyone believed he had perished in the River Downs fire that killed twenty-six horses. Many trackers came by the smoldering ashes of his barn that morning to inquire about him. Tearful voices and trembling hands pointed out the outlines of the stall where he routinely spent the night on guard duty, but the heat had left no trace. About 10:00 A.M., four or five hours after his usual morning round began, Pete came carefully out of a cement barn where he had never stayed before. To the amazement of all, he walked sorrowfully up and down the line of ashes, grieving for the horses he had been unable to save the night before.

Fred's Angels took him under their wings that fall, and Pete drowned his sorrow in hard work. Because no dogs were allowed on the grounds, Pete took guard duties seriously. No visitor went by the end of his barn without a challenge, and literally thousands came to know Pete. Tour groups on the Backside always stopped to hear his story. Pete loved to have his head touched and once he knew that no one was there to harm his horses, he was quite affectionate. The Angels tended to his every need, even placing him in his own hot tub to relax after hours.

One summer the Angels thought he needed company, so they bought a young mallard hen to keep him company. Pete spent a miserable summer. She followed him everywhere, pestering him constantly with incessant quacking. During the annual winter hiatus in Florida, Pete was relieved when the hen jilted him for a fancy drake in the infield pond. He remained a confirmed bachelor to the end.

He did suffer, like many trackers, from prejudice. Not considering himself to be "just a duck," but an equal member of the team, his pride was hurt when he went to eat with the others in the track kitchen. Ejected, he would stand at the door and loudly register his protest, but his big day came at a birthday party. The manager of the Pizza Hut allowed him to eat with the others at the table. Prejudice still showed when he got salad instead of Pizza.

At Tampa Bay Downs this last winter, Pete expanded his guard duties to professional comradeship. George Steinbrenner [the owner of the NY Yankees] hired a night watchman at his barn and Pete went to "talk" with him every morning at 3:00 A.M. for about fifteen minutes. The watchman reported he could set his watch by Pete's arrival and it was good therapy for him to have the duck to visit with him [which is what Pete intended!] Then Pete would make his long trip back to his barn to await the arrival of the Angels.

But Pete stayed in Florida. He died a hero's death. Long before daylight one morning, there was a loose horse running through the Backside. No one else was near so Pete did his duty. He went out and tried to stop the loose horse. His trampled body was found at daylight.

Burial was in the Forest Glade at the edge of the Backside. But his memory lingers on and his friendly but businesslike manner is missed at Beulah Park."

The next month, the Racing Digest carried a footnote to the "Requiem for Pete" story. "Trainer Fred Watkins, in order to replace super guard-duck Pete, has installed three ducks, two chickens and a cat. This shows how valuable Pete had become."

People may or may not agree with me on this, but my own belief is that inter-species communication was part of God's plan for us all. We humans have felt so superior because we talk in innumerable languages, words and sounds, and can articulate our every thought, have labeled most of living, moving things as "dumb animals," because they can't talk like we do. Expand that to include plants. We talk to other species with words, with body language, motions, and perhaps intuitive sensing of the others needs. While scientists may argue the whole theory, I just keep talking. Go ahead, talk to the animals!

CHAPTER 20

Spiritual Warfare On The Track

**"Finally, be strong in the Lord and in His mighty power.
Put on the full armor of God so that you can take
your stand against the devil's schemes!"**

[Paul, Ephesians 6: 10]

There are many books on "Spiritual Warfare" published and being published. I will not attempt rewrite any of them. One the racetracks, we are in the spiritual warfare of our lives!

The track has been termed by some as "The Devil's Turf." To go there with the message of Christ makes Satan mad. He tries by devious methods to stop the effectiveness of the Gospel. Sometimes he takes back a step of ours, but so far he is outpaced by far with the steps of progress in winning people for Christ. He uses the same methods on the track that he does elsewhere in the world, namely power, money, sex, sickness and combinations of all of them.

If you are not familiar with the passage in Ephesians started above, I will quote the rest of it. I think Christians especially ought to read this passage very often for Satan tries hardest to disrupt new Christians. We need to pray God's protection for our loved ones every day.

> "For our struggle is not against flesh and blood, but against the rulers, against the authorities, against the powers of this dark world and against the spiritual forces of evil in the heavenly realms. Therefore put on the full armor of God, so that when the day of evil comes, you may be able to stand your ground, and after you have done everything, to stand. Stand firm then, with the belt of Truth buckled around your waist, with the breastplate of Righteousness in place, and with your feet fitted with the Gospel of Peace as a firm footing. In addition to all this, take up the shield of Faith, with which you can extinguish all the flaming darts of the evil one. Take the Helmet of Salvation and the sword of the Spirit, which is the Word of God. And pray in the Spirit on all occasions with all kinds of prayers and requests. With this in mind, be alert, and always keep on praying for all the saints."

There it is. We are all in Spiritual Warfare! The best weapon Satan has is to persuade unsuspecting Christians that he does not exist, but that thought is not anything new. Christians have known it from the beginning, but they let their guard down sometimes.

The biggest effort that Satan uses is to attack the chaplains. He used health on me. When I would not quit when I had to travel around the track on crutches or a golf cart, he hit on my wife. Her health finally caused me to resign the job we both loved and re-enter to pastoral ministry. There I could be with her more, or call on parishioners to watch over when I had to be gone.

This is a practice used by organized worshippers of Satan. They are out there. A friend of mine was returning to Seattle on a plane one day. She was involved with Elijah House, which published the story. Dinnertime arrived and she was in a window seat. The man on the aisle side had to pass her tray across to her. He told the stewardess that he would not eat, for he was fasting. Thinking he was a fellow Christian, she opened up a conversation, asking, "Oh! You must be a Christian! May I ask why you are fasting?"

"No, I'm not a Christian! I belong to a coven of witches in Seattle. We've been trying to stop the effectiveness of the ministers in Seattle, but with little success. Now we are praying and fasting to hit the minister's wives! If Satan can break up the wives with sickness, affairs and unrest or divorce, we will hurt the minister's efforts!"

Are you still with me? It has happened to a lot of us. Three former chaplains left their wives and ran off with trackers. It hit the best-trained chaplain we had, who had more counseling education than any of us. He called our president to tell him that he thought it would make little difference in his ministry, but Dan cut him short. "It will be news on every track in the country within a week via the Horse Van Express! I want your resignation immediately!"

It happens out there in the churches as well, to the detriment of the message of Jesus.

We don't have to yield to temptation. Hebrews 2: 18 tells us "Because He Himself suffered when He was tempted, He is able to help those who are being tempted." But all of us, without exception, have failed to ask His help. "For all have sinned and fall short of the glory of God!" Romans 3: 23. All of us! The sight of money makes people want it. Two left the chaplaincy after using funds that were not theirs. And that happens in the churches as well. Read your newspapers.

Power? How can a servant of God desire power? Several chaplains decided that instead of being under the authority of RTCA, they would branch off on their own, sometimes in what they thought was competition. The Gospel was preached, but their solitary efforts always failed in the end. Power in the churches shows itself in church politics. That makes the newspapers as well.

One chaplain had witchcraft symbols painted on the door to his office, presumably to "hex" him. Strangers in her home attacked his wife when he was on the track. The War is on! People should pray for every Christian leader that they might be always encased in the full armor of God!

Since Christians have often criticized this racetrack ministry of ours as ministering to the wrong people, I want to talk with Paul when I reach Heaven to ask him about these verses concerning the armor. You see, since we are supposed to be facing the enemy, stopping the "fiery darts of the wicked," there is no armor for the back. Yet my back is often hit by the fiery darts of the righteous!

A female member of one cult got a job as a hotwalker on one track and started so called "Bible Studies" in her tack room. Only she offered the lonely grooms sex afterwards! It did not take long for Security to put her off the track!

Temptation is everywhere, not just on the track! Satan is trying to hinder the Work of the Lord!

I saw a sweatshirt in Cortland one day that said things pretty clearly. It read,

WHEN SATAN REMINDS YOU OF YOUR PAST,
REMIND HIM OF HIS FUTURE!

CHAPTER 21

Extras On The Track

**"Let us not become weary in well doing, for at the
proper time we will reap a harvest if we do not give up.
Therefore, as we have opportunity, let us do good to all
people, especially to those who belong to the
family of believers."**

[Paul, Galatians 6: 9-10]

Since I was the chaplain, there were a lot of opportunities
to serve God in what some might call "extras."
Weddings and funerals took place in different settings than a
church minister would ever see. The first year at River
Downs showed the need for a Vacation Bible School for all
the children of grooms, trainers, riders and others, who were
there on the track with their parents. Then I saw the need for
a Boy Scout Troop for the boys. When a ponyman came to
me with his wife in a Kentucky Hospital needing expensive
blood, I gathered some others and went into Kentucky to
donate blood for her. That led to an annual blood drive on

two of our three tracks. Sorry to say that the American Red Cross looked at the rec. room on the other track and told me it was definitely not a big enough area. Surprisingly, it was larger than either of the other two facilities, but they could not be swayed. I really don't think they liked being on a racetrack. All led to stories.

A very unusual wedding took place at a training arena in nearby Fox Chapel Stables. A newspaper covered it with an article and photos headlined, 'A Bluegrass, Baroque Blend." They were both former high school teachers who met at the school. The bride, who owned several horses, was an English rider and had a music master from the Conservatory. The groom rode Western and leaned towards Bluegrass for his style of music. He had a beautiful quarterhorse that he used in rodeos as a cutting horse. They were married on horseback, the groom in boots, a western suit and fancy cowboy hat, and the bride rode an American saddlebred with a sidesaddle. She had dressed like a sixteenth century horsewoman.

The wedding was to have been held outdoors in Winton Woods, but rain sent it into the arena. The rehearsal was outdoors, and her filly spooked, dumping the bride and wrecking an antique sidesaddle that was borrowed and would have to be rebuilt. But the actual ceremony went without a hitch, even to kissing the bride in her sidesaddle!

Two years later the groom appeared at my Chapel Trailer. When I recognized him and asked how he was doing, his answer was, "Terrible, Chaplain, I need Jesus in my life!"

We went on into the trailer and he blurted out his story with some tears. He had told me before the wedding that he had job security at the school for he taught a subject that no one else in the area could teach. But the school had given up his department because of budget cuts, and he was out of his job! He was a real macho type of guy and this was a real shock to his ego. She went with him with their horses in a trailer and tried to sell themselves as horse trainers wherever they went. They got as far as Texas before they gave up. He had begun to drink in his anxiety and his new insecurity. They came back east as far as her family property in Vermont, when his actions prompted her to throw him out.

He repented in tears and prayed to have Jesus forgive him for his many sins, and to come into his heart and life as Savior and Lord. I realized at once that since he was not a tracker where I could have daily contact with him, he would need more help and discipling than I could give him. I put him in touch with the leader of a local chapter of "Cowboys For Christ," a national organization of evangelical cowboys and horsepeople.

The most disturbing thing about his whole story was that he had traveled non-stop from Vermont to Cincinnati, Ohio just to find his way to the Lord! He knew I would listen to him and hear him out, but how many ministers, how many Christians did he pass by because he did not know if he could trust them? It is a shame to the whole church community that we seem so inaccessible or uncaring!

I lost track of him eventually, but I do know that he became a part of that chapter of Cowboys for Christ. Fellow horsemen ministered to him there.

Another wedding took place in the outer part of the HBPA office in Cleveland, where we held our chapel services. The groom was a former jockey and now was a trainer. His nickname was "Nutsey," because he had been told that he was "nuts" for riding bad-actor horses. The bride worked in the publicity department at Thistledown. The maid of honor was a trainer and the best man was a Jockey Agent. The General Manager, George W. Jones, was present and in the wedding pictures. After the wedding, one of the groom's friends dumped a feed bucket of oats over the couple!

One very memorable wedding took place in a barn during cold weather in the fall. The groom exercised horses for the bride's father, while the bride worked for her father as a groom. I had watched the romance grow for a long time.

Let me describe this barn. A former owner of Beulah Park had raced horses and had put in a cement floor in "his" barn. It was the only barn so equipped on the track. A barn has horses stabled along both walls with the floor between swept or raked a couple of times a day, whether dirt or cement. Up in the rafters in this drafty barn were huge, old cobwebs, all covered with dust and billowing up and down in the air currents. It was cold. The bride and groom wore down jackets. A bale of hay served as a kneeling bench. Every horse in that end of the barn had its head out of the stall over the webbing, ears pricked forward to catch every sound. I could see that while most of the guests were horsemen, some were evidently not. So I prefaced my ceremony with some extra words.

" I know that some of you think that this barn is a peculiar place for a wedding. You can look up and see the big cobwebs," pointing to them, as every head swiveled to look up. " Some of you wrinkled up your noses as you came in. Those of us who are horsemen have gotten used to it, but the smell of manure is in every stable. You can even see some dried manure on the boxstall walls if you want to look inside. Counter that with the sweet smell of hay and straw and the pleasant smell of contented horses that are also guests at this wedding. But just remember that the Lord and Savior, Son of God, God Incarnate, was born in a stable! It had cobwebs. It smelled of animals and manure. It was not a sterile place like a hospital, or like the prettied-up images of the manger scene on Christmas cards! It was a working stable! If one was good enough for the baby Jesus to be born in according to God's plan, then this horse barn is not only good enough, but just fine for a Christian wedding!"

As people talked to me that night and some in weeks after, they all said that the most memorable part of the wedding was my short talk on stables. We sometimes forget that most of us came from humble beginnings and we should not be afraid of working with our hands or the smells of a different occupation!

The most picturesque wedding I ever had was for a jockey and bride that took place in front of the tote board [a large, billboard sized electronic sign that flashed the numbers of the horses as well as the ever changing amount of money bet on each horse, and the changing odds before the race. It also showed the payoff for win, place and show tickets after the race was over.] It took place immediately after the last race of the day. The track was muddy after a morning rain, but the entire maintenance crew put a string of 4'x8' pieces of plywood from the winners circle to the walk-through gate to the turf track, which was just to the right of the tote board. They also ran a grandstand-connected microphone out to the rail for us to use. The television crew atop the grandstand stayed late and made a video for the couple. Two outriders in fancy uniforms rode their horses to the tote board and then faced each other, for a proper background. I walked out from the winner's circle trailed by the groom and his best man in their jockey silks. Then came a parade of all the jockeys at the track that day, all dressed in their colorful silks with their jockey whips under their arms. They formed a double line in front of the tote board and then turned and came up close to us before turning to face each other with about six feet between the rows. Then came the bride and her attendants in single file, in formal wedding attire, holding up their long dresses as they gingerly walked the wooden path across the mud. As they reached the end of the double row of jockeys, the jocks all raised their whips in an Annapolis style of bridal arch for the girls to walk under.

I spoke the words of the wedding ceremony into the microphone, holding it out to the couple for their responses.

After the ceremony, the remaining crowd in the grandstand gave a great roar of approval. The wedding party walked out under the arch of jockey whips and, two by two, made their way across the plywood to the solid ground of the winner's circle! Literally, it was a colorful wedding!

Everett and Charlet were at the first ever stable-area service at Beulah Park in the spring of 1976. Everett had been a groom for over forty years, since he was eleven years old. They lived in a stable tack-room. After one service, while the rest of us were talking with each other, I noticed Everett at the card table where I had left my Bible. He sat there touching the Bible and slowly turning pages. "I wonder if Everett has a Bible of his own?" I thought to myself.

Florence noticed him when I did, and turning to Charlet said, "Look at Everett reading Norman's Bible!"

Charlet looked, then said slowly, "Everett can't read. But he loves to touch and hold the Bible. At night, he'll ask me to read it to him."

They left for River Downs a few days before I did. When I drove through the gate a tracker flagged me down to tell me that Everett was in the hospital. He had not been well at Beulah and I had asked a doctor who owned horses to look him over, but now he was worse. The summer rolled on with Everett in the hospital much of the time. One late afternoon he showed up at the track. He'd given the nurses the slip and walked and caught rides back to the track. By this time he was sicker than before. Charlet got me and we took him back to the hospital. I let them both off at the door where she half carried Everett inside and I went to park my van. By this time it was evening and they had a tough woman guard doing her duty. I had come without a chance to wash the day's dust off my face or change. The guard stopped me and told me it was after hours and I could not come in. "But I'm their minister and I just brought two people here!" I sputtered.

"Which church are you from?" she asked, looking critically at me.

"I'm the Chaplain from River Downs!" That settled it in her mind. I did not get in!

I spent a lot of time in visits that summer, taking Charlet to see him, usually leaving her to get a bus back to the track. One time as I was leaving, Everett turned to Charlet and said, "I'm so glad Chaplain Evans came to live with us. I don't think I would have ever have found Jesus again!"

We talked of many things that summer. Everett knew or surmised that he was dying. He informed me one day that he wanted to marry Charlet. I had assumed that they were already married, and I knew he was not up to the simple task of getting a license. But to comfort a dying man, the nurses and his doctor set up a wedding! The nurses came up with a nice dress for Charlet and a white shirt for Everett. No tie. Everett had told me that he had worn a tie only three times in his life, all for funerals. I assured him that he would not have to wear a tie at either his wedding or his funeral. That pleased him.

His doctor stood beside Everett's wheel chair as his best man, and a nurse stood in with Charlet as maid of honor. It was really a mock wedding without a license, but Everett was very happy to feel married.

We talked about his funeral. He told me that his track family was closer to him that his own family and he wanted to be buried on the track. I gently told him that that would be impossible, but that if he was cremated, I could spread his ashes on the infield. That pleased him and they both agreed.

Cancer caught up with him in August. For a description of his funeral, I will copy an article by free-lance reporter Maryjean Wall that was published in the Horseman's Journal.

EVERETT WANTED TRACKSIDE RITES

"The flies. Like sticky pests they buzzed about. Biting flesh at every chance they always managed to escape just in time each angry swatting hand lashed at them in self defense.

Curiously out of place in such a gathering, the flies hung on with all the tenacity of uninvited guests. They did not share the reverence of the others, choosing instead to light then dart away in crazy sacrilege on the preacher's book.

It was the flies, the riveting of heavy summer rain on the roof of corrugated tin and the way the men seemed to think it proper to remove their hats this one occasion on entering this barn they call a "spit box" that stamped the funeral of Everett Cookendorfer forever and foremost among all funerals in the photographic bank of my brain.

But more than flies or rain or the imposing sense of something terribly out of place in this barn where people normally take their winning horses for routine drug tests after races, it was Everett that kept the men shuffling their feet uneasily in the dusty dirt while waiting for the ritual.

ASHES IN INFIELD

Everett, or what the men and women, about 30 of them, [a newspaper said over 150, my own estimate was about 100] thought they understood what had been Everett, the man who was their friend and fellow groom, rested atop a saddle towel spread over a 50-gallon drum placed smack in the path these people tread each time they cool out horses 'round and 'round the small square shed.

Reduced to a tiny box of ashes wrapped in fancy paper, Everett waited to be committed by the preacher to his final reward. His River Downs badge which Ohio law required that he wear on his outer clothing was affixed now to that part of the box facing the people.

["I'll take the ashes to the infield some evening when it's quiet," the preacher had said in an aside, "I'll take his stepson with me when nobody's around. It's too sacramental to do publicly."]

And the service begins.

"We are gathered here today not just to honor one who was a part of our lives for so long," intones the preacher, who is the race track chaplain, "but we are here to worship God."

It is Thursday, shortly before post time. As the loudspeaker crackles across the backstretch airwaves to "get your horses ready for the first race," words strangely foreign to the curse-worn airwaves of the spit box tumble forth from the group, with feeling.

BRUSHING OFF FLIES

Some of the younger people, Catholics probably make the sign of the cross as Rev. Norman Evans, a Baptist and known here as "The Revener," quotes from Psalm 23, the Gospel of John and other places he has marked in his black book.

The Revener still is brushing flies away when he closes his book to tell the men and women, all backstretch workers who have come to pay respects, that "it is only in Jesus that we can realize death is not an ending but a blessed beginning."

The Revener is dressed right well for a funeral, brown suit with white shirt and tie. But the rain has turned the paths and roadways of the barn area to a sloppy track and doused the Revener with mud up to his knees.

It was Everett's wish to go from the track, the preacher tells the congregation. "He said you folks here, this community in which he worked for 40 years, were closer to him than his own family. He wanted his funeral here and later on, his ashes will be sprinkled on the infield."

The Revener Evans explains how Everett, a man of 52

years, being sick in the hospital with cancer, missed River Downs' opening day for the first time this year, since coming onto the track as an exercise boy at age 10. In the latter stages the cancer spread to his brain and Everett, confused and frightened, had run away from the hospital several times ending up, always back at the track.

WIDOW CRYING

"Yeah, everybody knew him. He was a good groom," whispers one of the men in the back of the group. "He worked for nearly everyone. Used to exercise horses too, when he was younger."

Another groom, one of black complexion, nods. The black is Revener Evans' "unofficial chairman of the board of deacons" at the racetrack. He is losing out to glaucoma but still mucks stalls every day and helps pass out hymnals at the weekly backstretch services.

The deacon is equally proud that he can wear up to $1.50 in quarters in each ear ["I don't have any pockets"] and brags on abstinence from vegetables for 20 years ["but the Revener's got me taking those things-what'dya call 'em – vitamins, every day now."]

Everett's widow is crying. She is a plain looking woman dressed in pink pants and a matching top and wearing her straight brown hair tied back tight with a rubber band."

Part of Everett will always be near the stables. I spread his ashes on the infield as planned. But he's with Jesus now, and I hope Heaven's streets are not all paved with gold. There ought to be a stable there somewhere where someone who loves horses could slip away from choir practice for a while. I'm sure that Jesus, born in a stable, would understand one whose new birth was in a stable and who left one to come home!

The story is not over. I helped Charlet get a job in the

kitchen on the track, but there is more. After Everett's funeral and the spreading of his ashes, a couple of trackers came to me to say, "Chaplain, you are now a tracker yourself!" I had not taken Everett away from them but had been willing to take care of everything right before their eyes. I think the mud on my suit and the mud on my tie and white shirt, which I received when I slipped in a puddle while carrying Everett's ashes, helped. I do know that acceptance of my ministry, while good to date, improved afterwards. I was one of them!

A trainer from Kentucky came to me to talk. His wife of many years had just died and he was in distress. He went on and on about the fact that he could not look in a closet where her clothes were hanging without breaking down. I even went down to his farm at his invitation to see him. Harry had been around horses all his life, even to riding in parades in Cincinnati with Roy Rogers, before Hollywood changed his name. I told him that he needed to have a woman come to keep his big house and to pack his wife's clothing into boxes for Good Will. He finally agreed but asked. "I don't know anybody I could get. Can you help me?"

I thought of Charlet, introduced them and she agreed to go down for a while to help. I moved to Beulah Park soon after Charlet began working for Harry, so I did not hear from them for some time.

When I next heard about them they had just been married at Latonia Racetrack in Kentucky. Both the Columbus Dispatch and a Kentucky newspaper carried the story, plus Maryjean Wall did her usual good job writing it up for the Horsemen's Journal.

It seems that things had worked out with them better than expected! They had planned to get married during the winter of 1977, but a loose horse on the farm changed their plans. Two horses had gotten loose at the same time during a very bad cold snap. Harry got one horse back in the barn easily but the other led him on a long chase in the cold and during a heavy snowstorm. That horse, blinded by the snow, ran head on into a tree and dropped dead, while Harry froze both of his feet.

Harry was quoted as saying at the time of the wedding, "They wanted to take one off at the ankle and the other off at the knee, but they didn't, thank the Lord and my bride. If she hadn't taken care of me, I would have lost my feet. She bathed them three times a day in hot water and Ivory soap. I couldn't work the rest of the winter and most of the summer."

They went to Latonia the next winter and had their wedding in February. They were married in the Latonia Racetrack receiving barn, which receives all the horses that "ship in" from farms or other racetracks just for the day. An altar was built of hay bales, and the guests sat on bales of straw. Harry wore the same costume he used to wear in Cincinnati parades riding a Palomino that he claimed was a full brother to Roy Rogers' Trigger. The bride wore a long formal gown and a nice hair-do, and was topped by a fur coat. Chaplain Verne Musser, the RTCA chaplain in Kentucky, performed the ceremony. Two racehorses were expected to stand behind the altar of hay, but they would not stand so they were led in circles behind the wedding party. The riders, in their silks, were both jockeys, one a son of the best man and the other the son of the matron of honor. Twelve jockeys in their colorful silks were lined up in a double line as part of the wedding party. The best man was a former jockey.

After the ceremony, everyone went to the track kitchen for the reception. Sorrow and pain, healing and happiness, all took place here, just as out in the world, but these race-tracker-lives worked out joyfully when everything had seemed hopeless for both of them.

Carol and his wife Sylvia were both trainers at both Beulah and River Downs. I had often talked with them when one day Carol told me he was going to the hospital with Hodgkin's Disease. I went to see him in the hospital. His wife was sitting on the edge of his bed. Since they had not been out to a chapel service, I inquired if they had ever had a relationship with Jesus, or had ever attended church. Sylvia's face turned stony. She then bitterly told me why she had never become a Christian.

"When I was a girl, my best friend was the daughter of a deacon. He was dead set against dancing and forbid my girl-friend to ever dance. Well, we had a prom one night and she desperately wanted to go. We girls had set it up so that we would pick her up after her father went to sleep. She got out and enjoyed the prom until she fell and broke a leg! [A Freudian slip?] We took her home and got her to the door, but rather than wake her father, she crawled up stairs and into bed. She was so scared of her Christian deacon father that she laid there all night, dreading morning when her father would find out she had been to a dance! Now, if that's Christianity, I don't want it!"

"I wouldn't either," I told her, "but that's not what Christianity is all about. Jesus loves us, died on the Cross so forgiveness can be enjoyed by all who believe in Him, and love is what He has to offer!"

Both were rather startled, but as I talked with them they grew more relaxed and asked a lot of questions. Before I left, they both prayed for forgiveness and asked Christ to enter their hearts and lives. At a later visit, I handed Carol the first copy of <u>Life's Condition Book, the New Testament in Today's English Version, A Guidebook for Running the Race,</u> which I had just received. The American Bible Society had just printed several thousand copies for RTCA. A photo of a group of horses and their silk-clad riders close to the wire in color, made the front cover and spine of the Racetracker's Bible. I was pleased that the photo was one I had submitted.

Carol took the Bible and looked at it with interest. "Those horses look like quarterhorses," he told me. I had not dated my color slide from which it was made, and I had happened to shoot it during the American QuarterHorse Congress in Columbus. They had some national races mixed in with Beulah Park's regular thoroughbred races. The quarterhorse legs were slightly shorter and with a little more bone than the thoroughbred, with more heavily muscled hindquarters. But the thoroughbred people liked the Bible greatly, most not noticing any difference. In fact, Carol was the only one to speak about it to my knowledge.

Carol grew sicker as time went on. I was in Phoenix, Arizona, one January when a call came into the trailer park where I was staying overnight in a mobile home with close friends who were also members of the Ohio Council that backed me. It was Sylvia; Carol had died. She had called my wife who checked my itinerary for the trip, and then Carol used telephone information to track me down. "Could you fly right back to conduct his funeral?" she asked me. It was tough to tell her that I had several more days of scheduled engagements, but I suggested she have a local minister have the graveside service at his burial and then, when I got back, we would set up a good memorial service. That is the way we arranged it and a lovely memorial service was held. One lady came up afterwards and took my hand with both her own and told me it was the first "evangelical" funeral message she had ever heard.

The "Godincidence" [I don't believe in coincidence] of an event later on in Michigan was heartwarming. I was at a church one evening showing my slide presentation of the ministry on the racetrack. Many of the slides were of people, and I told their stories. I flashed a slide of both Carol and Sylvia on the screen. As I told their story, I heard an explosive sob-like noise from a few rows back. After the presentation, a man came up crying with joy. Carol had been his cousin, and he had been praying for years that our Savior, Jesus, could reach Carol and Sylvia. He had just heard that his prayers had been answered and he was so overjoyed when he saw their photo and heard my story he could not help his initial reaction.

Gale Osborne was once America's winningest trainer. When leading trainers in the nation were winning an average of twenty percent of their races, Gale was winning an average of sixty-one percent. He raced at Finger Lakes in New York in the summer and Beulah Park in the spring and fall. He began training back in the 1930's after a few years of riding in the bush tracks of Kansas and Missouri before he was old enough to be legal. He raced horses in the USA, Canada, Mexico and Cuba. His greatest horse was Strike The Anvil, who once ran a twelve race winning streak before retiring to stud in Florida. Strike The Anvil was still racing at Beulah when I began. He was what they call a "class" horse. While a lot of horses would prance around and work up a sweat before a race, Strike The Anvil would relax and come out onto the track walking very dignified, scanning the crowd in the grandstand to see how many were there, and then walk sedately into the starting gate and wait patiently while the other horses were loaded. When the bell went off he ran right past all the other horses to the finish line. He walked back to the winner's circle, unruffled, no sweat-lather, and posed. He'd done his job!

Gale died after I had left the track and I was flown back from New York for his funeral. The family decided since his life had been spent on the track, his funeral should be from there. They had it in the clubhouse before the first race of the afternoon. What the family had forgotten was that prior to the first race all the many TV sets around the clubhouse came on with the races of the day before. It was complete with the shot of the flag while the Star Spangled Banner was played, followed by the loud sound of the excited announcer calling the races! We were well into the service when the TV interruptions blasted forth. I stopped to laugh, telling the audience that I thought Gale would have been tickled pink! We went on, smiling and to compete with the TV, I used the loudest voice I have ever used at a funeral!

Area churches that I had enlisted in my ministry conducted Bible School on the track. I had preached in all those churches and they responded so well that one summer we had four weeks of Bible School conducted by four different churches. It made a big difference for these children, who, while usually helping with horse chores, had a lot of time to figure out their next mischief. One little boy, about six, had to park his Copenhagen at the door and get rid of his wad of snuff that was hidden inside his lip before taking part.

One year, I heard that the Racing Commission was going to vote at their big meeting in Columbus, on banning all children of racetrackers from being on the track. I went to that meeting and had a chance to stand and address the Commission on the subject. Telling them about my own children growing up on the farm and wanting to help us by the time they were five or six, I told them that racetrack children were with their fathers and mothers and it was far better that they be there than out on the street with no supervision. Telling them of our Bible School and the care all racetrackers gave those kids, I informed them that many future trainers would be ready to pass their license tests as soon as they were old enough. They had learned their lessons from their parents, while street kids usually had no idea what direction their lives would take. Thankfully, the Commission voted down the proposition to ban the children from the tracks.

I observed that many boys need more than the Bible School as they grew a year or two older. I visited the management at River Downs, and with their cooperation, we started a Boy Scout Troop at River Downs. Calling on the Dan Beard Council of Boy Scouts in Cincinnati, the Scout Executive for the area came out to River Downs and helped us set up the troop. Along with myself, two grooms and four trainers made up the Scout Committee of River Downs Troop and Pack No. 115, of the Boy Scouts of America. It was the first troop ever set up on a racetrack! The Council established that each boy could enter the troop where he lived from fall until spring, and regroup at River Downs in the summer. A donation was given that allowed all the boys to have official shirts and caps. They looked splendid when their group photo was taken in the winner's circle before the track closed, although a few Indiana boys had already started school back home.

The annual blood drives went well and every tracker could sign up five people who could receive free blood if needed, and every tracker in Ohio could have the same. I was out getting donors while the bloodmobile was parked in front of the kitchen one day when I asked a big black man from Cuba if he would give. He could not understand English yet, having only recently arrived on the infamous Mariel Boat Lift, when Fidel Castro emptied most of his prisons into the United States. Probably a political prisoner, he had all his front teeth knocked out during the interrogation before being imprisoned. He beckoned me to follow him and took me into the kitchen where we found a Hispanic jockey. After hearing what I wanted, he nodded vigorously and all three of us went to the bloodmobile. The Cuban was greatly disappointed because they could not take his blood. He had too recently been in a malaria region. But from that time on, even though we understood each other only by smiles and other body language, he was my special friend. I once pointed to my heart, clasped my hands as if I was praying, and then pointed up to Heaven. He nodded and with a "*Si! Si!*" and went through the same motions with a big grin, then hugged me.

Contact with people is essential in a ministry, the more the better and by various activities. Not all lead to an evangelistic encounter, but you usually have to be a friend first in order to be trusted and heard. I love people, and what a place to minister! Everyday I would meet many people who had never talked with a minister before! These were the glory days of my life!

CHAPTER 22

Working With Track Security

**"For rulers hold no terror for those who do right, but
for those who do wrong. " Do you want to be free
from fear of the one in authority? Then do what
is right and he will commend you."**

[Paul, Romans 13: 3]

"Funny, there's been no theft of any kind this year,
since you came to the track. No, wait, somebody did
report a feed bucket missing," the head of Beulah Park
Security told me one day when I greeted him in his office,
[which was right across from mine in Jordan Hall.] That
thought has been echoed throughout the nation where
RTCA chaplains have served.

I always had a good relationship with those on the security team at all the tracks. They man the gates, where you
either have to show your license or have somebody who has

a license sign you in. I had to be at the gate to sign in my visiting groups or someone that came to the gate and had to ask security to call me on the public address system. At Beulah Park, my office was right next to the gate, so it was handy. One day I saw the owner of the track being interrogated at the gate. I went over to greet him and he had to ask me to sign him in! The guard did not know him and was doing his job rather well! The owner was not too happy about it, but gave in with a grin when I laughed at the irony of it all.

Usually I went home on our chapel service night after the seventh or eighth race to eat early and get back. As I returned to my van late one afternoon, the head of security asked me to come into his office. "Are you busy? he asked.

"Well, what is on your mind?"

"We've had a grandstand bomb scare phoned in. If we try to evacuate in a hurry, there will be casualties on the stairs. What I would like you to do is let me put this walkie-talkie on your belt, pull your jacket down over it and go stand near the grandstand. We have every available person searching the entire grandstand. You just stand there and listen. If anything happens, you'll know where to be!"

"Sure! Anything to be of help," I told him and, thus equipped, went over to the space between the grandstand and the paddock. All was quiet on my radio. I was talking with two farriers there when a small man, a groom who was almost always partly drunk, came unsteadily out of the lower grandstand entrance with a pint cup of beer in his hand. He came up to the three of us and we were all talking when there was one word spoken over my invisible radio. The groom tipped his head, looked up at me with a concerned look on his face and asked, "Chaplain, are your pants wired?" The farriers were bent double with laughter! And most importantly, the bomb scare was another dangerous hoax.

Once I was in the jockey's room, which is where the

jockeys each have a valet who keeps their boots shined [no matter what kind of a track the day presents, boots are changed and cleaned after each race] and help with their clean colors and outfits. Every time you see the Post Parade, the jockeys are all in bright shining colors and clean white pants. That means a change after every race, and if it is a muddy track, perhaps a shower as well. This day I entered to share thoughts with the jockeys who were not running in the race. Jockey Mike Perrotta, who was one of my right hands in the jocks room was lying on his side on a wooden bench. "Hi! Mike, how are things with you today?"

"Not so good Chaplain, my back right here is killing me!"

Having been a sufferer of a "bad back" for many years, I looked him over saying, "You are in a good position right now to fix it."

Mike knew immediately what I was talking about and said excitedly, "Can you do it?" I arranged him on the bench and gave him what is called a "pelvic twist." "That's great Chaplain; now do it on the other side!" He was already rolling his body the other way, so I stepped around the bench to do it again. I had just given him the procedure when I noticed a big pair of shoes on the floor beside the bench. I was following the legs up to the face of a six and a half-foot Racing Commission Representative when the Racing Secretary's voice came over the sound system.

"Chaplain Evans, you are needed immediately in the Racing Secretary's office!"

"Oops" I said, "I've been caught practicing medicine without a license!" With laughs all around, Mike jumped up, told me his back now felt fine, shook my hand in thanks and rushed off to get ready for the next race. The State Security man asked me how I knew how to do that and I told him how it worked on me, but that I was very hesitant to use it on anyone else. Then I went on to answer the call and found a routine matter with which the HBPA wanted my help.

I asked a State man once [there were always two of them all over the track] how they approached someone who might have "inside knowledge" of something on the crooked side. He told me of a man who was getting a name for winning a lot of trifectas. [A trifecta means a bet is placed on three horses in the exact order of their finish. Long odds appeal to a few with more money than sound good sense, who think only of the big pay-off if they win.] The bettor, who was standing at the rail, showed him how he had marked his program. There had been changes in trainers and riders and he had wondered why until after a long study he was willing to gamble that the changes would work out a certain way. Sometimes he was right. The State keeps very close scrutiny over every aspect of racing. The state is involved at all tracks for the states get a percentage of the handle. The handle is the total amount of money bet that day. Some of it is bet many times, but it is the total from which the state and the horsemen get their share. The horsemen's share makes up the purses paid to winning horses in win, place and show, and sometimes farther at the big tracks.

I was in the private office of the manager at Beulah one day. While he was talking, his eyes were on a big array of changing numbers, which was connected to each mutuel clerk's machine. "Excuse me Chaplain," he said grabbing the telephone to security. "Get a man to window number — in the clubhouse, upper level. Someone is throwing hundred dollar bills on a trifecta on horses numbered [he rattled off three numbers.]"

"Sorry to interrupt, Chaplain, but those three horses are the longest shots in the race. Spomebody may be very foolish, or something may be wrong or somebody may be tampering with the horses! A plain-clothes security man will stand behind the person making the bet and follow him until the race is over. If those horses win, in that order, he will immediately be brought in for investigation!" No track and no state will allow anything scandalous to happen there if it is stoppable by any means. Neither will the horsemen; they follow the rules. There have been attempts by outside criminal elements to horn in on the money, but they have all failed or been exposed..

Did you ever think of the perfect answer to a surprise question, only too late to give it? That happened to me on television. A Cleveland station had invited me to be on a Sunday morning talk show. The host was very genial to us, for the show would be interviewing two oddballs at once; a racetrack chaplain and a priest who worked his wide parish with ham radio. All went well and we entered the studio [far from the first time for me] and sat down. Still relaxed, the program started. We were introduced and sat there expecting the questions we had just been told we would be asked. Never, ever trust a talk show host! The first thing he said to me was, "I've got a friend out at Northfield [a Cleveland standardbred trotting track] who tells me every race is fixed! What do you have to say about that?" I went from relaxation to an on-edge defense in a mini-second. In fact, I was mad! But I answered, at least to the satisfaction of all the horsemen who had been alerted to listen.

As I walked out the door, I slapped myself on the forehead and thought out loud, "Horse racing is more honest than television news!" Oh how I wished I had thought of that in the correct instant!

My reason for thinking television news is not balanced is an event at the Dallas-Fort Worth Airport. We had a bit of time before our plane left and I was in a big restaurant near a window and, being in Tex-Mex country, was enjoying my first taco salad. A large group of people in hot weather casual clothes was on a grassy bank outside my window. Some were laying on their backs, some sitting, refreshments at hand in a perfect picture of picnic relaxation. Suddenly, the group began to scramble onto their feet and pick up signs that had been lying in a pile. A local TV station truck was approaching. When the TV camera was turned on they were shouting and yelling, looking angry and shaking their fists at the camera. They were all aircraft controllers, who had been fired by President Reagan after they went on strike. The TV audience that night would have to believe, because of what they saw on TV news, that the fired controllers were ready to take on the whole Army! But, after the camera stopped, the signs came down and people started for their cars, waving goodbye to each other, just as if they <u>had</u> been on a picnic!

Security took care of licensing for our yearly ID badges [it was a separate badge for each track in the beginning of my ministry], as well as fingerprinting. At the beginning of a meet, long lines would form behind the registration desk as we all waited for our chance to give our ID information. One summer at River Downs when I was asked what I did, and told the secretary, "Chaplain," she said, "There's no category like that in my instructions!"

The man behind me spoke up to be helpful, saying "Yes, he's our chaplain; he works for God!"

The secretary made an instant decision and typed up my badge. After my picture was taken and the badge was processed, I saw to my amazement that under my job title was written, "Agent of God." Word spread and a lot of trackers came up to me to read my badge. Actually, that is exactly what I was, and it was a constant reminder to me to hustle for Jesus just like the jockey agents hustled for their jockeys.

How well I was accepted showed one day at Beulah Park. I was making a call on the offices, secretaries, accountant and the managers and owners offices. The owner of the track was in the manager's office and I greeted them and asked how everybody was feeling. The owner spoke right up and told me that Bob, the "money man," was sick, at his job in spite of being told he ought to go home, and that he, the owner, would appreciate it if I would follow him back to the "money cage" to pray with him! I followed him in a passage behind the office to a tiny room, enclosed on two sides with heavy wire-net protection, and two walls full of shelves jam-packed with bundles of money! I'd never seen so much at one time before! The owner unlocked the door and Bob, complete with a green celluloid visor like movie cashiers, looked up and said, "Chaplain, you've come!"

"Yes, Bob, I came to pray with you." There were mutuel clerks standing in line behind a small opening in the wire mesh, holding large handfuls of bills, waiting to get fresh packages of sorted bills for their mixed ones. They had to wait. I put one hand on Bob's head and took a hand in mine, and before I could start praying, Bob started praying. His voice was loud enough for all in the line of clerks to hear. When he finished his prayer, I began mine. When I finally straightened up, I saw open mouths all along the line of clerks. A prayer meeting in the money room! Unheard of!

A tragic event happened one year at River Downs. In the summer we had a lot of college kids and young men out of high school working on the track, usually as hotwalkers or grooms. They caused an influx of drugs that we saw little of the rest of the year. One young man, not older than nineteen or twenty, was using Quaaludes. He and another lad were off the track in a car, so stoned that his passenger had his head lolling out the window. The driver sideswiped a tree and the head was utterly smashed.

The young man's parents and their son were in my office the next day. It seems that the Quaalude pill dealer was an assistant trainer on the track. I had the barn number and the man's name as the boy, with a lot of tears, told his parents what had happened and how. I told them all that the next evening I was going to have a memorial service for the dead youth in front of my chapel trailer, and that I wanted their lad to be in attendance.

He was there in the front row of chairs when I held the service. Many trackers were there as we talked about life, and eternal life and how to have it. The young man actually stood up and told the story with tears of contriteness and sorrow.

Since the information I had about the drug dealer was not confessional but public, I told the head of security. He asked me if the lad would be willing to buy another pill from the dealer, and give it to me to give to security. I had to think hard about that. I didn't think it was in my "job description!" But because we were trying to stop the flow of drugs, when the boy consented, I gave him five dollars that the head of security had provided, and arranged a pass-by meeting in the winner's circle after the horses had left for the post parade. We met, shook hands and I had the pill in my hand right in front of many thousands of people. Security checked it in the PDR and found it was in fact, a Quaalude.

I waited. Nothing happened. News traveled fast on the track and I would have known at once if there had been any news on that subject. After a wait of a couple of weeks, I specifically asked the chief what they had done. Seems they had to catch him in the act of selling drugs and they hadn't figured out a way to do it. Seemed flimsy to me but I'm not in law enforcement. I was disappointed because I had gone out on a limb for them with no results.

Security was always friendly and watched out for me. I remember one churchman telling me that before I went into the track ministry, to always lock my car on the track, and I really should get a car alarm system installed. I very seldom locked my car on the track, for the trackers knew my car and would jump anyone messing with it! I did lose my CB radio in front of a church one night when I was the special speaker!

CHAPTER 23

A Dangerous Business

**"A horse is a vain hope for deliverance,
despite all its great strength it cannot save."**

[David, Psalm 33: 17]

When you are lying on your back, it's easier to look up. The racetrack is a dangerous place, and those riding horses in any capacity are in special danger. Only Lloyd's of London will insure jockeys. An ambulance follows behind every race. Ministering to fallen jockeys and other injured or sick horsemen is a big part of our work. When they are down in a bed with a broken bone or worse, they are especially ready for a loving approach to finding their salvation.

I once asked a former steeplechase jockey who was now exercising horses if he would tell a small group of boys who were on a visit how to ride horses. "It's really simple boys, you just keep your head in the middle and a leg on each side, but I've had twenty-three broken bones that came when I forgot to keep that position!"

Mike Perrotta was a Christian jockey who came regularly to our chapel services. He was a good friend and grew up less than a hundred miles from my hometown in New York State. The Columbus Citizen- Journal of April 1976 ran a small headline, "Injured Perrotta a Class Guy." He was injured in a fall about fifty feet from the finish line when his horse fell and threw him over the rail. Mike got a broken pelvis and cuts and bruises out of it. In seven years, besides the results of this fall, Mike had suffered a broken back, five concussions, numerous leg injuries and other assorted ailments. From his hospital bed, Mike said, "I wish I was out there riding today!" My hospital visits to him and his wife were always joyful because they both knew the Lord and were glad to pray with me.

One groom got kicked in the face when he was hooking a horse up to a hotwalking machine. It ripped up his face, and was so close to his eye that the surgeon had to rebuild a tear duct! The surgeon was proud of his handiwork! We had a lot of hospital time to pray together.

A young Christian couple came out of Washington State with a trailer load of five horses. Sue, the wife, was the jockey and her husband Wayne was the trainer. Sue was a good rider and had ridden both in Washington and New York. I was off-track one morning when Sue was working a young horse. For some reason the horse shied at the finish line and Sue was thrown over the rail and took out the finish line mirror. This mirror is right under the finish line so the judges can get a left side image as well as a right side photo in case of a close finish. The tall mirror was mounted on an upright plank. She took out both mirror and plank with a crash that was heard all over that area. Those who saw it and told me about it that afternoon were of the opinion that she would never walk again if she survived!

I went immediately to the hospital and knelt beside her

bed. She was the same age as my daughter. She had a concussion and eight broken ribs plus cuts from the mirror, and a lot of bruises. As I held her hand and prayed, I remember hearing myself say, "Lord, heal her so fast that the doctors will be amazed!"

She came back to their tackroom after only about three days, exercised a few horses gently at eight days and at the two-week checkup the doctor could not tell on the x-ray which side had been hurt! She then resumed racing again! Trackers had been helping Wayne with their two children, a boy age two, and a newborn. The two-year old already liked to help with the horses. I have a slide of him sitting on a bucket with a hose, cooling down a stallion's leg. The horse stood there, ground-tied, enjoying it.

A fourth generation tracker, a jockey was injured, not by a horse but by diving off a tree limb into a creek on a dark day. The streambed had changed since the last swimming season, and he broke his neck. His father, a valet in the jock's room, came to me with tears in his eyes, saying the doctors had told him that he could become a quadriplegic. After praying with the father right there on the spot, I hurried to the hospital. The young man had a "halo" brace on his head and was under traction. He was in intensive care, with curtains around the various beds. The first thing he told me was that a woman from a local church where he lived had been out to see him and he had accepted Jesus Christ as Savior and Lord! I stood there talking to him about the accident, then asked him if he could wiggle a toe for me. The big toe on his right foot slowly moved just a little. "How about a finger?" And a finger slowly moved. "Great! You are going to be well again! What do you want to do with the rest of your life, now that you know Jesus?" I asked him. "One thing for sure is that you're not going to sell pencils out of cup on the sidewalk! What do you plan to do?"

"I'd really like to ride again," he said. "All my family for generations have been on the track. It's all I know!" We prayed and together asked the Lord to heal his body and make him strong.

As I was leaving I heard a noise behind a curtain but did not understand the voice until the nurse asked me to stop and go into a cubicle where the sound originated. . "She's calling for you," she said. I pulled the drape aside and found a thirtyish lady with several tubes in and out of her body.

"I don't know who you are or what church you come from, but I want what you've got!"

Probably all instructors of hospital visitation would frown on my bedside manner that day, but I actually chuckled with a big smile as I took her hand. Without any preliminaries, I said, "Do you know Jesus?"

"I'm not sure; I know about Him."

"Would you like to be sure that you know Him?"

"Oh, yes!"

"Then pray with me," and I led her in the Sinner's prayer and she asked Christ into her heart. She'd had an operation through her nose to remove the pituitary gland and was quite discouraged. We talked for a while and I told her I'd check in with her in a couple of days.

She told me when I visited the two of them in the next visit that her husband had walked in that night and stopped in shock when he saw her. "What happened to you!"

She was radiant and told him, "I've been touched!" and went on to tell him what had happened. I continued to visit her until she left to go home, and had a note from her later.

Two and a half months later the jockey across from her attended the HBPA picnic for trackers. He was still wearing the halo brace and walking slowly, but he was there to lot of greetings and applause. His father was beaming. He went back to riding that winter in Florida.

My Sunday speaking engagements took me far and wide. I was due for a morning service well down in West

Virginia and one that night back up in Ohio. Rather than get up so early and drive the distance and then drive back all in one day, I told Florence I was going to take Saturday afternoon off and drive down leisurely, stay overnight and be fresh the next morning. I started down the pike and had gone maybe forty miles when I realized that I had left part of my luggage at home. The plan had to be changed. I turned around and drove home. Florence was on the phone and in tears when I entered the door. "He's just come in! she said and handed me the phone. It was Mike Perotta from the jock's room. Florence had told him that I had left for West Virginia and there was no way she could contact me. I was needed now and here I was. Godincidence again!

Kevin was an apprentice jockey who had ridden quarter horses in Texas and had started with thoroughbreds at River Downs that summer. At Beulah Park he had ridden four firsts, six seconds and two thirds out of thirty-seven starts, until that October day when his mount put him over the rail. The horse was a rather green two-year old in a maiden race [for horses that have never won a race] and it was only his second start. He had a five-length lead headed for a win when the horse veered into the rail at the eighth-pole.

As the crowd in the grandstand looked on in horror, he was loaded in the ambulance, and sirens screaming once out the track gate, taken to a hospital in Columbus. The jockeys wanted me there to pray with them for Kevin, and for themselves in the races still to be run.. We arranged to meet in the waiting room by Kevin's room after the last race and find out how Kevin was doing. About twenty five of us gathered. We were told that he was in critical condition and still in surgery. It took seven hours on the operating table to put him back together. He had a fractured skull, dislocated his sixth and seventh cervical vertebrae, chipped his teeth, broken his right leg, broken the bones around his left eye and crushed the left side of his pelvic bone. The surgeons had to wire his left eye in place, insert rods into his leg and remove his spleen.

We joined hands in the waiting room in a big circle and I led an impromptu prayer service. We all hugged and agreed to keep on praying for his recovery. And recover he did! He came back to Beulah Park to say thank you to everybody in the jock's room and kitchen, who had collected a sizable purse for him, and just to prove he was doing well. He had to wait, impatiently, for six months to ride again. That winter he frequented the Latonia track in Kentucky just to be with fellow jockeys and keep his mind on riding again.

A Jewish jockey broke a leg and was visited in the hospital. He and his brother had both been in our chapel services and his father was a good friend; one you could sit and talk to. Some trainers always went about in a mad, nervous rush and were hard to talk with for even a short time. The only time they relaxed was when they gathered to chat in the HBPA office, and I was a frequent visitor there. Irv, the father of the fallen jock, enjoyed a chance to visit with me. At the hospital, after I had prayed with the jockey and his girl friend, I said just before leaving, "Oh, here's something by one of you guys." I handed him an American Bible Society tract with Jesus' "Sermon on the Mount." He gave me a big grin as he saw what it was and started reading.

Many, many hospital visits were made for track injuries that kept the ambulance busy and the hospitals working. Many times I looked up the hospital social worker to tell them there was no money or insurance available for the person that I had just brought to the facility in my van. The HBPA helped in some cases, sometimes to help with bills, sometimes to send them home. I have taken more than one tracker to the airport and shepherded them through the process of air travel.

One thing was peculiar to racetrackers. If they were injured and went to the hospital, they always came to the track on the way home to recuperate. They just had to show that they were tough and that this was their real home. It never failed. One reason for quick recovery beside the prayers of friends is that the jockeys are among the world's best-conditioned athletes.

Sometimes, someone I had taken to the hospital was back at the track within hours. They wanted out. It was too different. Chaplain Cliff Holsema of Florida once told me about taking some elderly trackers to the hospital. "They usually beat me back to the track! The only way to keep them there is to put a muck basket full of horse manure under the bed!"

The jockeys are very much aware of dangerous conditions on the track. I came back from lunch at home one day just after the first race was over. As I was directed into a parking spot, the attendant, a constant attender of the chapel services, said, "You better get to the Jock's room Chaplain, there's trouble!"

When I walked in, I found that the jocks did not want to go out for the second race. The owner of the track was there, along with the manager. The head of security and the two men from the Racing Commission were also on hand. There were a lot of very loud conversations going on all at once.

It seems that the track had gotten lower at the center and rail than the ground at the rail itself, making the track like a shallow pond. Even with three or four sets of goggles to pull down as they became covered with mud, they could not see well enough to ride. They did not want to go out again, not necessarily out of fear but because reason told them it was too dangerous. The owner pleaded with them to race again, for if they did not race enough races, everyone who had paid to get into the grandstand would have to be given their money back. He shouted, "I'll give an extra $100 to every-one who will go back out and ride!

Most of the older jockeys just shook their heads. Mike

Perrotta came up to me and asked, "What do you think, Norm?"

I responded that I could not tell them to ride, but if they did, I would go out on the track and stand in the mud just off the winner's circle and pray for horses and riders all the way around the track. Mike nodded and thought it over. Ron Copeland then came up and asked me the same thing and got the same answer. He talked with Mike and then the two of them told the owner that they would ride. Little Reyes Matias, an apprentice from Puerto Rico, then spoke up loudly, "I ride! I ride!" Finally, enough "hungry" apprentice jockeys who were looking for a chance to show their talent, filled the number of jockeys needed.

I stood in the mud and prayed that no horse would go down and no jockey hurt as I had promised. They jocks had all heard by now about why I was standing in the mud and they all grinned at me or winked as they went by in the post parade, and slapped my hand when they came back. One jock said when every race was over, "We did it again, Father!"

Some of them had to ride "blind" and let the horse have its head, but no horse went down and nobody got hurt. They were all a muddy mess after every race, but came out for each post parade all dressed up in clean silks, pants and shined boots! Reyes Matias never forgot that day for it gave him a chance to ride. He actually won five races that day and after that was given rides by many trainers!

Sometimes "accidents" did not happen and for a reason. A sixteen year-old jockey came out of Michigan. As an apprentice, he had won two out of his first three races and thought he was going to be the next Eddie Arcaro. And he was a braggart. The jocks got sick of hearing him and putting up his arrogant manner. Someone from the jocks room tipped me off one day that the older jocks were waiting for a chance to "put him over the rail." They planned to crowd him into the rail when the chance was good, just to "teach him a lesson."

When I heard that I went to the ambulance drivers who always followed the horses around the track and told them to watch out for the boy and why. They were part of our security team so I knew it would get back to the chief. I then passed the rumor on to the secretary's office. Then I asked a jockey agent who had one of the veteran jockeys for a client, to sit with me on a bench just outside the jocks room. I told him of the rumor and that I had no idea who the planners were. I asked him to inform his jock that the ambulance, secretary and the chaplain were all watching out for the kid. Nothing happened. The boy? He soon grew too big to ride. He never knew anything about the planned "accident."

CHAPTER 24

Fire!

**"Likewise the tongue is a small part of the body,
but it makes great boasts. Consider what a great
forest is set on fire by a small spark.
The tongue is also a fire..."**

[James, James 3:5-6]

Fire on a racetrack is a thing of horror. In 1978, on the
night of May 19, a blaze swept through a number of
barns at River Downs, killing horses and hopes. I wrote my
account of the fire very soon after it happened, while names
and events of that terrible night were fresh in my mind. I
made a few copies on a mimeograph, letting the Racing
Secretary and the president of the Horsemen's Benevolent
and Protective Association each read them. Both counseled
me not to make it public, as there would be pending
lawsuits. I have no idea what took place between lawyers
for the Horsemen and lawyers for the Track management,
but twenty-five years later, I feel that I have waited long

enough. I shall use my 1978 manuscript with a few editorial notes from this side of the event. It needs to be told.

"FIRE!"
River Downs, May 19, 1978
Chaplain Norman B. Evans

Any event is seen differently by different people because of their varying positions, experiences and attitudes.

From being there, experiencing the event as the Chaplain, and talking with many who experienced it with me, I have attempted to tell the story of the May 19 fire from my viewpoint, as it affected me. Undoubtedly, the story is not complete, simply because so many of us were there and my narration cannot include everyone's experiences.

This is how I saw it.

<u>Cincinnati, Ohio – "May 19, 1978 "26 Horses Perish In River Downs Fire"</u> Cincinnati Enquirer.

The story flashed outwards from Cincinnati, diminishing in detail as the miles grew, to short statistical "fillers," and then disappeared. But to those who experienced that night on the Backside of River Downs, the details are indelibly burned into memories and we are not the same.

"We," because I was there. For two and a half years I've been the chaplain to the people on the Backsides of Ohio's Thorouhghbred racetracks, as a team member of Race Track Chaplaincy of America, Inc. I live on the Backside during the week, in a room that once served as the photographer's darkroom, in the Kitchen building. Because it has a sink, it's the best-equipped "tackroom" on the grounds and the only one not in a horse-barn. In fact, it was provided as an office for the chaplain, but I choose to live in it as well in order to be with my people.

For 55 years, the River Downs racetrack has stood on the banks of the Ohio River. Its old weathered barns had been succumbing gradually to the ravages of almost yearly flooding, dry rot, termites and winter winds, with destruction postponed by layer after layer of tarpaper and hot tar, sprayed creosote on the wood, with patches and props here and there to keep them tied together. Some of the barns are even older than River Downs, having been moved here second-hand from another racetrack when River Downs was just getting started. New, concrete barns have been gradually replacing them, usually behind schedule from the Horsemen's point of view, and even the Racing Commission's, that did grant extensions of time to the track when requested.

The Backside area is divided by a big ditch, with three roadways bridging it. [Later, the ditch, which drained the backside, had big concrete pipes installed and was covered over for all of its length.] On the East Side is the Horsemen's Gate with its Guard Shack, the sprawling Kitchen Building that also houses some essential offices. The main restroom/shower facility for the track, two tack-shop trailers, four large concrete barns, two newer wooden barns, a series of feed-trailers and a parking lot complete that area.

From the ditch west to the track's far turn are packed four rows of barns with roadways between. Two rows are new, concrete barns, but the alternate rows, with one exception, are all old wooden barns. Two barns in the first row are old horse barns that have been converted into groom's quarters by pouring cement onto the dirt floors in the stalls, paneling in places where boards were missing, with plywood, and making rough "barndoors" to fill in the stall entrances. There are tackrooms in all the barns with some folks sleeping on dirt floors. The new dormitory building has been on the drawing board for some time. It was scheduled to be finished before the 1978 season, but no start was made. They said it was a rough winter.

It was a rough spring. From the time horses came onto the track in mid-April, the horsemen had been complaining about the leaking roofs in the old barns. The shedrows were a mess with ankle-deep mud in many places. Grooms complained about having to "take a shower" while doing up a horse's legs. It became a concern, not just an inconvenience, when the leaking roofs let water run down through the electrical lights and fixtures. From his post at the gate, the night security guard could see electrical fixtures sparking in the first wooden barn; the groom's barn. The guard persuaded Maintenance to put another layer of tarpaper on that barn. In barn 53, Clifford Brafford had reported sparks coming from the light fixtures for a week. Bill McNerney, who lived in the same barn with his wife and four of his children, had also reported electrical shorts. After repeated complaint had failed to bring any repair, Brafford finally bypassed channels and brought the Maintenance man personally to his barn. He was told they would get to it in "three or four days." When Brafford pressured him he promised to start putting tarpaper on the barn roof on Friday morning at 7:00 A.M. That time never came for Barn 53, or for Barns 52 and 54 on either side of it.

I had heard of racetrack fires. Nothing carries more dread for a tracker than a barn fire. I had hoped that I would never see one. Back in 1973, five old barns had burned at River Downs. Many trackers had told me of that fire. Their stories of that night and the aftermath were part of the fear of fire that trackers keep suppressed in the back of their minds.

Thursday, May 18, was a different day for me. After making my rounds on the Backside early that morning, I drove across southern Ohio to a speaking engagement at Reno, just east of Marietta. [I hate to take speaking engagements that take me away from the track, but this one was to make up for one I'd had to cancel the year before.] After the talk, I realized that I could make just as good time going back by taking the Interstate and looping north, which also meant I could stop at my home in Grove City [near Columbus] and have supper with my wife. After supper, Florence asked me if I was going to stay overnight and go back in the morning. I had the feeling that I was needed at the track so after checking the mail, I continued on to Cincinnati.

It was quiet that night on the backside. Although the rain had stopped, it was sultry, a good night for mosquitoes. In the dusk, I helped a groom locate his trainer in a nearby trailer park. The groom was concerned about a sick horse. After spending a half-hour with the two men, I went back to my room, wrote three letters, did some reading, got to sleep about midnight. The Recreation Room had closed about 11:00 P.M. and all was quiet.

Security Guard Carrie Carias went off duty at mid-night. She had been the only woman member of the South Gate Fire Department just a year before at the Beverly Hills Supper Club fire. There was great loss of life at that fire. Something made her uneasy. Instead of going right home as she usually did, she stopped just up the road at 4 Acres Restaurant for a while. She was there at 1:00 A.M. when the alarm came.

I was aroused by the clatter of a horse running by my door a couple of minutes after 1:00 A.M. Half asleep, I thought, "Security will have to catch a horse." A crash followed – the horse jumped onto a car that was arriving. Ron Ennis was on his way back to the track, saw the sudden glare of the fire as the tarpaper roofs exploded into flame, and pulled into the gate to be met with a horse landing across his windshield. He thought he was, "A goner' for sure!"

Still groggy after only an hour of sleep, I was trying to sort out the meaning of the sounds, when sirens began to come closer. Awake now, I pulled my pants over my pajamas, threw on a jacket, slipped into my shoes and stepped out my door. The sky was red beyond the kitchen and it seemed like every horse on the track was screaming!

In my last pastorate, I had been the Fire Photographer with the local fire department. Automatically I grabbed my camera and headed to the barns. Flames were high in the sky, silhouetting the concrete barn in the second row on the west side of the ditch. As I crossed the ditch, a herd of loose horses thundered behind me on their way out the main gate. Florie, a groom, grabbed my arm as I got to the corner of the row of concrete barns and, as I gasped at the sight, sound, smell and feel of those kindling-wood barns going up, she sobbed, "Isn't it awful!"

The screams of 1,000 horses, the cries and yells of the Backside people and the roar of the fire combined with a blast of heat made the racetrackers dread of fire so real that the memory of that moment will always haunt me.

Barns 52, 53 and 54 were completely engulfed; blazing skeletons of flame and blast furnace heat! No one could get near to them! Had everyone gotten out? Of the twelve people sleeping in those three barns, a majority had been with me at the track service the evening before last. Were they safe? Looking down to the third barn, #52, I could see Big Jim's corner tackroom. It was an inferno! No one could be living there if they had not gotten out in time! Was Big Jim out? Johnny Morse was in the other end, along with Paul Hostedler, the McNerneys, and the grooms in Barn 54; were they out?

I took off at a run to get there, to find people, to ask, to look for faces in the red light of the fire, to count noses! Staying next to the concrete barns, I tried again and again to get past the fire, but was forced back by the heat each time. Breathing a prayer, "Lord, let them be safe!" I went back to try going around the other end. I got by the Spit-Box side, but the heat between the burning barns and the outside fence forced me back again. As I backed up I saw trainer G. L. Roberts, who had been able to get some horses out.

"G.L.! Have you seen Johnny or Big Jim?"

"I saw Johnny – he's out!"

"Thank You, Lord! Let Jim and the rest be out too!" Finally, I went back and circled the concrete barns and went through the last one to get to what was left of Barn 52. There was Johnny and I hugged him. Then Big Jim and I saw each other! We both cried as we embraced.

Barn 51 was the last barn in the row. It had been evacuated but the heat from Barn 52 was so intense that it could ignite at any moment. Firemen were dragging hoses between 51 and 52 through a hole they had cut in the chain-link fence and a truck had just pulled into the Backside through the Quarter-Pole Gate, when vegetation at the middle of 51 exploded into flame before my eyes. The kindling point had been reached. The tar was already bubbling and smoking on the roof, the flame from the burning vine just reached the roof edge and fire flowed like water both ways down the roofline. I yelled as loud as I could, over all the noise, to the firemen. Alert firemen heard me and opened up with hoses from both ends. Barn 51 still stood after the fire, but it would only have taken seconds more without being wet down, and it would have joined its mates.

The fire had started in Barn 53 where electrical shorts had been repeatedly reported. There was no fire alarm on the track that night [there is now!] Ed Finneran, the guard on duty after midnight, turned in the alarm by phone at 12:59 A.M. and went back to the barns, yelling as he got horses out. He worked like a madman! Without him, many more horses would have been lost.

Bill McNerney heard his pony scream and strike at the metal stall-gate. At the same moment, a daughter heard their dog. Bill went out barefoot, saw the fire at the other end of his barn, grabbed the dog to unsnap its chain, and the fire was upon him. All six of the McNernys got out, along with the pony, which managed to break out through its gate, though it was burned on its back. All five of his Thoroughbreds died.

There was confusion that night with people running back and forth, firemen trying to get set up and horses galloping in the dark. Some areas were bright with firelight and others in blackness cut with flashing lights. Someone called to me to say McNerney was burned – where was the ambulance? I ran back near the fire area to get the ambulance. I got him to set up near the Kitchen area where people could be brought for treatment. Bill's burns were not serious but he was near hysteria. Weeping in shock and loss, he cried, "Chaplain, I'm wiped out! Everything is gone! I've nothing left!" Suddenly he grabbed both of my arms, exclaiming, "But Chaplain, Praise the Lord! My family is all with me!"

Bobby Todd is a past middle-age groom, bent with arthritis and not the person that stands out in a crowd. He did that night. He led out horse after horse, even going into burning stalls. Part of the burning roof brushed him as it fell, setting his jacket on fire. He kept going until someone knocked him down to take it off him. At one point he came to Wayne Hanna's tackroom in Barn 54. Getting no response to his yell, he went in and shook him. Wayne was sleeping so hard that Bobby just grabbed him by the heels, snaked him outside, and went on to the next stall. When nothing more could be done, Bobby was taken to the hospital for treatment of burns on his arms.

[Two stories connected with Bobby Todd and Wayne Hanna are inserted here, twenty-five years later, because they relate to the fire. Bobby Todd and a big, much younger man named Jerry "Blue" Spencer, both African Americans, worked in the same stable. Blue picked on Bobby incessantly, calling him names [Bobby was known as 'Dirt-Man'] until one day Bobby turned on him. He picked up a pitchfork to even the odds and went for Blue. While not connecting with the pitchfork, the act was enough to get Bobby ruled off the track by the stewards. I asked the stewards for permission to speak for three minutes before they heard the case. I told them what Bobby had done to help a lot of trainers and owners during the fire, even endangering his life to save horses. When I faced Blue he admitted that he had been picking on Bobby, who was much older and smaller than he was. "Gentlemen, it is your decision. I just wanted to make sure you knew facts that might not be evident." They were both let off with a warning and continued to work in the same barn. Both came to me afterwards to express their gratitude for saving their jobs.

The other story concerns Wayne Hanna, whom Bobby could not wake up and then dragged out of danger. It seems that Wayne drifted to Ellis Park Racetrack in Kentucky, where he was arrested and put off the track for starting a fire. The news was in a horse paper that circulated at the tracks. Another groom came to me after it came out to ask me if I remembered a fire in a strawy manure pile at Beulah Park in the spring. I did remember, for a fire truck had to come onto the Backside and water it down. The groom told me he had been Wayne Hanna's roommate at Beulah and that Wayne had set that fire! What was the chance that Wayne had been involved with the starting of the fire in Barn 52 at River Downs? There was plenty of electrical possibility evidence, but…? Was Wayne really sleeping that hard, or feigning sleep to provide an alibi? We shall never know, but the evidence favors the electrical reasons for the fire.]

Around 2:00 A.M., I brought a paramedic and Trainer Stan Patton to my room where Stan's hand could be washed before treatment of a deep puncture wound. He'd been letting out horses as long as he could and had no idea when he had been hurt. Later, he told me the fire's spread was unbelievably fast. He'd run into a stall in the end of a barn which the fire had not reached, slipped a shank onto a horse and, turning, started out of the stall. The horse stopped at the stall opening. Stan turned and saw three walls of the stall all aflame! Again and again people were to tell how the stalls just burst into flame as the kindling point temperature was reached. A lot of folks, who were not treated for burns, had singed hair and eyebrows!

In the M.K. Essig stable in Barn 52, Big Jim Rice, Johnny Morse and Paul Hostedler had all been aroused by the sounds around them. They rushed out, checked on each other, and began turning out horses until the barn exploded into flames. The horse next to Big Jim's tackroom awakened him. Only a board partition was between them. Jim tried to get him out with a shank, but the horse, in its fright, refused to follow. Jim then tried to drive him out to no avail, and finally threw the water from his water bucket on him. Jim finally had to leave. Morning light showed the twisted remains of Big Jim's bed frame just three feet from the burned carcass of the horse. "He saved my life," he grieved, "but I couldn't save his."

Big Jim saved only what he was wearing, losing all he owned. John and Paul each dragged out one trunk as they left their tackrooms, but Paul let out horses with no shirt on. His right arm had second and third degree burns from the heat alone, for he was burned before his own barn caught fire.

There were many that let out horses that night. Some got there in time to save one, some many. It would be hard to get the names of all who risked their lives to get out horses, usually not even their own! The newspapers would use the cliché, "unsung heroes." No one seemed concerned about getting any credit. It is part of being a member of the Backside Community.

Some of those who let out horses were very much affected by the experience. Jackie Danner tried to get one horse out but he refused to come. In fear, the horse wanted to stay in his stall that had meant security to him. Jackie tried until the stall caught fire and the flames drove her back. Days later, she cried as she remembered the screams of the dying horse she could not save.

Her brother, Gary Danner, had been asleep in a concrete barn that opened out at the end of Barn 53. He ran out and turned out horses as long as he could, then returned to his own concrete barn that could not burn, finding a plastic manure tub 30 feet inside the barn melting and a wooden bench smoking. He turned on his water hose and began to wet down the stalls and piles of baled hay that were exposed to the heat, as did others in other concrete barns.

Mark Perry broke his right index finger as he turned out horses. He took one horse out three times before it would stay out. [It is horse nature when frightened to want the security of their stall, even if it means death. Horses are very lovable but horse sense is very overestimated!] On the other hand, some horses actually freed themselves by smashing through the webbing on the stalls. Two of those that managed to free themselves broke legs in the effort and still died in the fire. About 8:A.M. that morning, I saw Mark riding in from the track ponying a horse he had found. I intercepted him to ask how his finger was. He held up his right hand, pointing his splinted finger to the sky, holding the lead strap with three fingers. "We're tough!" he answered with a grin.

John and Mary Ricky lived in Barn 51 next to their three horses, with two dogs and four cats [one 20 years old.] Just a couple of days before, Mary had proudly shown me their horses. Nobody else's horses looked any better!

John is 79 and Mary 78, neither of them well. One of them is always with the horses. When one goes to the kitchen, the other is at the barn with the horses. They never leave their horses. After the fire, Mary told me they had seen other fires and always went to bed dressed in case they had to get up quickly. John has raced in Cuba, Canada, and nearly every track in this country. In fact, while a young man racing in Cuba, he met Mary, with a group of Gypsies. Falling in love, he bought her for $50.00! John has raced at River Downs since it opened and while the barns were being built. As the barns weathered and began to sag, so has John.

One of their dogs woke them up. John determined no one would turn his horses loose in the darkness to get injured and broken down running in terror. One excited thoroughbred can drag a man all over and even break away from most people, but John went barefoot out into the night with two horses on one shank in one hand and one in the other hand on a stall chain. When the loose horses ran by and around him, he had his hands full. But when he saw that the fire had been limited to three barns, and his Barn 51 was safe, [Barn 51 was the one that I saw catch fire and the firemen dowsed the flames quickly] John came in, still barefoot, with his three horses, all safe and unhurt.

As the sun came up through the morning mists and the rising smoke from three long rows of embers, John sat by his barn. Person after person came by to tell John and Mary they had been worried about them, or how glad they were that they were safe. John kept saying in wonderment, "I must be doing something right! I don't know what it is, but the Lord was sure on my side! He sure had His arms around me last night!" Mary leaned her head on my chest as she thanked God for bringing them through the night.

The Kitchen opened up at 2:00 A.M. that morning. No one went back to sleep. The place was full. Trainers and owners who slept off the track kept arriving. People talked. There was anger. There was shock. Some cried softly. Some were numb. I floated as I could to minister to hurting people.

Big Jim suddenly came to me, half-crying, "Paul was out, but nobody's seen him since the first ten minutes! I've asked everybody on the Shedrow!"

"You don't think he would have tried to get more from his tackroom…? I jumped up and went back to the fire. Rushing to the spot where Paul's room had been, I asked the firemen for light. They directed a spot as well as bringing hand lights and a pike pole. Trying not to feel or think, I began probing. One fireman ran over and told me they had taken two men to the hospital – could he be one of them?

"Two? I know of only one! Could you radio for the names?"

In a minute or so, I sobbed another, "Thank You, Lord!" He was OK, back in the morning with bandaged arms and ready to work. Paul's fiancee worked in my bank, so at 9:00 A.M. I called the bank and got her on the phone, just in case she had gotten the news about the fire and was worried about Paul.

I'm not sure of the time, but the firemen were still working hard when I began to see pony people and a few trainers, mounted on their ponies, slipping by the fire-trucks. The pony horses stepped over the hoses, around the flashing lights on the fire-trucks, past the fires and out the quarter-pole gap. Although they went out individually, they came back in a parade like I had never seen before. Out there in the dark they had somehow organized, covered the territory all the way to Old Coney [an entertainment park,] caught the loose horses, and now they came into the diminished firelight like a quadruple-length post-parade, minus jockeys! Grooms, trainers and all manner of horse-people ran up to the ponies and led away the thoroughbreds. They hung the horses on hot-walking machines until all were full. They were tied in washracks, even doubled up in some stalls. Over on the East Side of the Backside, people like Mrs. Hermon had been locating empty stalls and catching horses since the beginning of the fire. She had been so active back there that she probably reduced the total number of horses killed or injured. As it was, one had to be put down after breaking its neck running into a chainlink fence. Some said a dog that had broken its chain was chasing it. Others said the dog was only trying to get out of the way. I was not there, but I did see another horse being sewn up hours later after running into a bridge railing.

A girl told me she got up on a manure wagon on the East Side, the better to see everything that was going on. Suddenly a horse ran out of the darkness and, not seeing the manure wagon, hit it head on. Momentum carried the horse right onto the wagon and off the other end. The girl did a split second jump off to the side, escaping the horse by mere inches! The horse must have been injured, but which horse it was is not known.

Many of the loose horses had marks or burns from the fire, or were bruised and hurt from running into things in the dark. Horses that were not turned loose, from wooden barns that did not burn, or from concrete barns that could not burn, had sore feet and bruising from pawing and banging around in their stalls. One of the terrors of racetrack fires did not occur. Some old-timers will not talk about past fires, but some will shake their heads and tell you about "Flaming horses," horses running out of a barn streaming fire from blazing manes and tails, often setting new fires as they ran into other barns. We are thankful it did not happen this time!

The veterinarians worked all through the night, usually having no idea whose horse they were treating. All the horses on the hot-walking machines were given shots to keep them from going into shock. Treatment continued as morning came, for with the light, assessment of visible injury could be made. Some horses had escaped, but will never run again. Legs, lungs, spirit – all were hurt.

Like people, each horse is different. About 10:00 A.M., I noticed a horse in a concrete barn, whose stall was on the end next to the fire. He had been able to see the whole scene. He'd been hot as well, for I had been unable to get by his stall earlier in the night. Now he just stood in his stall, trembling like a leaf all over, head down and sweat dripping from his body. Two days before the fire, he'd won a $7,500 race. Ten days after the fire, he was entered and went off the 2 to 1 favorite. He ran in spurts, finishing dead last. He performed the same way in the next race he ran. If he were human, we'd call it a nervous breakdown.

As the pony people brought in the horses during the night, Lauri Workman released her horse to one of the many helpers in the crowd of horsemen, wheeled her mount and walked him over the hoses from a fire-truck. In a moment she disappeared in the darkness toward the kitchen. A few minutes later she reappeared on foot with a tray full of cold soda for the firemen. Then she went back to her pony and rode out again, looking for more horses. In the daylight the pony people made a last sweep, combing the woods and brush of the Ohio River bank as well as the infield.

A chill mist seemed to rise about 3:00 A.M. We had been busy and moving, often near the heat of the fire. Now, jackets were being zipped up. The fire was contained to the three barns shortly after the firemen arrived, but water was still being played over the burning coals. The burned out embers seemed to haunt people. After sitting in the kitchen for a time, they would rise and go back to the grisly scene. I stood there, contemplating how fortunate we were that there had been no wind that night. No barns had ignited from flying sparks; just the heat at the kindling point had ignited the barns on either side of #53. Everything had gone up with a roar, straight up in a horrendous blaze. As I pulled my jacket closer, I realized Big Jim, beside me, had only a tee shirt and was shivering.

We went back to my room and I gave him the only warm shirt I had with me. Florence had given it to me for Christmas. It fit him. I started back out the door, but realized that Big Jim wasn't following. I turned and saw Jim on his knees under a painting of Christ in Gethsemanae that hung on my wall. I went back in, sat on the bed, wrapped my arms around him and added my own thanksgiving. I cried again.

Sometime before daylight, eleven-year old Mark McNerney realized the extent of his own loss. Sitting with his folks in the kitchen, he said, "Dad! I lost my new boots! It sure hurts when I think how hard I worked to get them!" Mark had been working and saving, a quarter here, a dollar there, to get boots like he'd always dreamed of owning. He'd just succeeded in saving enough and had proudly purchased them only a few days before the fire. What could Dad say? He put his arm around Mark. In the daylight the family went out and poked around in the ashes. Mark's boots and his dad's had been sitting side by side. Dad's boots were burned to the nails, but Mark's were unhurt except for the smell of smoke! There are some things that we cannot explain; just accept them on faith!

No one could explain the duck, either. Pete, the white duck, lived in Barn 53. A lot of us grieved when daylight came, as Pete was an early riser, but was nowhere to be seen. His body would have been cremated in the fire, with no trace left. But about 10:00, Pete waddled out from the concrete barn across from #53! He had huddled in a corner of a concrete stall during the night! Much wonderment concerned how he had known when to leave and where to go!

A ripple of rage ran all through the night. Sometimes the ripple became a wave, along with the thanksgiving. It didn't have to happen! The knowledge that horses and people were living in firetrap barns that were behind schedule for being replaced, with leaky roofs and dangerous electrical wiring that should have been fixed, was bad enough. Add to it the feeling of being trapped economically so that you <u>had</u> to be there and emotions became explosive. It could have been the first row of barns where more than 50 former horse-stalls now housed people! Along with thanksgiving that the fire had <u>not</u> started there was the oft-expressed angry statement that had it been that building, "We'd have had another Beverly Hills!"

It was a warning. There had been warnings five years before with the other fire. How many warnings were needed? Some tracks have sprinkler systems in concrete barns, fire hoses hitched to hydrants at the end of each barn, fire alarms to wake up the Backside, fire trucks on patrol at night and decent dormitories for the trackers. But this takes money and in reality, few racetracks are operating in the black. In Ohio, the State makes more than the Track or the Horsemen. The State gets its money off the top, regardless of how the tracks and horsemen are faring with inflation and costs. The State shares in the responsibility to the people of the Backside, but time will tell if this fire will be enough to heat the grease that oils the wheels of change!

As daylight came, I made two phone calls. One was to Florence back in Grove City to alert her before she caught the radio or TV news. I broke down attempting to tell her what happened. I left messages with her to give to other Grove City people with folks at the track. Then I called Rev. Glen Ray of Anderson Hills, who was on my support council, to tell him of the need for clothing for those burned out. Calling his parishioners, he was there within the hour with the first of several batches of clothing. Some had new tags on them. Clothes began to come from many directions, so I turned the former First Aid Room into a free clothing depot. Those burned out soon had plenty of clothes so I opened it to any racetracker who had a need.

Beside the six McNerneys in Barn 53, Big Jim Rice, Johnny Morse, and Paul Hostedler in Barn 52, Weldon Scott, Jim Geerheart and Wayne Hanna had tackrooms in Barn 54. Jim Geerheart was just coming back to the track when the fire broke out, Wayne was dragged out by the feet by Bobby Todd, and Scott was roused by yelling and a car horn. All three lost everything. Scott was able to get some horses out before having to pull back, including one he groomed for Rudy Rosenhauer, named "Has Been." "Has Been" was in the fire of 1973 as well and is still going. Probably he is the only horse at River Downs that has escaped two racetrack fires!

Trainers who lost horses were Steve Cobb, whose horses were the only ones that did not get taken out of Barn 54, M.K.Essig and Jack Kordenbrook in Barn 52 [along with a Shetland pony belonging to exercise-boy Jimmy West] and R.B.Connelly, Clifford and Gary Brafford and Bill McNerney in Barn 53, where it all began. Gary had been through the former fire, had lost horses then, and suffered a nervous breakdown later.

The sight in daylight was worse than a horror movie. One groom told me he'd been in Vietnam, but was sickened when he looked at the smoking remains. A Cincinnati Enquirer photographer stood beside me about 9:00 A.M. He asked me if any horses had been killed in the fire. I told him over 20 at that time and he asked me where they were. "You're standing about three feet from one of them," I replied. I pointed down at the almost unrecognizable form at his feet. He jerked back in horror. Later, he told me that he was so unnerved by the sight that he had to get away from his work that weekend. The trackers could not get away, yet were affected more.

The trackers remembered the screams in the night as trapped, crazed horses caught fire and burned. They had to sleep there again that night - if they could sleep. Troubled sleep. Fearful sleep. What if the "barn" dorm should go up with them sleeping? Some went out to the groom's parking lot by the river that night. Mosquitoes drove most of them back within a night or two.

Smoke rose in many small columns where feed and wet down, partly burned boards still smoldered. Scattered in the black ashes were 22 black lumps that had once been horses. Beautiful horses. Valuable horses. Loved horses. Almost every one was a charred black heap with white bones sticking out where feet and legs had been burned off up to the knees or above. Almost every belly had burst open as the heat boiled the body fluids until the pressure forced the intestines to break out and show white against the char of the burned skin and hair. Halter buckles lay black and burned on grisly skulls, cooked eyes looking out of bone sockets. People stared. People cried. People raged.

A dozer with a front-end loader began to pick up dead horses by 10:00 A.M. There were more tears and groans – some turned and left when the charred carcasses began to drop into the waiting dump truck. The job went fast. I had been asked at daylight to photograph the scene by the Horsemen's Benevolent and Protective Association. I made them a set of over 30 8X10's, printed in my own darkroom. By the time I had finished, I refused to make more. I never want to see a burned horse again!

Surprising to some, training started at 7:00 A.M. Those not directly affected by the fire started going to the track. Horses came and went to the gap, going by the smoking rubble, casting apprehensive eyes at the sight and smell of burned flesh. Post Time came at 2:00 P.M. Some races had short fields due to dead horse entries or some scratched horses that had run loose during the night. Neither the Track nor the Horsemen could afford <u>not</u> to go to the Post. Feelings were swallowed and the show went on, although not without dissent or resentment.

My day continued on the track until near noon. All night long I had been ministering in every way I could. Clothes were coming in and I had moved grooms into my room/office. Near noon, I sought out John Spicer, Ohio HBPA's Vice President. I was scheduled to speak that night at a Father & Son Banquet at Ironton. Should I go or stay?

John said to go ahead. But first I went to the church in Anderson Hills to thank them for their efforts and tell them of continuing needs. Pastor Glen was out, but I talked with Connie Deweese, church secretary. [She also organizes the Bible School we have for track children in the summer.] Away from the crisis, I kept breaking down trying to tell about the fire. As I left the church I noticed a lady setting up a garage sale. Racks of clothing were in the garage door. On impulse I stopped. Telling her who I was, I asked that she take any leftover clothes across the street to the church. When I began to break down again, I turned away and went back to my car.

Home about 2:00 P.M., I finally got to take off my pajamas and shower. At 3:00 P.M. we left for Ironton. After a time on the road, Florence gently asked, "Tell me about it."

I tried. It took awhile. I had to talk about it or the sight, sounds and smells of the fire, the horses and people would keep tearing at me, awake or asleep. I spoke that night to over 200 men and boys. My voice broke and my eyes were wet. Sunday I spoke three times in two more churches. Would I ever get so I could tell my people's story without breaking?

Monday morning I hurried back to the track. There was to be a Horsemen's meeting. I had called to check on things and knew that I had to be there. Tempers were on edge. There had been arguments and a fight late Friday night among people traumatized by the fire. They were like tight strings, still in shock, and having to endure living conditions that would have to be experienced to be understood.

Out of the shouting of the meeting did come some positive things. A fire siren was mounted on the Horsemen's Gate Guard Shack. There was no P.A. system at the track that night. They had one, but it was removed in 1976, when people who lived up on the hill over the Backside, in their "nice" houses, complained about the noise. Ifs we had had one the night of the fire, more people could have been aroused and more horses saved. The first barn, the groom's barn, now has a tank truck and fire hose parked by it every night. The electricity was turned off for a time in all the old barns until they were rewired, although misunderstanding about that brought a near riot the first night it was done. The grooms had not had it explained to them and it caught them unprepared. I sent for the HBPA officers and stood on a manure wagon trying to keep the tempers down. That was another late night for me, as I dared not go to my room until the entire crowd had dispersed. Many stayed to talk with me after the near riot was over and we could talk peacefully.

There were many in the first chapel service after the fire that gave their thanks for being alive. They praised God. Over and over, people who had not done much talking about God in public, have been doing so since the fire. Many are more vocal now than ever before about their love for Him. My ministry continued on the River Downs Backside among people whom the Lord loves. We are not the same.

POSTSCRIPT

A speeded up building program did take place on the River Downs Backside after the fire. All the old barns were replaced by concrete barns. A new, two-story concrete dorm building went up. The big ditch was filled in. Many improvements happened. The chaplain had a donor who provided a Chapel Trailer to live in and hold services from, outside when possible.

All this, except the Chapel Trailer, cost the Track money. The Manager, Mr. Bataglia, called me in one day to tell me that they did not see how they could continue to keep Race Track Chaplaincy of America, Inc. in their budget. I smiled and asked him how he would handicap a horse in a given race from the Racing Form. He looked puzzled until I told him the Past Performance lists in the form were the first thing a handicapper looked at. I was willing to list my Past Performance for him. For one thing, I mentioned the fire. He had come in just before daylight and had seen me in action. I also told him I believed that I might have saved him damage to track buildings or worse when I faced an angry crowd with Post-Traumatic Stress Syndrome a few nights later. If I were a horse, he would have to put his money on me! We stayed in the budget!

Rewriting this has been both hard on my emotions and therapeutic for me. Many of my racetrack readers will remember that night in May of 1978 and I know it will be talked about again. For those readers who have never gone through a racetrack fire, be thankful and pray that you never will!

CHAPTER 25

Past, Present And Future

"Now to Him who is able to do immeasurably more
than we ask or imagine, according to His power that is
at work within us, to Him be glory in the church and in
Christ Jesus throughout all generations,
for ever and ever! Amen."

[Paul, Ephesians 3: 20, 21]

Call it a promise, call it a blessing, call it a benediction,
the verses above ring with enthusiasm! "With God, all
things are possible!" [Matthew 19: 26.]

The possibility of a nationwide chaplaincy on the racetracks, one which is also spreading across border lines,
seemed nearly impossible over thirty years ago. It just
seemed at that time that it was not only an unthought-of
place to minister, but where would money come from to
support such a ministry? Now, while RTCA always has to
be careful in its budget, over forty chaplains are serving on
tracks all over the country!

I have been a bit hard on the average church, but I want to give a rousing commendation to churches, denominations and individuals that have not adhered to the old concept about staying away from questionable places. The American Baptists and the Southern Baptists, plus the Assembly of God have all set apart persons in their main offices to be liaisons with RTCA. They attend all the annual meetings and support all the chaplains, their own in particular. Their input over the years has been tremendous! A lot of churches have RTCA as part of their regular or special mission giving. Individuals, many from within the industry, have contributed out of their own pockets, and sometimes enabled RTCA, especially in some struggling years, to end up in the black.

One group of special closeness to me was the Ohio American Baptist Women. They decided that my chaplaincy would be the beneficiary of their 1979 State Project. At their annual meeting that June, with a goal of $5,000, they presented me with a check for $8,853.78! I stood before them in tears. That money was tithed [10%] to RTCA for expansion work, part of it went to support the chaplaincy at Thistledown [now with its own chaplain,] and the balance would provide a seminary intern for three years to assist me in the summers at River Downs!

Those interns sure learned a lot during their summers. One told me as he was going back to seminary in the fall that he was sure glad he had been there before his senior year. "Now I know what to study and how to act when I have a church of my own!"

Not all denominations are cooperative. A very successful trainer at Thistledown had a brother in Cleveland who paid frequent visits to him at the track. He was the pastor of a church from a denomination known for its mission work in the hardest situations in the world. I sought an appointment with him at his office. It was a small church that had a hard time raising enough funds to pay the pastor a sufficient salary. He was very open to the thought of becoming a part-time chaplain at Thistledown, but told me he could not do it. When I asked him the reason for his inability to come to RTCA as a chaplain, his answer was simple. "I would be kicked out of the denomination!"

While all nations and ethnic cultures and colors coexisted at the track, that denomination preferred to minister to them where they lived, far away from Cleveland, and preferred that they stay there instead of becoming close neighbors! Truly, we are a people with many "blind spots" that most folks do not even know they have!

Beulah Park had a chaplain one-year from a denomination that was well-known in America and around the world. He was liked and did a fine job, but he called in to say he could not come back. His district minister had told him that if he went back, they would force him out of their ministry!

When I retired in 1988 with health problems, I had my eye on the harness track near by, Vernon Downs. If I had been well I might have gone there myself to be their chaplain. Close by, in the same denomination to which I just referred to, was a young pastor with a farm background. I knew him well, having baptized him years before and had known both his father and grandfather. Vernon Downs was just over a couple of hills from him. He had also visited me in Ohio and had spent a day with me on the track. He was enthusiastic about the prospect of spending at least a couple of days at the track in ministry. He ran it by his area superintendent and was told that if he took the position, he would not be raised to the step of full ministry in the denomination. I was very disappointed for we had an opening and promises of support, but I could not find them a part-time chaplain.

I had another dream. In western New York are the Buffalo Raceway and Batavia Park. They ran alternate dates, when one shut down the other was running. A part-time chaplain who lived in between could minister to the same racetrack folks at both tracks on a year-round basis. This time I made an appointment with the Bishop of that denomination to make my case for an expanded ministry for someone with a relatively small church in the right location. He heard me out and I think he really liked the idea, but his final response was like a blow to the stomach.

"The problem is that the two tracks are in two different districts. You would have to sell the idea to both districts and then have both district superintendents meet to arrange a mutually agreed upon pastor. It would then have to come to me for final approval and then you could only be assured of one year at a time!" Since it takes time and funding to train and introduce a chaplain, that denomination ceased to be a source of chaplains. It was too bad, but that much organization can be too much for practicality!

I do know that my ideas can be controversial. One example of this occurred at a conference in Oregon. A young pastor told me he was starting a church in the state, and he was at a point where he could use some advice as a church planter on how to reach more people.

"If I had it to do over again, I'd go looking where nobody would expect me. Do you have anyone in your new congregation that has an alcohol problem?"

"Yes, I think I do."

"Does he still visit bars to drink?"

"I think so."

"Well, ask him to take you with him the next time he goes! You'll have to drink milk out of the carton to keep the rest of your congregation satisfied, for news of your being there will spread fast. Most all of the people in that bar have a need for someone to listen to them. What does the proverbial bartender know? You have the training and the loving care that people need! Listen to them and be their friend. I think you will find some response. They cannot call you worse things than the Pharisees called Jesus when He ministered to a drinking population!"

I know of one minister from the Dakotas who liked his coffee. The only place in town where he could stop for a coffee break was the local bar and grill. It was usually full of ranchers and townspeople that were not attending his church. He became their friend. But, while he became their pastor, marrying and burying, they would not come into his church! Finally, he installed a closed circuit television in the bar and piped all the church's Sunday Services there. A crowd always gathered every Sunday at the bar, and he had two congregations! And the Word was brought forth!

I tried to get him into considering a move to RTCA as a chaplain, but he was called elsewhere. He was the type that is needed, not only in the racetrack ministry but also in most of our churches! Jesus ordered us to "Go out into the highways and hedges and bring them in!" [Luke 14:23.]

In the verses in Ephesians that come before our introducing verse [14-19,] which speak of things to happen in our lives, they also speak of our past and present. In verse 17, Paul speaks of the past by referring to our "being rooted and established in love." [vs. 17]

Now being "rooted" speaks to my farming and forestry knowledge and experience. Some of our plants have shallow roots as well as some trees. Others have "tap" roots that go down into the earth a great distance. Alfalfa is one of the greatest hay crops for farmers [and much is used on the horsetracks] and has roots that have been measured to go down thirty feet! Not only are they "established" as Paul says, but they go way down beyond the topsoil into the subsoil, where alfalfa draws up trace minerals unavailable to most crops. More commonly found in suburbia is the lowly dandelion. It sure is rooted and established! It has a taproot with fine little rootlets growing from the main root, so that when you try to pull one up or cut it off, the fine rootlets grow a new plant back. When a historic hurricane hit New

England years ago, the beautiful maple trees were practically all blown over. Only young trees and saplings made it. The mature maples were much heavier in the top and the shallow roots could not hold against the wind. The American elm tree survived because it had taproots.

RTCA has been rooted and established in love. It was love that brought our churches into being, usually a long time past in our history. The Love of God and our love for Him prodded our early settlers to meet together in homes and then to construct a church building. RTCA was founded in love by a racetracker who loved his people and wanted them to know Christ. The ministers who responded [after Salty had spent two years trying to get them interested] were already rooted and established in love and they saw the need to spread God's Love! As individuals we need to put down our taproots deep into the Word and be firmly established in Jesus. Then the storms of life will pass us by without our being upended.

If anyone has not been established in love, there's no time like the present to put down your roots and accept God into our lives. Now is the perfect time for accepting His gift!

Paul speaks of our present when he prays that:

> "Out of His glorious riches He may strengthen you with power through His Spirit ...so that Christ may dwell in your hearts through faith...[and that you] may have power, together with all the saints, to grasp how wide and long and high and deep is the Love of Christ, and to know that this Love that surpasses knowledge – that you may be filled to the measure of all the fullness of God."

What a wonderful portrait of the present-time Paul presents! And it is available to us! It is really there for us just as Paul prayed for the Ephesians! Even though it is seldom achieved, we all should strive to be open to the fullness of God's love. Most are too afraid to really trust God to fill them.

You know, God's love is like Shadberries. They may be called Juneberries in some places, or Serviceberries in others. Here in central New York State they live around the forest edges and areas going back to woodland after agricultural abandonment. They bloom earlier than choke cherries or wild apples. The tree is not a commercial tree except as a landscaping ornamental. Its wood is the hardest wood in New York. The fruit looks something like blueberries, except that it has a purplish cast and grows on bushes that can become forty feet tall in maturity. The berries are ripe and ready to eat about the third week in July at my hilltop elevation.

We used to plan retreats for visitors during the shadberry-picking season at our big primitive campsite. I had told everybody how wonderful the shadberries tasted and was excited to show them what they had been missing all these years. When the caravan of visitors arrived and were setting up their tents and getting settled in, I would take a dish and go get some shadberries. No more than half the berries that I picked went into the dish, the rest went into me! I would then bring the dish to the crowd for this exciting moment of superlative taste testing! I always told them to eat them like this, "Take a small handful at a time, see, like popcorn. Put them all in at once!" and I would demonstrate, with a look of extreme satisfaction. Talk about the " Fruit of the Spirit, love, joy, peace," all going over your taste buds and tricklng down your throat, leading to great contentment!

Then I would hold out the dish with great excitement so they could share this wonderful gift of God! Invariably, they would reach out very tentatively with a thumb and forefinger, pick up ONE berry, look at it closely, put it up to their mouth, bite it IN HALF [!], roll it around in their mouth and then spit out seeds that I never knew were there!

That's the way God's love is! It's so great we cannot even comprehend it in any part of its totality! But are we willing to accept it? To dive into His love and let it fill us? No! We almost without exception are afraid of too much of God's love! "It might make us different! It might even change our minds about some things! It might even make us love our neighbor [even if he lives on a racetrack, under a bridge, or on the wrong side of town!] No, no, I'll take just a little of that great love, maybe that's all I could stand. I might even be so satisfied with more that I would give up something, and I would never want to do that!"

If only we had eyes to see into what God would bestow upon us! Look at our title verse again. This is our future! Here it is in The Living Bible version.

> "Now glory be to God who by His mighty power at work within us is able to do far more than we would ever dare to ask or even dream of – infinitley beyond our highest prayers, desires, thoughts or hopes."

This could be our future if we just accept more of the Love that God would share with us!

Martin Luther King is famous for many things, but when we think of him, we remember the "I Have a Dream" speech, in which he dreamed of the time when children of all colors could learn to accept each other and be safe. Then, maybe adults would accept each other.

I have a Vision of when we all can accept God's Love like I eat shadberries! If we all accepted His Love, my Vision would make Martin's Dream come true! Join with me in the Vision, join in God's Love! Let us go out "into the highways and hedges" looking for forgotten and rejected people, letting God's Love flow out through us like a river, so that they too will share in my Vision!

Printed in the United States
23974LVS00002B/226-318

9 781594 674075